Saint Joan
Fifty Years After

Louisiana State University Press/Baton Rouge

Saint Joan
Fifty Years After

1923/24—1973/74

Edited with an Introduction by
STANLEY WEINTRAUB

ISBN 0-8071-0208-3

Library of Congress Catalog Card Number 73-77657

Copyright © 1973 by Louisiana State University Press

All rights reserved

Manufactured in the United States of America

Type set by George Banta Co., Menasha, Wisconsin

Printed and bound by Halliday Lithograph Corp., West Hanover, Massachusetts

Designed by Albert R. Crochet

Acknowledgment is made to the following persons and publishers for the reprinting of copyright material:

"The Prophet and the Maid," by John Mason Brown, copyright © 1951 by the Saturday Review Associates, Inc. "Shaw, Robertson and 'The Maid'," by T. S. Eliot, reprinted from *Criterion* by permission of Valerie Eliot. *"Saint Joan* in Paris," by Daniel C. Gerould, reprinted from *The Shaw Review* by permission of the editor. "Shaw on *Saint Joan,"* by James Graham, and "Pirandello Distills Shaw" ("Bernard Shaw's *Saint Joan*"), by Luigi Pirandello, copyright © 1924 by the New York Times Company. "Bernard Shaw's Saint," by J. H. Huizinga, copyright © 1959 by Meridian Books, reprinted by permission of Harper & Row, Publishers, Inc. "Shaw's Joan: The Hero as Saint," extracted from A. N. Kaul, *The Action of English Comedy: Studies in the Encounter of Abstraction and Experience from Shakespeare to Shaw,* copyright © 1970 by Yale University. "St Joan: The Theme and the Drama," by Desmond MacCarthy, and "An Irish Joan," by T. C. Worsley, reprinted by permission of *The New Statesman.* "The Saint as Tragic Hero," by Louis L. Martz, reprinted by permission of the author. "Shaw and Sainthood," by Hans Stoppel, reprinted by permission of *English Studies.* "Joan as Unhappy Trotzkyist," extracted from Arland Ussher, *Three Great Irishmen: Shaw, Yeats, Joyce,* copyright © 1952, reprinted by permission of the Devin-Adair Company. "Bernard Shaw's Other Saint Joan," by Stanley Weintraub, reprinted by permission of the author. *"Saint Joan:* A Modern Classic Reconsidered," by E. J. West, reprinted by permission of the Speech Communication Association. "That Sure Mark of Greatness: *Saint Joan* and Its Imperfections," extracted from J. I. M. Stewart, *Eight Modern Writers,* copyright © 1963 by Oxford University Press, reprinted by permission of The Clarendon Press, Oxford.

CONTENTS

Saint Joan
Fifty Years After

Introduction

Writing from "the Joan of Arc country" to actress Mrs. Pat Campbell in 1913, Bernard Shaw prophesied, "I shall do a Joan play some day, beginning with the sweeping up of the cinders and orange peel *after* her martyrdom, and going on with Joan's arrival in heaven." He would, he said, have God threaten the English with eternal damnation for their share in her betrayal and burning, but Joan would stay the judgment by bringing forth a fragment of burnt stick. "What is that? Is it one of the faggots?" God would ask, and Joan would reply, "No, it is what is left of the two sticks a common English soldier tied together and gave me as I went to the stake; for they wouldn't even give me a crucifix; and you cannot damn the common people of England, represented by that soldier, because a poor cowardly riff raff of barons and bishops were too futile to resist the devil."

English drama would have to be rescued ("by an Irishman, as usual"), he went on, from the disgrace of having nothing formidable to offer about Joan except Shakespeare's "piffling libel" in Henry VI; Shaw imagined the Bard "running down bye streets in heaven" to avoid a confrontation with the Maid of Orleans. A decade later he felt he would have no such problem. His Joan, newly written, was neither piffling nor a libel. In fact he had based his play on the transcripts of the trial and rehabilitation hearings themselves, Englished in 1902 for the first time in the nearly five hundred years since Joan's execution.

Criticism of the play in the half-century since its first production has generally sustained Shaw, although with reservations based upon everything from religion and politics to rhetoric and polemics, and this

3

volume attempts to sample the first fifty years in the existence of a play that has been called in the recent *Oxford History of English Literature* not only Shaw's outstanding work, but "conceivably the finest and most moving English drama since *The Winter's Tale* or *The Tempest.* It owns that sure mark of greatness: a stature that remains intact after every consideration has been given to its evident and undeniable imperfections."

Joan was written entirely in 1923, three years after the Maid's long-delayed canonization. Although Shaw had considered a Joan play for years, the words came rapidly once he began, and the ending he imagined to Mrs. Campbell—perhaps its real moment of conception for him—became the still-controversial Epilogue. "As I wrote," he told Theatre Guild director Lawrence Langner, "she guided my hand, and the words came tumbling out at such a speed that my pen rushed across the paper and I could barely write fast enough to put them down." Whatever the source of his inspiration, the play had *popular success* written all over it. Shaw had not had a box-office triumph since *Pygmalion,* nearly ten years earlier, on the eve of the war of 1914–18. The war had embittered his soul, and *Heartbreak House* and *Back to Methuselah,* the major works to come out of the war years, left little room for hope about humanity. But, however tragic, the new play was on the upswing: a species which could manifest a being such as Joan, whatever her fate, was not altogether lost.

Offered the play after its noble and money-losing effort in staging the *Methuselah* cycle, the Theatre Guild was galvanized into action and began rehearsing *Joan* in November, 1923. Remembering its unhappy experience with the lengthy *Methuselah,* the Guild early in its planning decided to write to Shaw urging him to make some deletions and appealing to his humanity as well as his desire for a good box office by observing that many potential theatregoers dwelt in the suburbs and would miss the last train home. Shaw cabled laconically:

THE OLD OLD STORY BEGIN AT EIGHT OR RUN LATER TRAINS AWAIT FINAL REVISION OF PLAY.

After the final dress rehearsal the Guild cabled Shaw again entreating him to cut the play:

JOAN OPENS FRIDAY EVENING. CONSENSUS OF OPINION AT FIRST DRESS REHEARSAL FATAL DROP OF INTEREST DURING TENT SCENE AND BEGIN-

NING TRIAL SCENE. WERE YOU HERE SURE YOU WOULD AGREE WITH US.
WE WILL NOT DROP ONE LINE WITHOUT YOUR CONSENT BUT FOR GOOD
OF PLAY AND TURNING POSSIBLE FINANCIAL LOSS INTO ASSURED ARTIS-
TIC FINANCIAL SUCCESS STRONGLY URGE YOUR CABLING CONSENT OUR
EXPENSE FOLLOWING OMISSIONS. . . .

Shaw's silence on the matter was total, and the play, as written, and
directed by Philip Moeller, had its first performance on December 28,
1923, at the Garrick Theatre in New York. The public liked the play
better than the critics, whose notices were mixed, and Langner sent a
personal cable, entreating Shaw to heed critical comment about the
play's length:

ONE CRITIC COMPARING YOU WITH SHAKESPEARE SAYS THAT JOAN CAN-
NOT BE SUCCESSFULLY GIVEN UNTIL AFTER YOUR DEATH BECAUSE IT
CAN THEN BE CUT. SPLENDID OPPORTUNITY TO PROVE AGAIN THAT YOU
ARE GREATER THAN SHAKESPEARE BY CABLING THE GUILD TO USE ITS
DISCRETION IN MAKING SOME OMISSION OF UNESSENTIALS. GUILD HAS
DONE SPLENDID WORK. SURE YOU WOULD AGREE IF YOU WERE HERE.

Shaw refused, and when Winifred Lenihan, the Joan of the production,
was pressed to send a cable asking him to "agree to some omissions" in
order to keep the play running, he cabled her:

THE GUILD IS SENDING ME TELEGRAMS IN YOUR NAME, PAY NO ATTEN-
TION TO THEM

Then he sent the Guild a long essay in which he set out his ideas about
the play, which he encouraged them to offer to the press in his own
defense. The Guild did not, but Shaw afterwards frugally incorporated
the essence of it into his preface to the published play. The key issue in
the proposed article was addressed to the apparent villains, the critics.
He was not in the "popular entertainment business," he insisted, where
the play is tailored to the audience's attention span and to the needs of
critics to rush back to newspaper offices and feed clamoring compos-
itors. What was more important was that he was "intensely interested,
and to some extent conscience stricken, by the great historical case of
Joan of Arc. I know that many others share that interest . . . and that
they would eagerly take some trouble to have it made clear to them
how it all happened. I conceive such a demonstration to be an act of
justice for which the spirit of Joan, yet incarnate among us, is still
calling." His play was not for "connoisseurs of the police and divorce

drama" or devotees of "the lilies and languors and roses and raptures of
the cinema," but for another breed of playgoer whose neglected needs
had brought the Theatre Guild itself into existence. When it came to
entertainment, Shaw declared, people had to learn their places just as
they did elsewhere, for when a man went to church and disliked the
service or the doctrine, he did not ask to have it altered to his taste.
Instead, he went elsewhere. So with his play:

> However, even at the risk of a comprehensive insult to the general public
> of New York, I must add that the limitation of the audience to serious,
> intelligent, and cultivated Americans means that *Saint Joan* must be re-
> garded for the present as an Exceptional Play for Exceptional People. It has
> cost a good deal to produce it for them, and is costing a good deal to keep
> the opportunity open. This will not matter if they seize the opportunity
> promptly with a sense that if they do not, they will miss it, and discourage
> the Guild from future public-spirited enterprises of this class. The solvency
> of a play depends not only on the number of persons who pay to witness it,
> but on the length of time over which their attendances are spread. Even a
> million enthusiasts will not help if they arrive at the rate of ten per week.
> *Saint Joan*'s present prosperity cannot in the nature of things last many
> months.

Despite the critics, the play was successful enough to be moved to
the larger Empire Theatre to accommodate the crowds. It ran for 214
performances, by which time it had also opened at the New Theatre in
London, where Joan was played by Sybil Thorndike. There it would
run for 244 performances and result in that most unlikely of English
events, a Shavian apotheosis. A. B. Walkley, who had worked with
Shaw on the London *Star* in the 1880s and to whom Shaw had dedicated *Man and Superman* (Walkley nevertheless condemned it), had
long been drama critic of the prestigious *Times,* and when *Saint Joan*
was announced for production he had written an extraordinary article
which the *Times* had had the bad taste to publish. Although he had not
read the play, and could not have seen it, he protested at length that
the subject was far too solemn and serious to be tampered with by an
irreverent jokester. When the play opened he found himself writing
reluctantly that in Shaw's hands the story of Joan "remains a lovely
thing, lovely in simplicity, lovely in faith." Even the Nobel Prize
committee could no longer look away, and Shaw received the Prize for
Literature in 1925, an honor almost certainly owed to *Joan.* To the
consternation of the grantors, he wrote to the Royal Swedish Academy
to "discriminate between the award and the prize. For the award I

have nothing but my best thanks. But after the most careful consideration I cannot persuade myself to accept the money. My readers and audiences provide me with more than sufficient money for my needs; and as to my renown it is greater than is good for my spiritual health. Under these circumstances the money is a lifebelt thrown to a swimmer who has already reached the shore in safety." At Shaw's request an Anglo-Swedish Literary Foundation was funded with the prize money, "to encourage intercourse and understanding in literature and art between Sweden and the British Isles."

Although he had written forty plays and would write fourteen more before his death, after 1924 Shaw remained, as far as the world was concerned, the author of *Saint Joan.* Yet he would disclaim about Joan, "I have done nothing but arrange her for the stage. There really was such a woman. She did and said all these things. Make your offering at her altar, not mine."

Criticism over the years has tended to focus upon the historical validity of Shaw's *Joan* as much as the play's theatrical values, for an event that has occurred but rarely in art has apparently occurred with respect to *Saint Joan.* Shaw's Maid has become the popular image of Joan of Arc, who is no longer the Joan of history or hagiology but the Joan of Shaw's *Saint Joan* much as the *Henry V* of Shakespeare has eclipsed the Henry V of history. Literature at its most triumphant can achieve such effects, just as it can raise to near-actuality in the popular mind a character entirely the product of the novelist or playwright. But Joan, too, has been interpreted according to the winds of political and social change, and becomes, in a number of the views in this volume, a precursor of, or spokesman for, concepts which would have baffled the historical Joan even more than the ideas of nationalism and Protestantism Shaw sees being played about her person by individuals who themselves are more articulate than they would be in real life in order that they may understand themselves sufficiently to enable the audience to understand. The critics of Shaw's *Joan* have been Protestant, Catholic, and freethinking; they have been capitalist and Marxist; they have represented nations and languages in which Joan has been presented in translations whose nuances of interpretation have been in themselves a kind of criticism. Fifty years are but a beginning with a modern classic. As Warwick suggests in Shaw's play, we have not heard the last of her.

I/Mr. Bernard Shaw Talks About St. Joan

One of the most interesting of the experiences that have fallen to my lot was the painting of two portraits in oils of Mr. George Bernard Shaw during my recent stay in London. The various sittings were more interesting to me than any Shaw play or preface could be, for, while we feel vividly the personality behind the plays and writings as we sit in the theater or read, here was the actual man in front of me, electrifying in his presence, immensely alive, gesticulating and laughing as he busily talked as good "Shaw" as he ever committed to paper. Paint can, at best, show but a pale shadow of flesh and blood; Mr. Conrad tells me that he thinks it possible for a writer to capture only about thirty per cent of the beauty of his dream, however successful he may be; and Mr. Shaw, though he has revealed enough of himself in his work to make the entire intellectual world regard him as his own superman (though he applies that name to one of the opposite sex), is personally far beyond what his writings lead one to expect.

Our sittings concluded, the present talk occurred on a final visit to my studio just previous to my departure for Paris. Mr. Shaw was rehearsing "Back to Methuselah" at the Court Theatre near by, and spent an hour and a half before my fire one evening until the time for the rehearsal arrived. He spoke of the many previous histories and plays based upon the life of Jeanne d'Arc, referring particularly to those of Schiller and Anatole France. In many of these accounts the fact that

Outlook, CXXXVII (June 25, 1924), 311–13. The author was an artist who had visited Shaw in hopes of having him sit for a portrait.

Joan is revealed as a lovely and spectacular sort of cinema heroine is partly excusable because they were written before the discovery or general dissemination of some of the actual records of her trial, which came to light in the forties of the last century. Even after these documents were known many writers and artists preferred to pamper the public taste for a vision of Joan as a lovely, insipid slip of a girl, divinely guided, but possessed of mental and physical attributes utterly incongruous with and unfitted to her achievements. His own conception of her personal appearance, as set forth in the play, he got from a contemporary Gothic statue that he found in one of the French towns where much of her time was spent at the height of her success. The natives of the place believe it to be a portrait of some saint, but nothing could be more probable than that the artist was influenced, even if it was intended to be the saint in question, by the physical attributes of this most dominant woman. He believes it to be an actual portrait of her. She is large and strong, and has a wonderful face. It is quite handsome, but far from pretty, and it is the face of a born leader. The eyes are very far apart with an expression of will and strength, the cheekbones high and broad, the nose long and vigorous, and the mouth firm and of generous size. Certainly the Joan of Boutet de Monvel[1] would meet with greater sympathy from the average public than a picture of her as the Amazon that she undoubtedly was; a screen version of her with Mary Pickford in the lead would prove to be a greater popular success than if the part were taken by Ellen Terry at her best. Anatole France, he said, was biased in his account of Joan by his opposition to feminism. He thinks that no woman could possibly be capable of the great things she accomplished, and, in this state of mind, blinded himself to the facts.

"Of course Anatole France is Anatole France. His book is immensely worth reading because he wrote it. But he has the facts about Joan all wrong."

I asked what he thought of Mark Twain's Joan.

"Much, much better," he said. "Mark Twain was a man of genius, but hardly one to write reverently of mediaeval times. He went for his

---

1. Louis Maurice Boutet de Monvel drew a striking representation of Joan for his book *Joan of Arc* (1907). [Ed.]

information to the same sources that I used, but the author of 'Inno-
cents Abroad' could not treat the subject with entire seriousness. Take,
for example, his 'Connecticut Yankee at King Arthur's Court.' What a
piece of Philistinism! But his book on Joan of Arc is an excellent thing,
and the truest account that has previously been given of her.

"The records of her trial reveal Joan as being as far as possible in
character from the namby-pamby picture card that usually represents
her. She was a strong-minded, scheming woman, shrewd, and of the
fanatical sort that could easily conceive that any pet idea had been a
divine revelation to her. She bullied every one who opposed her—
prelates, statesmen, and soldiers alike—and was undoubtedly, most
cordially hated by all of the people in authority with whom she came in
contact. Imagine her popularity with the dignitaries of the Church
when she insisted on eliminating them utterly from the office that was
the chief source of their power, and insisting that she was ·in direct
communication with God! If this attitude were to spread, the Catholic
Church would soon lose its hold on the people, and many of its leaders
would lose their jobs. She was more of a Protestant than either Huss or
Luther. No priest or bishop could stand between her and God. She was
probably also the first Nationalist and by her constantly repeated
doctrine of 'France for the French' threatened the whole fabric of
feudalism, which made her an abomination to the various lords like the
Earl of Warwick, whose authority would be swallowed up in that of the
King if Joan's dream came true. She insisted that the English had no
right on French soil, and exhorted the soldiers that they should not rest
until the last Englishman was driven out. The French soldiers had no
such feeling, and did not readily comprehend this new doctrine, as they
had always done their fighting impersonally and blindly under any lord
who happened for the time to be in the ascendency. So to these two
powerful classes, and to the generals as well, this obstinate daughter of
a small-town *bourgeois* seemed ridiculously presumptuous when she
suddenly appeared, voicing the heresy of direct divine revelations,
preaching nationalism, and demanding that she be taken to the Dauphin and put in command of an army, over the heads of Church, lords,
and seasoned soldiers to whom fighting was a lifelong profession.

"But, as everything else had been tried without success to stem the
tide of the victorious English, and soldiers and leaders alike were at

their wits' end, Joan soon acquired several influential followers who were convinced in her favor by a blend of superstition and shrewdness, seeing that the Maid could revive the flagging spirits of the soldiers by the belief that in her they had a supernatural leader inspired by Heaven. To begin with, she was of the type of strong-minded executive woman who has no sex appeal, even though handsome. You have known women of this kind, I am sure. The common soldiers, with whom she associated constantly, thought her supernatural because they felt no sex impulse toward her. Knowing their usual sex-mad tendencies during long terms of absence from feminine society, they could not explain the lack of any sex feeling toward Joan, who was constantly with them, and in men's clothes, except on the grounds of the supernatural. She was quite willing to impress them so, as it increased her power over them and kept her free from unpleasant annoyance. Various other seeming miracles caused the spirit of superstition to mount to some of those higher in authority; these Joan eagerly and craftily used to her ends, and proceeded successfully with her task of walking roughshod over the heads of all the dignitaries who, in protecting their own interests, naturally opposed her. Her constant reiteration that her every act was directly commanded by God was helped along by her somewhat hysterical termperament, that made it easy for her to convince herself that such was the case. This fanaticism spread to the soldiers, and caused them to follow her blindly with a fatalistic confidence that has often been effective with armies, the Moslems, for example.

"So, by dint of persistent bullying of nearly every one with whom she came in contact, she finally found herself at the head of an army. She was endowed with a certain elementary strategic sense, similar to that possessed by Napoleon in such abundance, though it was not at all trained, as his was. It caused her to realize that Orleans was the key to the whole military situation, and, blind to all else, she made for this objective, often throwing the most ordinary military caution to the winds. She did not fight actually—at her trial she said she had never taken a human life—but she always led her soldiers personally into the thickest of the fighting, carrying a white banner that made of her a conspicuous target, and her soldiers would follow her anywhere. The banner she never allowed out of her hands except on one occasion, when one of her chief lieutenants persuaded her to allow a subordinate to carry it after him as he crossed a moat to capture a castle. But this effort of precaution for Joan's safety she promptly defeated. Seeing her beloved emblem going into the action without her, she rushed after it into the moat in spite of a hail of stones and arrows, and struggled with the carrier for the possession of the banner in a way not at all in keeping with the usual conception of her dignity. She hampered this particular operation most seriously, and when subdued was hurried back from the moat to save her life. Luck was a considerable element in her favor on numerous occasions, and when it came she was not slow in making the best use of it. In another battle an arrow passed completely through a fleshly part of her neck without doing her any harm. She didn't even retire from the fight, and all who saw the incident, friends and enemies alike, thought it a miracle and were convinced that she was supernatural. When she arrived before Orleans, she demanded of Dunois, the commander stationed there, why he did not proceed immediately and recapture all of the fortifications. He called her attention to the utter folly of attempting this with the force at their disposal, pointing out to her that his reinforcements and supplies had been lying in ships in the river at some little distance, unable to join him because of a constant adverse wind. Almost as he spoke the wind suddenly changed to the exact reverse of its former direction, whereupon Joan remarked, 'But the wind is not as you say. Now are you ready to proceed upon Orleans?' Aghast at this new miracle, as they chose to interpret it, upon the arrival of the reinforcements and supplies the successful attack upon Orleans was launched, with the soldiers willing to follow the white banner and its invincible bearer into the very jaws of death.

"Then she insisted on crowning the Dauphin, a weak and vacillating person, in full state of Rheims Cathedral. She was even able to instill in him a semblance of courage that in time enabled him to do some creditable fighting. Her dream then was to take Paris; but evil days began to come, her fickle followers losing faith when every fight did not achieve a victory. From a supposedly supernatural leader they would not accept defeat. A serious wound that she received finally burst the bubble of the miraculous, and Joan suddenly found herself almost without friends.

"Her stubbornness at the trial cost her her life. Most patiently the

Church authorities in the tribunal before which she was tried endeavored to have her say the things that would make it possible for them to save her from the stake, but she constantly insisted that God had ordered her in every act, and persistently stuck to it. This was heresy, punishable by death, as the Church taught that communication with God could be had only through its priests. In vain they explained it to her again and again, and finally caused her to understand that persistence in this course meant death, but that her life would be spared if she would recant. Like the sensible person she was, she eagerly reached for the document of recantation to sign it, but, its contents being read, it was revealed that the alternative was imprisonment for life. She flew into a rage, seized and crumpled the document, and repeated again all of the statements to which the Church objected. There was no saving her then. According to the law of the Church, a relapse into heresy was unforgivable, so she was given into the hands of the Earl of Warwick's soldiers, and burned.

"Her idea in wearing men's clothes was a sensible one; she was a soldier, and could not be bothered with skirts, and as she associated with soldiers constantly it was really more modest to dress as one of them, instead of unnecessarily drawing attention to the difference in sex. But this was one of the counts against her in the trial, and was interpreted by the Church as wanton immodesty."

I asked Mr. Shaw how she could be canonized in view of the fact that the Church had condemned her to death.

"Oh, that was all satisfactorily arranged," he said. "No detail as important as that would be overlooked. The Inquisition was carried on by a so-called 'secular arm' of the Church, and in this case the English soldiers really burned her. So that lets the Church out nicely."

I could not repress an expression of my admiration for the dramatic conception and structure that his talk suggested to me, adding, more in jest than in earnest, that I was sure, with his marvelous skill, that he could have adopted precisely the opposite view of the whole situation and have made the play equally absorbing. The effect of this banal remark upon Mr. Shaw was most interesting. A look of mild pain and surprise came into his face; he evidently thought that I doubted his sincerity, and seemed at a loss for a reply, but when I protested laughingly that his whole conception seemed utterly logical and convincing to me he was satisfied.

"A straightforward attempt to tell the truth is usually misunderstood," he said. "The French people are indignant in the belief that I have belittled their national heroine. Roman Catholics protest that I have written 'St. Joan' as an attack on their Church. Neither was intended or achieved. I have merely written a play based upon the facts as they exist."

I told him I would get the book as soon as it appeared and read it with much interest.

"Why spend your good money?" was his laughing reply. "Just tell your friends you had it all from Shaw. There's much more swank in that."

II/Shaw on *Saint Joan*

For some weeks past a fierce controversy has been raging in Paris about Bernard Shaw's latest play, produced in New York some time ago, the heroine of which is Joan—Sainte Jeanne—Jehanne, Maid of Orleans, national heroine of France. The whole trouble, which has degenerated into an embittered quarrel, started through a dispatch in *Comoedia* from its New York correspondent, M. Thomas, which implied that the author had insulted Joan, thereby showing himself not only sacrilegious but also boorish and ungallant. A reply to this allegation was immediately forthcoming from M. Augustin Hamon, who in collaboration with Henriette Hamon, is the translator of most of Bernard Shaw's plays into French. M. Hamon took up the cudgels so vigorously that the argument quickly developed into a general discussion on the merits of Shaw and the Shavian theatre, chiefly between M. Thomas, M. Gabriel Boissy, and M. Hamon.

The latest contribution to the discussion is a letter which appears in *Comoedia* from no less a person than Mr. Shaw himself, in which the writer, with his usual wit and verve, hits back hard—or, at any rate, he seems to hit back hard, for it is not always the blow which resounds the most that counts. The letter is addressed to the London correspondent of the Paris theatrical publication in reply to the following questions:

1. What do you think of the criticisms of *Saint Joan* on the occasion of its production in New York?

2. What are your own ideas about Joan of Arc?

New York *Times*, April 13, 1924, Sec. 8, p. 2.

3. Is one justified in calling your play an attack on patriotism and religion?

4. Do you think the translation of your works recently produced in Paris faithfully reflects your thought and spirit?

Mr. Shaw writes:

"All that I know about the discussion in France concerning my play, *Saint Joan,* is that M. Thomas, writing from America, declared that I had insulted Joan. This is precisely as if M. Thomas, having seen the Sistine Madonna at Dresden, had reported that Raphael had carica- tured the Holy Virgin. I concluded that he had not seen my play or that he did not understand English. When my translator intervened, M. Gabriel Boissy adroitly came to the assistance of M. Thomas by remind- ing us that he had served his country heroically during the war. There was nothing more to be said. M. Hamon and I took our hats off: the bands played 'The Marseillaise': M. Thomas and his eloquent defender embraced, and the incident was at an end. In future I will not attempt to contradict any declaration, even if it is wrong, made by a Frenchman about my works, for, if asked to say whether he has been present at the play, he has only to reply: 'No, but I was at Verdun,' to seduce me to silence.

"When you ask me for my opinion about Joan of Arc, I must point out to you that, since the report of the legal case against Joan and her rehabilitation by Quicherat, there has been no room for opinion: the facts are too simple. All controversies raised with regard to the subject are nothing but attempts to obscure the facts in order to satisfy one opinion or another, whether party or not. Much fiction has been added with the intention of rendering the operation easier and more plausible. Anti-feminist opinion has refused to accept Joan as a political and military genius, in spite of her campaign on the Loire and of her policy which brought about the coronation, which would have confirmed the reputation of any adventurer of the male sex. Anticlericals and Protes- tants have refused to believe that the proceedings against her were honest and her execution inevitable. Psychologists have attempted to prove that she was insane. Romanticists insisted on the fact that she was a heroine of striking beauty; the name of Shakespeare is attached to a dramatization of Joan as sorceress and prostitute; Voltaire made of her a heroine of licentious and scandalous extravagance: Schiller represented her as amorous of Dunois. Anatole France took pity on her, on the marionette which she was in the hands of the soldiers and priests. Nothing remains of what Joan really was, and that is exactly what I have undertaken. No French writer seemed capable of the necessary detachment to do this, and perhaps it is just as well that this act of respect—for that is what it is—should come from the country which Joan defeated.

"Besides this you must have observed that the Frenchman, while abundantly recognizing the talent of his country, cannot admit French genius, just as Rodin was a Frenchman of genius, and both were obliged to go to London in order to find recognition. I am quite aware, of course, that Joan is widely celebrated in France as a saint, and that a number of equestrian statues have been set up in her honor, but the real woman in her is still as unpopular in her own country as she was when the Burgundians sold her to the English and the latter delivered her to the French Church and the Inquisition to be burned.

"France knows very little about Joan of Arc. Instinctively she disguises her in her own eyes. She was a saint, and France does not now know what a saint is; she adores St. Paul Bert and St. Louis Pasteur. Joan was the first great Protestant, and France has never shown herself friendly to Protestantism, although a great part of her population adhered to it with ardor. She was a great nationalist. And less than 45 per cent of the citizens of the French Republic are French. Joan was also a masterful woman, a capable woman, and, as France is the land of masterful women par excellence, the French groan under the tyranny of their wives and their mothers, and they cannot stand the thought that Joan, even at the age of 18, possessed more mastery than most women of brains possess at 50; in fact, this is why the French and the English so thoroughly agreed upon burning her. I will have to overcome all these prejudices and weaknesses when I show France her national heroine without fear or favor, as she was. I love the real Joan, but the conventional Joan of the stage makes me sick.

"The people who, as you told me, see in my work an attack against patriotism and religion, know nothing about it and are probably utterly ignorant about patriotism and religion. Of course, I make an exception of your military hero critics, who may be excused on account of shell shock. But you must understand that I do not write for those whom nothing interests but an eternal variation of the eternal triangle. The protagonists of my play, although they appear on the stage as soldiers and feudal noblemen, are in reality the Church, the Inquisition and the Holy Roman Empire. All united irresistibly to destroy a warrior saint. I have not belittled Joan, as would have been the case if I had turned her story into a melodrama about a wicked Bishop and a virtuous virgin. I have carried the tragedy completely beyond the taste of lovers of such melodrama and probably beyond their comprehension.

"They like duels and divorce cases, and cannot conceive a human being taking interest in the Middle Ages or in the Church or the empire. The inquisitor, in my play a very amiable gentleman, delivers a speech of six minutes without making a single illusion to any of the subjects forming the theatrical fare of ·all the public markets of the boulevards. The New York critics declared that the public would never stand such lengths, and that if the play was to be saved, all long speeches, all references to the Church, and the epilogue dealing with the history of Joan after her torture, must be cut without pity. Not a word was cut. Nevertheless, the play had an enormous success and had to be transferred to a larger theatre, able to hold the crowds desirous for the sake of Joan of Arc to listen for three and a half hours to a dialogue dealing with religion and with the politics of the Middle Ages. They were only too glad to escape from the divorce cases and scenes of adultery and prostitution which appear to be the Alpha and Omega of the drama in the eyes of the boulevardiers. The poor boulevardier suffers horribly when he has the misfortune to be present at one of my plays. If he is a journalist, he fills the papers with his lamentations and imagines to himself, poor devil, that I write with the sole end of annoying him.

"I have met with this sort of opposition in New York and London, and I will have to cope with it in Paris, for Paris is today not only as uncivilized as New York or London but is suffering from a special kind of Eighteenth Century provincialism—which is, by the way, not without its charm. You were good enough to say that I have obtained right of citizenship in Paris, but I assure you that you are mistaken. The theatrical movement which I represent has reached certain sectarian theatres in Paris: it has even touched the Comédie Française, but not through me. My plays have given an impulse to drama in America and

Germany, and the Paris stage has been reached by the American and German influence (via Russia). This is so true that even were I to say today, as I said thirty years ago, that the well-written plays of Scribe, Augier, Dumas *fils* and Sardou have the same connection with real plays as a toy rabbit with a live one, it is doubtful whether M. Thomas himself would exclaim: 'Was it for this that I shed my blood at Verdun?'

"In any case, I doubt whether the French stage will show me the same politeness I have received from most other national theatres in Europe until I have been dead for one or two hundred years. M. Gemier is a remarkable man. He has turned the Odeon into a theatre of our times; but I notice that he does not yet dare risk a more recent play of mine than *Arms and the Man* which dates from 1894 and is looked upon here as a mitigated classic suitable for girls' schools, like Racine's *Athalie*. It seems to me that the theatre in France addresses itself less and less to an intelligent public; the public is, in fact, so stupid that an explanation of the play must be printed on the program to help the spectators understand what they see.

"The other day I saw a program of *Arms and the Man* which carefully explains that the tragic figure of my play is a buffoon who must not be taken seriously. It is pitiful, because an appreciation of my plays has in a way become a proof of civilization, and up to the present France is almost at the bottom of the form. Nothing, however, can be done. I have educated London, I have educated New York, Berlin and Vienna; Moscow and Stockholm are at my feet, but I am too old to educate Paris; it is too far behind and I am too far ahead. Besides this, my method of education is to teach people how to laugh at themselves, and the pride of Paris is so prodigious that it has beaten all its professors from Molière to Anatole France and might even beat me.

"I doubt whether I shall be on good terms with the Parisians. You see, I know France much better than they know it and I love it all the better. It was not a Frenchman but an English poet, William Morris, who said to me that France was the most beautiful country in the world. I found her so; but the Parisians do not appreciate her. One ought to drive them all out and replace them by the English, who really appreciate the country. Still, the English would spoil things for me, because France is the only country in Europe where I can always remain a simple Mister, where I am not worried by request for auto-graphs, invitations to banquets and requests to inaugurate statues. She is like a delightful and peaceful backwater where I can rest without being pursued by my own reputation or any other modern reputations.

"When you ask me, Do you think that the French translation of your works given recently in Paris was the truthful reflection of your thought and your spirit? you expose yourself to the suspicion that you wish to translate them yourself. According to all French writers who cherish this ambition or were disappointed in it, my friends Augustin and Henriette Hamon are the worst translators on earth, entirely without any qualification for the work which I asked them to undertake at a time when the idea of writing for the theatre had not yet entered their heads.

"If a Frenchman says to me that the translations of Hamon are infamous, I can evidently not contradict him. I can read French easily, I can speak it after a barbarous fashion provided I am not asked to go more deeply into grammar than the present of the indicative; I can understand it when it is spoken as badly as I speak it, that is to say, by everybody except the French. How, then, could I venture to object if a Frenchman, a man of letters, says to me that Hamon is totally illiterate? But when, as generally happens, the gentleman who denounces Hamon shows the most disastrous and complete incomprehension of my works and sometimes undisguised hostility toward them, I begin to ask myself whether Hamon has not made enemies for himself by attempting to be too faithful to me instead of turning my works into Parisian articles, like the others think they could do so adroitly.

"My plays are mixtures of seventeenth century rhetoric, of modern thought and of that barbarous English humor which shocked Voltaire in Shakespeare. They are full of politics, religion, biology and all sorts of terrestrial things except adultery. They contain no traitors, no duels, no misunderstandings nor dramatic plots; and when the question of pas-sion between the two sexes arises, it is the real thing, not the conven-tion which holds its stead on your modest boulevards. The mate-rial which serves your talented dramatic authors for the construction of a whole play would not last me thirty seconds; the old-fashioned dénouements are mere phrases in my plays, at half a dozen a page.

"What is the result? When my poor friend Hamon has a translation of one of my works produced, your critics and your theatrical people cannot believe their eyes. They say: this thing is not the theatre; this is not a play; you must have translated it horribly. You see, their thoughts, just like their stage props, are two hundred years behind the time. Hamon, who is and always has been an advanced thinker, is like an intruder on a strange planet. The better his translation is, the worse it seems. When he says that my technique is at bottom that of Molière he makes things worse, because the theatrical people do not like Molière and would reject his works with contempt if they were submitted as new by a new writer. Molière, you will remember, won a place for himself on the French stage only by playing his own plays in his own theatre. Where would Sacha Guitry be if he had not a great actor, a charming and intelligent actress, and (consequently) always a theatre in his pocket? I have no such advantages. My father is dead and my wife is not an actress. Hamon, too, is an orphan. What chance have we in Paris, which, like Jerusalem, strangles its prophets? After all, why should I trouble Paris? I am not Alexander: I do not dream of conquering more worlds. If Paris perishes in ignorance of my works, the loss will be for Paris and not for me. I do not say that the loss would not be serious; for I am as indispensable as Bergson for a complete modern culture; but France will accept me at second hand if not at first hand. And thus all is for the best in the best of all possible worlds."

This rather violent diatribe will probably cause less impression than might be expected, because those arguing the case today are far more interested in what they themselves have got to say than in anything Mr. Shaw may say. The Frenchman likes to be master in his own house and choose his pleasures, artistic or otherwise, as may best please himself, for he believes that it is better to reign in hell than serve in heaven, so that all the very best advice, even from so high a source as Mr. Shaw, leaves him utterly indifferent. The French would, I am sure, even be willing to admit that Mr. Shaw is perfectly right when he tells them that the loss is theirs, not his. They just don't want advice from foreigners, that is all. This attitude may be annoying to the foreigner (including Mr. Shaw) who unselfishly desires to improve the mind of the French. But it is, after all, an attitude which perhaps finds its justification in results, for while it withholds some things which are good, it raises a barrier against a great deal more which is bad. And that which is really good filters its way through, anyhow.

Another thing for which Mr. Shaw does not allow—and, indeed, it is difficult to see how a professional iconoclast like him could allow for it—is the religious veneration of the Frenchman and his passionate love of everything which is connected with the idea of *patrie.* He may care little for religion, the fact that Jehanne has been made a saint of the Church may mean nothing to him; but if he thinks that she is in any way being attacked he is up in arms at once to defend her against all comers—and especially against all foreign comers. She is sacred to him because of his chivalrous love of France. Probably, indeed, it would be impossible to please a good Frenchman at all by a play about Joan of Arc, just as it would be unthinkable to please a good Catholic with a play in which the central figure was the Virgin Mary. Even if there were no intent at disrespect, it would create a disagreeable feeling.

It was not very long ago that Barbey d'Aurevilly fought a duel with an opponent who had insulted the Virgin in his presence. That may have been a pose—but it is the same pose which took the cadets of Saint-Cyr into action in August, 1914, wearing white gloves and brilliant red and white plumes in their *képis.* It may be a pose, and Mr. Shaw may laugh at it. But it is there, and because of it, whatever may eventually be the case concerning the rest of his works, his "Joan" will never go down here.

I should like to add in conclusion that I have not seen the play, nor have I read it. I don't have to. I know the French.

III/Bernard Shaw's *Saint Joan*

The audience bewildered me.

At the première of *Saint Joan,* by George Bernard Shaw, I felt myself a real foreigner, suddenly brought face to face with this mysterious America of yours. Though it was not altogether bewilderment, I felt, as I went home from the play, that I had learned something interesting and unexpected about the psychology of the American.

During the first three acts of *Saint Joan* I noted with great satisfaction the rapt attention, the shrewd and intelligent smiling, the hearty laughter and the sincere applause with which every shaft of wit or irony in this admirable and inimitable Shavian dialogue was welcomed by an audience keenly aware of the artistic treat that was spread before it. But then came the fourth act, which seemed to me the best in the whole play—the trial and condemnation of the Maid—where Shaw's dramatic power rises to its height, and where he really succeeds in awakening a deep and intense emotion. I had been expecting, in view of the preceding cordiality of the audience, to see people jump to their feet and break into unrestrained applause. Nothing of the kind! I looked around the theatre in surprise. It was as though I had been suddenly transported into a world wholly unknown and incomprehensible to me. The spectators sat for the most part in silence.

For a moment or two I was oppressed with a sudden sense of mortification at my own incompetence. But then my own feelings were

Originally titled "Pirandello Distills Shaw," in the New York *Times Sunday Magazine,* January 13, 1924, pp. 7-12. The translator is unknown.

so great that I could not help asking a question that was a question half
of protest to the friends about me. Had that scene been a failure? Had
no one been moved by that almost divine explosion of passion in the
Maid just before she was dragged away to the stake? I received in reply
a suggestion that few had applauded for the very reason that the
emotion in the audience was so great. And then, indeed, I was more
surprised than ever.

I am sure that, had an act as powerful as the fourth act of *Saint
Joan* been produced on any one of the numerous Italian stages, all
the people present would have jumped to their feet, even before the
curtain fell, to start a frenzied applause that would have called the
actors, and possibly the author, to the footlights, not once, but many
times, to receive the gratitude of the audience for the anguish it had
suffered, and its joy for having witnessed such a triumph of art. But
here, on the other hand, a certain sense of modesty seemed to be
uppermost. A certain sense of shame at being deeply moved, a need of
hiding emotion, and of getting rid of it as soon as possible. To applaud
would have meant confessing this emotion to one's self and then
publicly to others; and few seemed willing thus to betray themselves.

But then, to tell the truth, I was not as well satisfied as I had been at
the applause during the three preceding acts, though these, in a somewhat different way, were just as deserving. As an Italian, I could not
think it fair that an author should be applauded when he makes us
laugh, and rewarded with silence when he brings tears to our eyes.
Perhaps the reason is that it is harder to make an Italian laugh than it is
to make him weep.

At any rate, I have a strong impression that for some time past
George Bernard Shaw has been growing more and more serious. He has
always believed in himself, and with good reason. But in a number of
plays, after his first successes, he did not seem to believe very much in
what he was doing. This, at least, may properly be suspected, since it
cannot be denied that in his eagerness to defend his own intellectual
position against the so-called 'bourgeois morality', he not infrequently
abandoned all pretensions to seriousness as an artist. Now, however, he
seems to be believing less in himself, and more in what he is doing.
From the epilogue of this drama on Joan of Arc we may gather almost
explicitly the reason for which Shaw wrote it. This world, he seems to

say, is not made for saints to live in. We must take the people who live in it for what they are, since it is not vouchsafed them to be anything else.

In fact, as we look carefully and deeply at this work of Shaw, taken as a whole, we cannot help detecting in it that curious half-humorous melancholy which is peculiar to the disillusioned idealist. Shaw has always had too keen a sense of reality not to be aware of the conflict between it and his social and moral ideals. The various phases of reality, as they were yesterday, as they are today, as they will be tomorrow, come forward in the persons who represent them before the ideal phantom of Joan (now a Saint without her knowing it). Each of these type persons justifies his own manner of being, and confesses the sin of which he was guilty, but in such a way as to show that he is unable really to mend his ways—so true is it that each is today as he was yesterday, and will be tomorrow as he is today. Joan listens to them all, but she is not angry. She has for them just a tolerant pity. She can only pray that the world may some time be made beautiful enough to be a worthy abode for the saints!

This new tolerance and pity rise from the most secret depths of poetry that exist in Shaw. Whenever, instead of tolerating, instead of pitying, he loses his temper at the shock of reality against his ideals, and then, for fear of betraying his anger—which would be bad mannered— begins to harass himself and his hearers with the dazzling brilliancy of his paradoxes, Shaw, the artist properly speaking, suffers more or less seriously—he falls to the level of the *jeu d'esprit* which is amusing in itself, though it irremediably spoils the work of art. I may cite in point a passage in the second act of *Saint Joan* where the Archbishop expatiates on the differences between fraud and miracles. 'Frauds deceive,' says he. 'An event which creates faith does not deceive, therefore it is not a fraud but a miracle'. Such word play is for amusement only. A work that would do something more than amuse must always respect the deeper demands of art, and so respecting these, the witticism is no longer a witticism but true art.

In none of Shaw's work that I can think of have considerations of art been so thoroughly respected as in *Saint Joan*. The four acts of this drama begin, as they must begin, with Joan's request for soldiers of Robert de Baudricourt to use in driving the English from 'the sweet

land of France'. And they end, as they must end, with the trial and
execution of Joan. Shaw calls this play a chronicle. In fact, the drama is
built up episode by episode, moment by moment, some of them rigor-
ously particular and free from generality—truly in the style of the
chroniclers—though usually they tend to be what I call deliberate
'constructiveness'. The hens have not been laying, when suddenly they
begin to lay. The wind has long been blowing from the east, and
suddenly it begins blowing from the west. Two miracles! Then there
are other simple, naïve things, such as the recognition of the 'blood
royal' in the third act, which likewise seems to be a miracle.

But these moments are interspersed with other moments of irony and
satire, of which either the Church or the English are the victims.
However, this attempt to present the chronicle inside what is really
history does not seem to me quite as happy as it was in *Caesar and
Cleopatra*. In *Saint Joan*, history, or rather character historically conceived, weighs a bit too heavily on the living fluid objectivity of the
chronicle, and the events in the play somehow lose that sense of the
unexpected which is the breath of true life. We know in advance where
we are going to come out. The characters, whether historical or typical,
do not quite free themselves from the fixity that history has forced upon
them and from the significant rôle they are to play in history.

Joan herself, who is presented to us as a fresh creature of the open
fields, full of burning faith and self-confidence, remains that way from
the beginning to the end of the play: and she makes a little too obvious
her intention not to be reciting a historical rôle and to remain that dear,
frank, innocent, inspired child that she is. Yes, Joan, as she really was in
her own little individual history, must have been much as Shaw imagined her. But he seems to look on her once and for all, so to speak,
quite without regard for the various situations in which she will meet
life in the course of the story.

And she is kept thus simple and unilinear by the author just to bring
her airy, refreshing ingenuousness into contrast with the artificial,
sophisticated—or, as I say, 'deliberate' or 'constructed'—complexity of
her accusers. There is, in other words, something mechanical, fore-
ordained, fixed, about her character. Much more free and unobstructed
in his natural impulses, much more independent of any deliberate
restraints, and accordingly much more 'living' (from my point of view)

is the Chaplain, de Stogumber, the truly admirable creation in this drama, and a personage on which Shaw has surely expended a great deal of affectionate effort.

At a certain moment Joan's faith in her 'voices' is shaken. And this charming little creature, hitherto steadfastly confident in the divine inspiration which has many times saved her from death in battle, is suddenly filled with terror at the torment awaiting her. She says she is ready to sign the recantation of all that she has said and done. And she does sign it. But then, on learning from her judges that the sentence of death is only to be changed into a sentence of life imprisonment, she seizes the document in a sudden burst of emotion and tears it to pieces. 'Death is far better than this!' she cries. She could never live without the free air of the fields, the beauty of the green meadows, the warm light of the sun. And she falls fainting into the arms of the executioners, who drag her off to the stake.

At this moment Shaw carries his protagonists to a summit of noble poetry with which any other author would be content; and we may be sure that any other author would have lowered the curtain on this scene. But Shaw cannot resist the pressure and the inspiration of the life he well knows must be surging in such circumstances in his other character—the Chaplain. He rushes on toward a second climax of not less noble poetry, depicting with magnificent elan the mad remorse, the hopeless penitence of Stogumber, thus adding to our first crisis of exquisite anguish another not less potent and overwhelming.

Rarely has George Bernard Shaw attained higher altitudes of poetic emotion than here. There is a truly great poet in Shaw; but this combative Anglo-Irishman is often willing to forget that he is a poet, so interested is he in being a citizen of his country, or a man of the twentieth century society, with a number of respectable ideas to defend, a number of sermons to preach, a number of antagonists to rout from the intellectual battlefield. But here, in *Saint Joan,* the poet comes into his own again, with only a subordinate rôle left, as a demanded compensation, to irony and satire. To be sure *Saint Joan* has all the savor and all the attractiveness of Shaw's witty polemical dialogue. But for all of these keen and cutting thrusts to left and right in Shaw's usual style of propaganda, *Saint Joan* is a work of poetry from beginning to end.

This play represents in marvellous fashion what, among so many elements of negation, is the positive element, indeed the fundamental underpinning, in the character, thought and art of this great writer—an outspoken Puritanism, which brooks no go-betweens and no mediations between man and God; a vigorous and independent vital energy, that frees itself restlessly and with joyous scorn from all the stupid and burdensome shackles of habit, routine and tradition, to conquer for itself a natural law more consonant with the poet's own being, and therefore more rational and more sound. Joan, in fact, cries to her judges: 'If the Church orders me to declare that all I have done and said, that all the visions and revelations I have had were not from God, then that is impossible. I will not declare it for anything in the world. What God made me do, I will never go back on; and what He has commanded, or shall command, I will not fail to do, in spite of any man alive. That is what I mean by impossible. And in case the Church should bid me do anything contrary to the command I have from God, I will not consent to it, no matter what it may be'. Joan, at bottom, quite without knowing it, and still declaring herself a faithful daughter of the Church, is a Puritan, like Shaw himself—affirming her own life impulse, her unshakable, her even tyrannical will to live, by accepting death itself. Joan, like Shaw, cannot exist without a life that is free and fruitful. When she tears up her recantation in the face of her deaf and blind accusers, she exemplifies the basic germ of Shaw's art, which is the germ also of his spiritual life.

IV/A Super-Flapper

Mr. George Bernard Shaw's play, *Saint Joan,* at the Garrick Theatre, brings us a Shavian Joan. She is a super-flapper, a pert hoyden, who skips about and calls the Dauphin "Charley" and Dunois, the Bastard of Orleans, "Jack". The play is tedious and loquacious, a mere historical scaffolding upon which the dramatist drapes the old Shavian gonfalons of wit and skilful lampoonery. Humanity, insists the amiable G. B. S., was the same in Domrémy as in any village today; militarism—that is always the same; the English, well they never were anything anyway and they haven't changed; the Talkers—they will talk on forever; and as for St. Joan, surely her conduct needs explanation: we will begin with the "Voices". And they have set speeches, one for the hour, another for the quarter and a different one for the half hour. Poor Joan! She hasn't a chance so far as the play goes and she is acted at the Garrick by a very young and wholly inaedquate Irish-American actress, who is never for a single thrilling instant either the peasant maid of Domrémy, or the Maid. This Joan never heard Ste. Catherine, Saint Margaret and the archangel Michael speaking to her out of the green branches over her head; she was never the Maid glorious in white armour on her black charger leading her men to battle, crowning the Dauphin at Rheims, dying amid the flames at Rouen. We cannot even think of this "flapper" as the Joan of Bastien-Lepage. Neither the splendid production given the play by the Theater Guild, nor the notable cast, can galvanize it into life. If Mr. Shaw, the protagonist of

Untitled in the original. *Transatlantic Review,* I (March, 1924), 73–74.

Shavianism, had been willing to sink the protagonist in Mr. G. B. S., the artist, while he wrote *Saint Joan,* the result might have been as satisfying on the boards as Chesterton's life of St. Francis of Assisi is between boards. Many critics have praised the play but a few have been honest and cried loudly like wise children: "The king is naked."

Much is made in the play of the fact that Joan wears men's clothing. What she actually wears resembles a rather modest Coney Island bathing suit. The epilogue brings Joan back to the Dauphin in a dream or vision twenty-five years after the flames of Rouen. One by one her old friends and enemies drift back into the bedchamber of the Dauphin where Joan has appeared. Some are still in the flesh, others are out of it. The last to appear is a man pulled by a Shavian time-machine out of the future, the year 1920. He tells Joan that she has been canonized. Since she is a saint and can perform miracles, she offers to come back to earth in the flesh. Her offer is not well received. Warwick goes; the Bishop of Beauvais goes; Dunois goes; one by one they all slink away. The soldier who had given her the sticks tied together for a cross on the day of her burning stays awhile. Then he is startled by the chime of the clock and is snatched away to hell. The Dauphin turns his back upon Joan and goes to sleep. Mr. Shaw means to tell us, doubtless, that if the Maid came back today she would suffer martyrdom again; that there is no green island or quiet valley of this savage planet that is yet ready to receive saints and angels in mortal flesh.

V/*St Joan:* The Theme and the Drama

St Joan is a play of many and splendid merits. It is immensely serious and extremely entertaining; it is a magnificent effort of intellectual energy and full of pathos and sympathy; it is long but it never flags; it is deep, and I am by no means sure that I have got, or that I am going to get, to the bottom of it; it is a play it would be disgraceful to treat inadequately—I shall return to it next week. I intend now to make only a few preliminary remarks. We are lifted on waves of emotion to be dashed on thought. Only a languid mind could fail to find in it intellectual excitement, only a very carefully protected sensibility could escape being touched and disturbed—but I must add a proviso to that. The theme of the play is religion; therefore to be touched and disturbed by it in any appreciable degree the spectator, some time or other, must have experienced religious emotions himself; and further, having done so, he must not loathe them as some people loathe amorous emotions after having been dipped in them. He may distrust religious emotion, dislike exceedingly many of its manifestations (as, indeed, I do myself), but he must know what kind of a feeling it is and how it can draw and drag at the heart; otherwise he will neither apprehend the whole, nor feel the force of its most dramatic moments.

Of course much remains which a spectator who lacked such experience could and would enjoy; but *St Joan* is not a chronicle play. It is not primarily an historic drama. It is a religious play. Mr Shaw, need-

The New Statesman April 5, 12, 1924; reprinted in MacCarthy's *Shaw* (London, 1951), 162-70.

less to say, has a very powerful and dramatic imagination, but the historic side of it is not the strongest. Has he a love of the past? I believe he would scout the idea. The question would seem to him equivalent to asking him if he had a love of bric-à-brac. I do not believe he cares a dump for things that are dead, gone and changed. The first thing he invariably does when his setting is in the past, is to rub off his period the patina of time (*vide* Caesar and Cleopatra); he will scrub and scrub till contemporary life begins to gleam through surface strangenesses and oddities. He is confident that he has reached historic truth when he has succeeded in scratching historic characters till he finds beneath a modern man in fancy dress. He is careful of historic facts in this play; he never introduces anything equivalent to making Cleopatra play billiards; but the play is full of spiritual anachronisms. The atmosphere is not that of the Middle Ages. Let me give some examples: when Joan is told that her voices are the work of her imagination, she replies, "God speaks to us through our imaginations." No idea could be more foreign to the Middle Ages than that, or more typical of the latest modern religious 'heresy', of which Mr Shaw himself is the exponent. Again, the Earl of Warwick is a purely eighteenth century nobleman; he is not even a Renaissance character. I think he is closely related to General Burgoyne. The delightful study of a common English type, Warwick's clerical secretary, is brother of our old friend Britannicus—of the Bishop of London, and many a shell-making patriotic parson. But does all this matter? To my mind not a bit. It merely substitutes another kind of interest, and one, too, closer to the emotions of the majority of people. Mr Shaw would jump at the definition of his St Joan as 'a modern heretic'. I can fancy him saying: 'Why, trying to pick a hole in my work you have blundered on my central point.' I know I have. Twice in the course of the play Joan is defined as 'a Protestant'. The essence of Protestantism is that the authority of the individual's religious experience is final for him. No matter if disagreement and chaos result, it is the highest duty of everyone to obey, like Joan, his 'Voices'. He must listen attentively, he must live so as to sharpen his hearing; but when he is sure of what they say he must obey. God does not speak through tradition or organized religions, but is resident in the hearts and minds of men. In fact what we call our hearts, our minds, are, according to Mr Shaw, the spirit of

God Himself, a baffled, disturbed, struggling but inevitably emerging force, and—this is the accompanying emotion of such convictions and the source of their consoling and sustaining power—a force necessarily triumphant in the end. The confusion of voices does not matter; it is inevitable. In so far as the voices are genuine they are efforts, some of them perhaps futile, of the Spirit of the Universe itself to find a way. The first duty of man is to make himself a channel for its passage. If he does so he is a 'saint', and though he may be burned, he will have a strange power even over those who burn him or mock him. And what is the test of 'genuineness'? That is the crux. Organised religions say—we and our traditions; the statesman says the test is, do these saints or do they not threaten the social order; the people, whether they do or do not protest against our tyrants; the nationalist, whether they do or do not inspire patriotism; the soldier, whether they do or do not make for victory; the Gallios, whether they do or do not make for pleasure and peace. The Church is prepared to accept a canonised Joan once her dynamic and incalculably disruptive force has spent itself or been destroyed; while the fairer of its spokesmen are prepared to admit, even as they condemn her, that she may be better and more religious than themselves; the statesman that she is far from ignoble; the soldier that she alone could put the right spirit into fighting men, and they are ready to use her as long as desperate courage is a means to victory. But none of them want her back.

Joan, or rather the spirit within her, is shown in conflict with each of these powers and different points of view, and this conflict is the essence of the drama. But I must repeat for the sake of emphasis that this is not primarily an historical play. It is the tragedy of Joan herself of course as well, of a real girl whom we see before our eyes, who did the things we hear of on the stage, who triumphed, then failed and was burnt. But its central theme is wider; it is the struggle of religious inspiration against the world, down the ages, which, Mr Shaw would assert, was always essentially the same struggle, whether the world's antagonist is Jesus, Joan, Huss, Galileo, or one of the many lesser men and women. It is a struggle which cannot be won in any complete sense and yet can never be lost. The spiritual and intellectual anachronisms are therefore in a sense artistic merits, for they help to generalise the case. The last words are the cry of Joan as she appears in the King's dream, when each of her different opponents in turn acknowledges the

beneficence of her inspiration, then wills that after all she shall never
return again; 'O God, when will your world be fit for saints to live in.'
She is left as alone as she was in her defeat, as alone as she was, in spite
of appearances, in her victory.

The extraordinary intellectual merit of this play is the force and
fairness with which the case of her opponents is put; the startling
clarity with which each of them states it, and consequently our instan-
taneous recognition of its relation to the religious instinct. One of Mr
Shaw's most remarkable gifts has always been this rare generosity. It is
odd, but he has never drawn a wicked character—plenty of characters
who do wicked things, but not one wicked man. He has never believed
in the devil, only in blindness, inertia and stupidity; faults so widely
spread it seems a failure of common sense to distinguish particular
people by special abhorrence.

The other extraordinary intellectual merit of the play is the intensity
of its religious emotion and the grasp the dramatist shows of the human
pathos of one who is filled with it, as well as showing his or her
immunity from requiring anything like pity. It is probably I think, the
greatest of Shaw's plays. How these qualities are brought out, how the
dramatist has put his theme in perspective and how his intentions were
interpreted I will discuss next week.

There is no longer any doubt about the reception of this play. Last
week I reserved all discussion of its dramatic qualities and the acting,
and confined myself to an exposition of its theme. One point, however,
I must repeat before adding further comments. The object of the play is
to show Joan, or rather the spirit within her, in conflict with those who
at first make use of her and then destroy her, and although the tragedy
we watch is the tragedy of the girl we see before our eyes, who has a
close resemblance to the real saint (though it is not hard to imagine a
closer), the aim of the play is not primarily a reconstruction of the past,
nor its primary aim to move us to pity. As the epilogue, to which
several dramatic critics have objected, shows, the essence of the theme
is the struggle of religious inspiration against established religions,
against the patriot, the statesman and the indifferent—above all,
against the Catholic Church, the strongest of them. In a sense the play
can be described as an exceedingly powerful Protestant pamphlet, the

essence of Protestantism being reliance upon internal authority (Joan's faith in her Voices) as against the authority of tradition and a corporate religion which also claim inspiration. Mr Shaw states the case of the Church through the mouths of the Bishop of Beauvais (admirably acted by Mr Eugene Leahy), the Inquisitor and the Archbishop of Rheims (Mr Robert Cunningham's ecclesiastical aplomb and deportment are perfect) with extraordinary fairness. Although the spectacle of the heresy-hunters in the trial scene is painful and odious in the last degree, the gentleness of the Inquisitor's address adding a peculiarly sinister quality to it, the speeches of both the Bishop and the Inquisitor make it quite clear that they are not actuated by cruelty, but that the Church itself is at stake in this argument. Joan must submit. The impulse of the sceptic is to shout 'So much the worse for the Church. If it can only preserve itself by torturing and burning a girl like Joan, in the name of everything that is good, let it crumble and fall.' Both the Bishop and Inquisitor assert that in that case much worse barbarities, let alone utter confusion, would be let loose on the world. Mr Shaw presents their case, but because the play does not recall vividly the atmosphere of the Middle Ages, the strength of that case is hardly felt by the spectators. The mad credulity of the times is, it is true, suggested by the ease with which, in the first scene, the Sire de Baudricourt is convinced that Joan is inspired, for that the hens should begin to lay eggs as soon as he has granted her request to send her to the Dauphin with men at arms, is proof for him that her Voices are from God. In Scene 2 her recognition of the Dauphin, and in Scene 3, by the bank of the Loire, a sudden wished-for change of wind, has the same effect on others. What more, you may say, could Mr Shaw do in the short space allowed by a play? But the effect of these incidents on the atmosphere is neutralised by his peculiar dramatic methods of making each character speak with a self-conscious awareness of the orientation of his own point of view, which is utterly foreign to the times. The method has enormous advantages, but it has that drawback. Further, none of these miracles suggest by their nature the vital importance of holding the fort of authority against heretics—they are harmless. To reinforce emotionally (intellectually Mr Shaw has done the Church ample justice) the case of Joan's persecutors, we could have been reminded with advantage of some of the horrors and absurdities which the hundreds of 'inspired' men and women were perpetually sacrificing their lives to propagate. Not many years after Joan's execution Gilles de Rais (he appears in Scene 2), under whose special protection the Maid was placed and who had won the name of a knight without fear or reproach, was attempting to get into touch with supernatural powers by cutting out the hearts and gouging eyes of innumerable children.

This, however, is minor criticism, for in the trial scene we are, after all, reminded by the speeches that the Church is engaged in a life and death struggle with paganism, witchcraft and State religion; only what has gone before has not made that fact as vivid as it might be. The only point at which it seemed to me a false note was struck was the moment when Joan recants her recantation. Her submission when faced with death is very moving, but when her sentence is changed to imprisonment for life she bursts out into a speech about nature and freedom, the hills and the sky, and tears up her recantation. This speech is the false note; to Joan the Mass and the Church were infinitely more important than lambs and larks or communion with nature. Mr Shaw has made her out more of a modern Protestant than any facts warrant. The speech, too, lacks that verbal beauty which alone could make it dramatically moving. The substance of poetry is often present in Mr Shaw's work (vide Scene 3, the kingfisher, the boy, and the general), but verbal magic never.

The most admirable and perfect scenes in the play are the two which immediately precede the trial scene, magnificent as that is, in spite of this one false note. They are discussions or conversations, and they are splendid examples of the critical truth that such scenes can contribute to dramatic effect as directly as scenes of action. Without them the trial scene would lose half its significance. In the first of them, the Earl of Warwick's tent in the English camp, the Earl and the Bishop of Beauvais decide the Maid's fate between them. Their reasons are bitterly antagonistic, and the point of view of the all-too-simple patriotic Englishman, Captain de Stogumber (Mr Lewis Casson played him to perfection, and Mr Lyall Swete as Warwick brought out the points of his part excellently), acts as a foil to these two subtle minds. The Bishop sees that Joan in her success has begun to act independently of the authority of the Church; the statesman that her mystic devotion to the King is a political heresy as dangerous to the real rules of the land, the aristocracy. If the land belongs to the King, and the King is to give it to God and hold it for Him, where do the great territorials come in? At the bottom of the religious nationalism of the Maid lies an appeal to the people. In Scene 5 in the ambulatory of Rheims Cathedral, after the coronation of the Dauphin, we see the Maid among her friends, who are soon to become her passive enemies. The archbishop reproves her for her independent pride—she is no longer the submissive daughter of the Church; the King wants to make a treaty with the English (God's enemies to Joan for the time being); the general, Dunois (Bastard of Orleans), explains to her that he knows exactly how much their own joint success has been due to her miraculous aid and how much to human agency and his own generalship. If she persists in moving on Paris in obedience to her Voices, he will not risk a single soldier's life to help her, or to save her. The time for reckless courage is over; he is grateful and admires her as a soldier, but she must be put aside as an instrument which has served its purpose. We know what is going to happen, of course, the tragedy which is to come. There is a fine dramatic irony therefore in these scenes, beside their effectiveness in bringing out the theme of the whole play—the conflict between religious emotion and the world. In the latter scene Miss Sybil Thorndike is at her very best. She is an actress with a very definite personality. It is difficult to judge, after seeing her, what latitude of interpretation the part actually allows. All that can be said is that her personality emphasises the insistive, energetic, almost pert traits in the Maid as Mr Shaw conceives her. Some of the critics and some of the public have refused to accept a Joan who calls the Dauphin 'Charlie', and shows so little superficial reverence for that semi-sacred personage. There is an excuse for this dramatic exaggeration. We know that the Maid 'theed' and 'thoued' the Dauphin and addressed him as *gentil Dauphin,* but that these peasant phrases and 'angelic familiarities' expressed the attitude of mind which Mr Shaw's paraphrases of them suggest, is doubtful. Still in any case the latter do convey what he wants to convey, the fearlessness and complete disregard of worldly estimates on the part of one who is filled with a divine mission. That the Maid sometimes answered her accusers with tartness is a fact, and Miss Thorndike does so most effectively; but the sweetness and simplicity of the Maid's replies and demeanour in the trial scene she does not bring out. Her distress, her alertness, her courage, she does drive home, but whether the fault lies in the part itself or in the interpretation, 'the angelic side' of the Maid is obscured. Mr. Shaw so dreads the sentimental (when it is not a brusque denial of sentiment, itself sentimental), is so desirous that our response to beauty of character should be as ascetic as possible, that I am inclined to lay the blame on him in the first place, but there is no doubt that Miss Thorndike stresses this aversion to anything which might move us, first by its loveliness, only afterwards by its significance.

In a cast which is remarkable (and thanks to Mr Ricketts the costumes continually delight the eye), no part is more excellently played than the Dauphin (Mr Thesiger). I do not know enough history to check the portrait, but the one scene in which the Maid's power of inspiring others did not seem convincing was the dialogue between her and the Dauphin.

↙ EDMUND WILSON

VI/*Saint Joan:* The Unexpected in Shaw

No one was ever more perturbed than Bernard Shaw by the disgraces
and the failures of humanity; they have indeed been his chief preoccu-
pation; but no one has ever been clearer than he as to exactly what is
causing the trouble and exactly what is necessary to prevent it. His
plays, though they have constituted exceedingly complex presentations
of the conflicting prejudices and interests of society, have almost invariably ended cheerfully enough with a precise indication of the solution—and the preface has usually supplied an even more explicit analysis concluding with a clause by clause program for action.

In *Major Barbara*, for example, we have at the end a sort of allegori-
cal group of Religion wedded to Culture taking over Industry; in
Androcles and the Lion, Brute Force and Humanitarianism defying
Tyranny; and in *Getting Married* the unknown spiritual quantity which
will satisfy the whole set of ill-balanced marital equations is definitely
discovered, just before the curtain, to be that of "Christian fellowship."
A constructive critic was precisely what Mr. Shaw was—constructive
almost to excess.

In Mr. Shaw's world before the war there were no insoluble problems. Political and economic salvation—which implied all other
kinds—were unarguably to be effected by Socialism and Socialism was
to be effected through the orderly process of education and penetration
undertaken by the Fabian Society. There was much indignation in

Originally titled "Bernard Shaw Since the War," *The New Republic*, August 27, 1924,
pp. 380–81. Retitled by the editor.

39

Shaw but no real pessimism. And it was impossible for him to take
other dramatists seriously when they wrote in scepticism or despair:
Shakespeare's tragedies, for all their genius, he has always regarded as
fundamentally unsatisfactory because they offer no constructive criticism of life and Molière's masterpiece, *Le Misanthrope,* he has charac-
terized as the author's "dullest and worst play" because, like *Hamlet* or
Antony and Cleopatra, it presents a desperate impasse of character
which is obviously insusceptible of being resolved by the application of
a Shavian formula. For all his intelligence, the tendency of Shaw has
always been to simplify too much—to substitute a sort of Puritan
morality having its sanction in the Bible, which he was reacting against.

All this does still, of course, to some extent hold true. In the preface
to *Back to Methuselah,* for example, he seems to suppose that the "Life
Force" presented in that "Metabiological Pentateuch" somehow constitutes a substitute for that religion which he finds so disastrously lacking
in the modern world. But, on the whole, he has unmistakably since the
War shown signs both of a longer view of human affairs and of a deeper
feeling for human nature. His latest plays do fall short, to be sure, of
the electricity and vividness of the old ones, but on the other hand, if
they are somewhat less sharp, they are also somewhat less cocky and, in
any case, present a relief from the sterile formula of such comedies as
Misalliance and *Overruled* which no amount of intellectual energy
could make either convincing as life or acceptable as art. For one thing,
both in *Heartbreak House* and the last section of *Back to Methuselah*
there appears, however unwinningly conveyed, some genuine feeling
for the disappointments and enthusiasms of lovers—a subject which,
with scarcely even an exception in the instance of *Candida,* he has
insisted upon regarding as a lot of romantic nonsense intended to
stultify what at its best could be conceded as hardly more than an
agreeable biological necessity. *Heartbreak House* is perhaps the first
play of Shaw's which actually has any heartbreak in it, and it differs
also from almost all its predecessors in failing to end with quite the neat
Q. E. D. which has usually closed his demonstrations. Just as in some of
his political speeches after the War and his published lecture on Rus-
kin's Politics he seemed finally to have become capable of doubting the
ultimate efficacy of the methods of the Fabians—so in *Back to Methuselah* he takes us for the first time beyond the best that Socialism may

be expected to do, through the regression of European society to a sort of unorganized Arcadia and to the final enfranchisement of the human spirit as a set of vortices in space—a solution which disposes of the problem of life only by announcing it all to begin over again and a triumph which must be admitted to give rise to feelings of horror and despair.

Now in *Saint Joan* we get no such ultimate victory of the saint as we did in *Androcles and the Lion:* on the contrary, what is unexpected in Shaw, we find the forces of tradition and authority represented as equally intelligent and morally admirable with the heretic and the rebel and, instead of being left with the reassuring inference that the catastrophe of Joan—like the disillusionment of Major Barbara or the embitterment of Vivie Warren—is merely a sacrifice which will immediately bear fruit in a more intelligent program of social reconstruction, we are left with the moral that the same thing may happen again. "My God! my God! why hast thou forsaken me?" cries Major Barbara in her hour of anguish; but immediately afterwards she readjusts her ideas of God in such a way as still to find Him at the helm of her readjusted world. "How long, O Lord, how long?" cries Saint Joan; but they are her last words in the play.

Not that Shaw has been seduced from his rôle of social critic by the purely pathetic possibilities of Joan. He has managed one or two capital dramatic moments, of a kind rather rare with him, in which it is predominantly the personality of Joan which holds us—such as the scene in which she rouses the Dauphin and his partisans to follow her lead against the English. But primarily *Saint Joan,* like Shaw's other plays, is a criticism of society—only longer-sighted and less hopeful than has been his wont. Most of the really thrilling passages are those in which we feel the great forces of human history at work—the scene in the tent between Warwick and Cauchon in which the Bishop prophesies the downfall of Europe as the result of the disruption of the Catholic Church and the latter scenes in which we realize Joan's predicament caught between the institution to which she is dangerous and the nation which she has helped to defeat. I do not see how those critics who have objected to the Epilogue can really understand what the play is about: if the Epilogue were to go, the tent scene would have to go, too—as would also the Inquisitor's speech and a great deal more;

we should, in fact, have to have a different play built on different lines, and with Joan's individual tragedy and not human history as its theme.

Saint Joan, like Shaw's other plays, however—though in a somewhat less degree than many of them—is not free from the characteristic over-rationalizations of the social historian turned dramatist. Shaw is reported to have said that every time he saw a play of Tchekov's he felt like throwing all his own into the fire and it is quite easy to see why: Tchekov is able to have his characters convey to us their aims, their prejudices and their places in society not only with an incomparable economy which is no less telling than Shaw's prolixity, but also without ever doing violence to the likelihood of the way in which they are made to reveal themselves: whereas Shaw has been largely restricted to having his characters make out logically reasoned cases for them and defend them with debaters' skill. This is true even in the case of Saint Joan, who sometimes seems disconcertingly out of key with the naive faith of the middle ages. In one passage particularly she is allowed to rationalize her point of view beyond all bounds of probability or dramatic propriety. When Baudricourt assures her that her divine Voices are the products of her imagination, she replies all too sensibly, "Of course. That is how the messages of God come to us." And Shaw has overexplained not only in the case of Joan but also to some extent even in the cases of those other characters who may more reasonably be supposed to have understood what they were doing: the Bishop of Beauvais and the Earl of Warwick are made perfectly aware both of the functions they fill in contemporary civilization and of their subsequent places in history and even designate the tendencies they are discussing and which were then in their infancy with names like Protestantism and Nationalism which could only have existed when these were mature. Shaw says in this connection:

> It is the business of the stage to make its figures more intelligible to themselves than they would be in real life; for by no other means can they be made intelligible to the audience ... the play would be unintelligible if I had not endowed them (the Earl of Warwick, the Inquisitor and Bishop) with enough of this consciousness to enable them to explain their attitude to the twentieth century ... beyond this neither drama nor history can go in my hands.

This last sentence, though evidently not intended for one, reads like a confession of limitation and I believe, in fact, that this over-explicitness marks Shaw's worst weakness as a dramatic artist—his imperfect grasp of "character in action." The business of the dramatist should be precisely, as Tchekov does, to find a means of making things intelligible without suggesting to the audience that it is hearing a book read instead of witnessing a real event. To have kept out the language of written history would have been to heighten the illusion of reality, and to have heightened the illusion of reality would have been to intensify the drama.

But even if *Saint Joan*—like *Back to Methuselah*—had never been intended by its author to be acted, it would still be a work of extraordinary interest. What these later plays of Shaw's remind one of rather than of any other acted drama are the series of *Dialogues Philosophiques* which Renan wrote in his old age; these two bodies of work present some striking resemblances and it is interesting to compare them: both are dramas of ideas and in some cases of the same ideas but, beside Renan, who has traveled in his life-time over the whole geography of ideas of humanity and who has learned a polite hesitation about preferring one to another, Shaw even in his later and more tolerant phases shows a little provincial and harshly Protestant: such historical values as the point of view of the mediaeval church with which Renan was familiar from boyhood are brought to our attention by Shaw at this late date with something of an air of excitement and surprise and the scepticism of all politics and politicians at which Renan had arrived before the end of the last century comes to Shaw in *Back to Methuselah* as the last disillusion of old age. Yet beside Renan, Shaw shows a kind of fire which sometimes gives a superiority to limited ideas over more learned and wiser ones. Shaw's demonstrations and programs and systems are probably much less important than his critics think them. What is important is the imagination with which they are illustrated and the intensity with which they are expressed. It is these which have really spoken to us in Shaw and which continue to speak to us even now that his brand-new, one-hundred-percent-efficient social system has begun to lose credit not only with us but with the inventor himself.

🖋 J. VAN KAN

VII/Bernard Shaw's *Saint Joan:*
An Historical Point of View

I

The appearance of the long-awaited chronicle play is greeted as an event both in the English world of letters and in the literature of Joan of Arc.

Bernard Shaw's *Saint Joan* is the first serious attempt to give a dramatic rendering of the figure of France's sublime heroine based upon a truly historical foundation. For as such none of the early or later French dramatic—we might even add epic and lyric—renderings of this marvellous material can be reckoned. They are all, without exception, products of an imagination which has refused to be bridled by rigid facts; which always interweaves real events with the dreamings of the writer, and which frequently, for the sake of harmonising the combination, has even invented the events themselves. Moreover, with the exception of Charles Péguy's *Mistère de la Charité de Jeanne d'Arc,* none of them is a work of art of any importance, which in itself is sufficient reason for not dwelling upon them.

Neither does the First Part of *Henry VI* come under consideration from this point of view. Shakespeare reproduces the English conception of the Maid of his own day; and that conception was no other than the obstinate echo of the representation that had been needed to lend its great political significance to the trial of Joan of Arc, and at the same time render the abominable legalised murder acceptable to those in

Fortnightly Review, CXVIII (July, 1925), 36–46.

sympathy with England and Burgundy. This representation had been purely political, and in Shakespeare's day its reproduction was not based upon historical research. The only ground for what was offered as history was tradition; and this tradition itself was drawn from political sources and also—but in a much smaller degree—from hate and vengefulness.

Schiller's creation can lay as little claim to being historical. Schiller approaches his heroine with love and reverence—for which we shall always bear him gratitude after the atrocious coarseness of Voltaire— but his representation ranges so freely through the realms of fantasy that the portrait he created of her whom he has christened for all time, and especially in Germany, the "Maid of Orleans" has often nothing more in common with historical actuality than the unhistorical title.

It is very striking that the first attempt to mould the imposing tragedy of the Sublime Maiden into dramatic form, with material that is borrowed from history itself, should come from across the Channel— from the land that was once the land of Warwick, and which aspired to the dual kingship, but which has now long been the land of Southey and Andrew Lang; the country that in its oldest and in its newest cathedral seeks out beautiful spots in which to honour the memory of her against whom its forefathers perpetrated the most cruel of injustices.

II

Shaw wished to create an historical work, and it is an historical work that he has accomplished. But this historical work is yet, above all, a work of art. It goes without saying that the fundamental lines, however essential, may not hamper the imagination of the artist, or dictate the setting or development. Historical facts, worked out dramatically, must necessarily be modified in many ways. A poem remains essentially historical as long as the representation is rooted in actual events, even if these actual events, for the sake of drama and its exigent demands, are moulded into a modified form. The spirit of the actual events is not outraged even if they are apparelled in a different way, provided that the arrangement and decoration are borrowed from the arsenal of history. It would therefore be narrow-minded pedantry, even a misunderstanding of the artistic conception, a confusion between art and

history, if we were to demand of the artist that he should keep the
events entirely intact. The poet may mould facts in his manipulative
fingers, but the material itself must not be the fruit of his imaginative
creation. Should this be the case the poem forfeits its historical character, and with it the artistic advantage in view, which in the present case
is very great: the story of Joan of Arc is so moving, so sublime, that the
poet who paints her with the brush of actual fact has everything to gain
by so doing.

III

It is just because Shaw's creation is an historical work that it deserves
historical criticism.

This criticism wishes to be, first and principally, appreciative; to
express how much it values the serious historical structure of the
chronicle play, the deep and accurate study that the poet-scholar has
made of the literature relating to this intricate problem. Every page of
the tragedy bears the mark of this. But it would also call attention to
certain historical inaccuracies which are the cause of small, but nevertheless unnecessary, blemishes in the character of the Heroic Maid, and
which distort the surroundings over which she spread her angelic light.

After what I have said above it will be understood that the last thing
I wish to do is to cavil at such alterations as the drama renders
necessary, and which do not violate the spirit of the facts, such as the
individual arrangement and the concentrated representation of things
which in reality took place in a different and more spacious form than it
is possible or desirable to reproduce on the stage. It is perfectly legitimate to combine incidents from the two journeys to Vaucouleurs, from
Joan's two visits to the King's castle at Chinon, and from various
sittings of the Court of Justice at Rouen. It is also defensible to bring
into conscious expression tendencies towards Protestantism, National-
sim and the defence of a privileged position, which were then no doubt
nascent in men's minds, although the conscientiousness is anachronism.
Pardonable also are small anachronisms which the poet draws from his
own knowledge of the future course of events, such as the characterisa-
tion of the Crown Prince by his royal father as "a horrid boy. He hates
me. He hates everybody; selfish little beast" (Sc. II, p. 3). Charles VII

could not have spoken like that in 1429 of his five-year-old son. But this liberty is allowable, as by its means the poet can tell us something characteristic which he could not do otherwise.

It is less pardonable to raise La Tremoïlle to the command of the army. The programme of the New Theatre even represents him as Constable of France. The Constable was Arthur de Richemont, and the commander of the army that was operating in the middle of France, in so far as the command was concentrated, was Charles de Bourbon. George de la Tremoïlle was neither, nor was he a Duke; nor, of course, was his wife a Duchess (Sc. II, pp. 35,38). He was Sire de la Tremoïlle, Baron de Sully, and was not raised to be Count until the Day of Coronation. Neither was Sire de la Tremoïlle a diplomatist (Sc. II, p.34), and it sounds strange to hear this description applied to him by the man who, with the King's mother-in-law, Yolande, held the whole diplomacy of the disorganised kingdom in his own hand.

But these are only external details. Of far more importance is the excessive exaggeration in the drawing, or rather in the caricaturing, of the King. Certainly Charles VII was weak-willed; but only in an unhistorical caricature could such words be put into his mouth as "I never asked to be a King" (Sc. II, p. 24). "If you want me to be crowned at Rheims you must talk to the Archbishop, not to me" (Sc. II, page 26). "I am not such a fool as I look" (Sc. II, p. 30). "If we go to Rheims and have a coronation, Anne will want new dresses" (Sc. II, p. 31). Who is Anne? Shaw must know as well as anybody else that the Queen of France was called Marie (of Anjou); and in 1429 no one but the Queen had any right to clothes at the King's expense.

Charles VII was by no means a dignified King, but only a caricature could use such coarsely sacrilegious expressions as "I thought I should have dropped when they loaded that crown on to me. And the famous holy oil . . . was rancid. Phew!" (Sc. V, p. 50, *cf* also p. 59, "Oh that oil!")

Another exaggeration that far exceeds the bounds of reality is the atmosphere of noisy hilarity and flippant disrespect for all sense of dignity which Shaw represents as reigning in the Court of Chinon. "All the ladies explode in uncontrollable laughter," and "a roar of laughter breaks out as Gilles joins in the laugh and jumps down from the dais" (Sc. II, p. 26). Even the Court of the Roi de Bourges was not a Court of drunken grooms and rough wenches. The unfortunate result is that amid all this noisy buffoonery, the solemn tension and spiritual expectancy, the atmosphere of religious conviction and universal good will which the presence of the Saint had called forth, which had overmastered the King and transformed the whole train, is completely lost. Yet Shaw was not unconscious of this atmosphere. Dunois speaks later for all when he declares: "I have not forgotten . . . how our hearts changed when you came!" (Sc. V, p. 61). But nothing of it is apparent in Scene II except at the very end, in the cry of "To Orleans!" raised by all the knights, which, after all the nonsense that has been going on, has rather the effect of a church bell ringing in a jazz band.

In another instance want of respect for the King has brought the author to an unseemly handling of his subject which cannot be historically justified. The late-born child of an insane father and a mother of sullied reputation, there was every reason to throw doubt upon his royal origin, and this doubt was, indeed, whispered by the people. It is therefore historically possible that it should be touched upon by Poulengy in his conversation with Baudricourt (Sc. I, p. 8), although the tenor of the conversation is little consistent with the reserved character of Bertrand de Poulengy. But it is impossible that this most painful subject could be alluded to in the King's presence, or that the King himself should refer to it in public. The King's defiant exclamation to the assembled Court: "Who dare say now that I am not my father's son?" (Sc. II, p. 26) is quite unhistorical.

IV

I now come to the exalted figure of Joan of Arc herself. There must always lurk a personal element in the vision one has of personalities, past or present. In the poet's vision of such a marvellous personality as that of the Maid that personal element may be very strong. Far be it from me to make it a reproach against Shaw that his vision is different to mine. But everyone's vision must be born of, and led by, the facts of history. In my opinion Shaw does not always take sufficient account of these facts. It is an error to lay in the mouth of Joan the bellicose tirade "I am a soldier . . . I dream of leading a charge, and of placing the big guns" (Sc. III, p. 36), and further on, "I am a soldier and nothing else"

(Sc. V, p. 57). Undoubtedly she was a soldier, and we can believe that she may have said of herself "Je suis chef du guerre."[1] But she was anything but a soldier by choice who dreamed of the joy of fighting and waging war. She was a soldier from stern necessity, a soldier "toute preste à faire paix." The soldier was—I say it emphatically because this side of Joan of Arc is still much too little felt—an angel of peace.

Neither is it right to lay in the mouth of Joan words which have a tang of boastfulness: "And what is that? Less than my father's poorest shepherd" (Sc. II, p. 31). Shaw's intention when he wrote these words is plain. He meant to protest against the idea, current for long but now exploded, that Joan was the daughter of poor peasants, who had herself worked as a peasant on the land and herded her father's sheep. Researches, those of Siméon Luce in particular, have raised it above all doubt that Joan came of the very well-to-do peasant class. Shaw states this with emphasis and elaboration through the mouth of Baudricourt (Sc. I, p. 7; see also Preface, pp. xii-xiii), and he returns to it.[2] But his method is not happy. Anything with the least hint of boastfulness was worlds removed from the Maid.

It is one of the marvels of this peasant girl that she, in the entirely strange surroundings of the Court, immediately found the correct and natural way to behave. "Elle possède, sans l'avoir apprise, la langue qu'il convient de parler aux grands."[3] This has not been sufficiently understood by Shaw. He gives her the *naïf* awkward speech of the peasant girl who comes straight from the land, first to the Commander of Vaucouleurs and then to the King's Court. She says to the King such things as "Thou needs new clothes" (Sc. II, p. 29). At the first acquaintance she addresses Baudricourt and Poulengy by their Christian names (Sc. I, p. 12 and IO ss.), and the King she almost immediately calls Charlie (Sc. II, p. 29). This sounds very different to the real "gentil Dauphin."

There is another point of great importance. I mean the interpretation of "the voices." Everyone is free to interpret and explain in his own

1. In a letter to the Duke of Bedford, March 22nd, 1429. But we must not forget that the authenticity of the passage may be doubted, in view of Joan's formal denial at her trial on February 22nd. (See Champion, *Procès*, Paris, 1920, t. I., p. 41; Quicherat, *Procès*, t. I., Paris, 1841, p. 240.)

2. And once more: "I am no shepherd-lass" (Sc. VI, p. 82).

3. A. Desjardins, *Vie de Jeanne Darc*, 2ᵉ éd., Paris, 1862, p. 38.

way the voices that from her childhood had guided Joan. Shaw is
perfectly free to interpret "the voices" as the product of Joan's imagination, the echoes of her own common-sense, or even of her own
wilfulness. But it is in contradiction to all the facts to impose this
explanation upon Joan herself. For it is as certain as anything historical
can be certain that Joan was absolutely convinced that through "the
voices" the Saints, as animate beings outside herself, spoke to her. It
never for a moment entered her mind that "the voices" could come
from her own spiritual power. It is therefore in flagrant and serious
conflict with history when Shaw makes her answer to the opinion
expressed by Baudricourt: "They (the voices) come from your imagination," "Of course, that is how the messages of God come to us" (Sc. I,
p. 11); or when he makes her say to Regnault de Chartres: "They (the
voices) are only the echoes of my own common-sense" (Sc. V, p. 65); or
to the King: "If you prayed from your heart and listened to the trilling
of the bells in the air after they stop ringing, you would hear the voices
as well as I do" (Sc. V, p. 60). In these passages it is not Joan but Shaw
who speaks. Joan would sooner have let her tongue be torn out of her
mouth than pronounce a naturalistic explanation of what she, in the
certainty of her faith, held to be the actual voices of Saints dwelling in
another world. This is the greatest and really capital lapse from history
of which the play is guilty.

I should like to call attention to another inaccuracy. I may begin by
saying that for a long time Joan has been regarded as one of the
pioneers of the Protestant idea of liberty of private opinion. In Shaw's
drama this so-called Protestantism in the Maid again plays an important
part. I, for my part, do not believe in it in the least, and I repeat the
words of Andrew Lang, a great student of Joan of Arc and a Scottish
Protestant: "She was as sound a Catholic as man or woman could be in
matters of faith."[4] But in this matter there may be a difference of
opinion. It is historically established, however, that in the tragedy of
the Maid the contrast between authority of the Church and private
judgment was first formulated by the judges at Rouen after they had
been primed by the University of Paris. It was the most dangerous
snare that the prosecution spread, and it is unhistorical to make it

4. A. Lang, *The Maid of France* (London, 1913), 251.

appear as if, even before the catastrophe of Compiègne, anything whatever had been noticed in Joan that had the least suggestion of pro-Protestant tendencies. The words which Shaw's Archbishop addresses to the Maid on the day of Coronation in the cathedral: "The voice of God on earth is the voice of the Church Militant. If you perish through setting your private judgment above the instructions of your spiritual directors the Church disowns you" (Sc. V, p. 65) are expressions which Shaw has borrowed from the legal proceedings at Rouen, and which he anachronistically uses in anticipation. In July, 1429, no one thought or spoke thus in the camp of the Armagnacs—not even the bitterest ecclesiastical foes of the Maid, to whom Regnault de Chartres undoubtedly belonged.

V

This transplacing of things that occurred later to an earlier time is not the only instance of the kind that we find in the chronicle play. The whole of Scene V is unhistorical in this respect. Undoubtedly, even before the Coronation, the atmosphere of silent opposition was spreading, and in this the envy, jealousy, and small-minded self-seeking of the Government and army leaders who were thrown into the shade by Joan found their secret means of action. These secret forces were to grow even more sinister during the ten months of reaction between the day of glory at Rheims and the day of disaster at Compiegne. But at the Coronation no one would have dared publicly to set himself up or to express himself as antagonistic to Joan, neither the Archbishop-Chancellor nor the newly created Marshall Gilles de Rais, and least of all the King or Dunois—apart from the fact that the latter would certainly not even have thought of doing so.

In another important instance this method of anticipation gives the wrong value to a cardinal point. Shaw makes it appear as if in the summer of 1429 the Earl of Warwick had already formed the plan for getting Joan into his hands and then having her condemned by an ecclesiastical court. Even before the Coronation Warwick is in negotiation about it with Cauchon. "Some of Charles's people will sell her to the Burgundians; the Burgundians will sell her to us; and there will probably be three or four middlemen, who will expect their little commission" (Sc. IV, p. 41). Again, on the day of Coronation Dunois is made to say: "The lucky man that makes the capture will receive sixteen thousand pounds from the Earl of Ouareek" (Sc. V, p. 63), and then Cauchon will see to the rest, Cauchon who "is coming to business in the English camp" (Sc. IV, p. 42) and who "knows his business" (Sc. V, p. 64). Now there is no historical evidence whatever of such a plan having been formed to secure Joan through the treachery of the Armagnacs; and Cauchon's business, directed towards a process of law, does not begin till after her imprisonment in Compiègne. It has even been ascertained upon good authority that the plan for transferring the prisoner from Jean de Luxembourg to the English for the price of ten thousand pounds originated in the Paris University, whose messenger Cauchon was on his visit to the Burgundian camp, which introduced the negotiations. Of course, Warwick eagerly entered into this plan. However this may be, even if the plan for selling Joan was originated by the English, this is certain, that the obvious instigation for the plan lay in the capture at Compiègne and not at an earlier date.

VI

In Scene VI Bernard Shaw rises to his full power. All the available material of the procedure is concentrated in masterly dramatic style into one sitting, which the poet places on the ultimate day of May 30th, 1431. The great dramatist in his supreme effort is here at the same time an accurate historian. Not that I should care to take the responsibility of all the representations given, and, in particular, not of those which interpret the clauses in the proceedings which brought the Saint to the stake, as anything more than an ecclesiastical dressing—*pour le besoin de la cause*—of a legalised political murder, or those which show the majority of the judges as anything more than conscious liars and deliberate murderers.[5] But eminent historians think otherwise on this point, and Shaw may allow himself to be convinced by them and their arguments. At all events it is a satisfaction to one's sense of historical

5. *Ibid.*, p. 232.

justice that Shaw does not conclude his last act without having exposed the treachery of the Inquisitor and the Archbishop in all its cynical monstrosity (p. 94).

I should like to call attention to one more point, because on it there is a great deal of misunderstanding. I refer to the connection between the seventy (why does Shaw speak of sixty-four?) counts and the twelve articles. Shaw also represents it as if the seventy points of accusation, being too long and too learned for all the members of the Court, are reduced—cut down to twelve (p. 73). This is not correct. The twelve articles are not the abstract of the seventy articles. Each document fulfils a separate and different function.

The seventy points form the accusation required by the Ecclesiastical Public Prosecutor (the Promoter); the regular proceedings were opened by the exposition of these. The twelve points, on the other hand, form a document which, according to usage in trials for heresy, was sent at a later stage of the proceedings to theologians and lawyers, to gain their opinion. As regards the exact nature of these points, the accusation proffered would naturally partly determine them, but by no means exclusively or even in the most important particular. The twelve points of this document are especially based upon the replies made by Joan in the process of examination. The misunderstanding has arisen out of the original text of the report of the proceedings of April 2nd, which at the first reading is misleading.[6]

And now a small error of Shaw's connected with the above-mentioned misunderstanding can easily be corrected. It was the business of the Promoter to compose the accusation; in accordance with this rule of procedure the seventy articles were the work of the Promoter d'Estivet, not of de Courcelles, as we read in Shaw (p. 73). It is true that de Courcelles—which probably misled the author—read out the articles in the sitting of March 27th. The twelve articles, on the other hand, are not the work of the (vice) Inquisitor Jean Lemaître (see Shaw, p. 73), but probably of the Assessor, Nicolas Midi.

6. See the text in Champion, *o.c.*, t. I., p. 269; Quicherat, *o.c.*, t. I., p. 327.

JOHAN HUIZINGA

VIII/Bernard Shaw's Saint

I

THE PLAY AND ITS PERFORMANCE

If there had been one miracle too few to warrant the canonization of Joan of Arc, it might have been brought forward that she has been able to wipe the grimace from Shaw's joking countenance and to force that acrobat, eternally turning somersaults about the crossbar of his ingenuity, to his knees for a moment. No one has the right to demand from the master of satiric comedy that he should refrain from every witticism and comic effect throughout a sixty-two-page Preface and a performance of three hours and a half. But, even aside from the effect of the play itself, the mere fact that this time one can read the Preface with hardly a shrug of the shoulders is proof that something unusual is happening. Shaw, in whose hands Caesar and "the man of destiny" grew small and foolish, has now experienced the power of the heroic, and whether he would or no, has written in the humble service of his incomparable subject.

The more one thinks about it, the greater the miracle seems. A person with the limitations of Shaw, that man with the utterly prosaic mind (in the good sense of the word) who appears so alien to everything that seems to us to be noblest in the Middle Ages and most essential in

Reprinted from *Men and Ideas,* trans. James S. Holmes and Hans van Marle (New York, 1959), 207–39. First published as "Bernard Shaws heilige," *De Gids,* LXXXIX (1925), 110–20, 220–32, 419–31.

the history of Joan of Arc—the Catholic faith, late Gothic life, the pure, clear tone of the French spirit—what will such a person make of it all?

What he has made of it is certainly a peculiar product, and there are any number of objections, from both the artistic and the historical point of view. Meanwhile, the play is traveling through the world, and it attracts people (not only because it is Shaw), moves and affects them—and uplifts them. Shaw has once more posed a problem: this time, in spite of himself, the problem of his success. There is perhaps sufficient reason to offer a historian's marginal notes on this play that everyone has seen or read, or both. For the most part these notes have to do with Shaw's conception of the historical figure of Joan of Arc, but as a result they unavoidably touch on an evaluation of the play and its performance as well.

The task that Shaw has set himself approximates the highest task the human mind has succeeded, a few times, in accomplishing: the creation of tragedy from history. Who, aside from the Greek Tragedians and Shakespeare, has actually succeeded in bringing before the eye in one close-knit image, and in its most essential and exalted significance, something that once actually happened? (Or is reputed to have happened; it makes no difference whether the subject is the Seven against Thebes, sunk into the shadows of legend, or Henry VIII, dead by Shakespeare's time no longer than a good half century.) Shaw has attempted the task, completely aware of its requirements. And attempted it with material that has increased the demands, because it is historically so extraordinarily detailed, so sharply delineated, and so fully documented, and because the mere historical account is itself so chock-full of the transcendent emotions that drama attempts to arouse: the classical combination of sympathy and fear, the shuddering admiration for the hero, the being carried away by the sweep of inevitable events, the indefinable yet so clearly conscious catharsis. In *Hamlet* all the tragic element is the work of the poet; the dramatizer of Joan of Arc may be happy if he does no more than to allow the organ tone of history itself to reverberate as purely as possible.

In constructing his tragedy, Shaw comprehended one important principle: that, in Hegel's phrase (it is rather a surprise not to find it quoted in the Preface), the truly tragic is not to be found in the conflict between right and wrong, but in that between right and right. Joan of

Arc surrounded by nothing but cowards and rascals might be a romantic figure, but not a dramatic one. Yet Joan as the superior being
crushed between two tremendous and necessary powers, the Church
and the interests of the State, is the very personification of the tragic
heroine. In its deeper foundations, history is much closer to the tragic
conception of the past than to the romantic. In the historical analysis of
a conflict the sense of an awesome inevitability, of the relative justness
of both sides, always appears as the final result. The romantic emotion,
that is to say, the polarization of the pathetic, the passionate, the
personal in events, is a sentiment of a more superficial sort.

Speaking generally, then, it was not necessary for Shaw to do violence to history in presenting the judges as limited but respectable
persons, and Pierre Cauchon, the bishop of Beauvais, with even a touch
of greatness (whether he as a person deserved it will be discussed
below); in depicting Dunois, the Bastard of Orléans, as a normal egoist
of good will; and in attempting to convince us of the justness, on a
lower level, of the archbishop of Reim's anxious diplomacy and the
excusability of Dauphin Charles's defeatism. In doing so he could, with
some justification, feel that he was the mouthpiece of history. And he is
no little proud of the role. In his opinion, he has captured the historical
essence of the events. The words he puts into the mouths of his
personages Cauchon, the inquisitor Lemaître, and the Earl of Warwick
as personifications of the Church, the Inquisition, and Feudalism "are
the things they actually would have said if they had known what they
were really doing. . . ." As for Saint Joan herself, the play "contains all
that need be known about her." Does Shaw really think that we do not
want to know anything more? Does he not understand that every word
she spoke, every detail of her appearance and her actions is dear to us?
If not, then he does not know the true nature of historical interest. But
in the last analysis it is not a view of the past which Shaw is concerned
with, but the lesson that the "case" of Joan still has to teach. "If it were
only an historical curiosity I would not waste my readers' time and my
own on it for five minutes." Here is the usual misconception of the
nature and value of the historical sense: the things of the past, as we
observe them, are of themselves nothing more than curiosities, unless a
pragmatic application to the questions of today can be deduced from
them. History, however, takes its revenge on Shaw.

It goes without saying that no blame is due the dramatist for his deliberate abbreviation of the reality of history, for instance, his condensation of the questioning, the sentence, the abjuration, the relapse, and the execution into one single scene. That he gave Warwick the place where the regent Bedford should have stood had good grounds dramatically, since he wished to personify the old aristocratic principle in resistance to the emergent monarchy, and for that the noble Warwick was more suitable than Bedford, a prince of the blood royal. That the honor of holding the cross before Joan, due Brother Isambard de la Pierre, is enjoyed by Martin Ladvenu will cause a twinge of pain only to a scholar at home with all the details of the story. For all his vagueness I prefer the unknown Master John Tressard, the royal secretary, who said, bitterly weeping, "we are all lost, for it was a good and holy woman that has been burned," to Chaplain de Stogumber, the jingo *avant la lettre* whom Shaw has built up out of the single phrase *quidam cappellanus Cardinalis Angliae* ["a certain chaplain of the cardinal of England"] from the record of the rehabilitation trial. But it is Shaw's perfect right to create such a character if it is necessary for the play.

Nor do inadvertent inaccuracies affect the play's worth. If Shaw thinks that it sounds better for the dauphin to say, "Anne will want new dresses," we are happy to forget that the queen's name was Marie d'Anjou, and even more so that it was not until ten years after 1429 that the Bastard of Orléans became Dunois. It is merely the schoolmaster in me who cannot refrain from mentioning such trifles.

Regarding faithfulness to history, however, Shaw pretends to much more than a painstaking accuracy in details, which he thinks of little matter. "The ideal biographer," he says (and that is, in a sense, what he considers himself), "must understand the Middle Ages . . . much more intimately than our Whig historians have ever understood them." The Middle Ages were a period "of which the thinking has passed out of fashion, and the circumstances no longer apply to active life . . ." But Shaw knows them, thanks to the progress in the field of historical studies: "I write in full view of the Middle Ages, which may be said to have been rediscovered in the middle of the nineteenth century after an eclipse of about four hundred and fifty years . . . Now there is not a breath of medieval atmosphere in Shakespeare's histories." Is there, then, in *Saint Joan?* Here one's eyebrows rise automatically.

At this point we approach the almost bewildering questions raised by Shaw's play. For it is not only a question of the extent to which the play breathes a medieval atmosphere, but also of whether the presence or absence of such an atmosphere detracts from the play's dramatic effect and value. On this last point one's immediate response is a very definite Yes.

Today's general reader has his mind's eye too sharply focused on the differences in times for him to be able to endure any gross internal anachronism. Joan of Arc is too firmly anchored in French history of the fifteenth century to be able to serve as a timeless dramatic person-age such as Phaedra or Alcestis. The drama of Saint Joan must trans-port us to the Middle Ages as we see them. Does Shaw's play do this? I should not dare say No straightaway, but even less so Yes. The arch-bishop of Reims strikes one as remarkably Anglican, and seems a cousin to the bishop in *Getting Married.* In the English production, which was rather over-acted compared with the Dutch, the dauphin is all too much the spoiled Eton boy. The comic element in La Hire is quite acceptable and in no sense disturbing, but the whole tone of the dialogue, the sheerly farcical effect of the page who pounds for silence with the halberd is all too Shavian to seem medieval.

Yet is it actually the lack of a sense of the time that hampers us? Is it not rather that this lack is inseparably linked with a dramatic deficiency of a much more serious sort: the lack of a high style? I do not mean literary style, of course, but dramatic style. Shaw's play would have gained nothing and would have lost a great deal if the dialogue had been filled with archaic grandiloquence and Walter Scott-like solem-nity. And it is a moot question whether that would have made it more "genuinely" medieval. The fifteenth-century *novella*, Villon, and Joan herself in her answers to her judges are testimonies enough that collo-quial speech in those days could be as fluent and free as our own. What we miss is something else: the transportation of our minds into a sphere where each emotion and passion has acquired a higher potential, each word affects more deeply and resonates more fully than in everyday life. There is, says Shaw, not a breath of medieval atmosphere in Shakespeare's histories. No, perhaps not, in the technically historical sense. But there is an abundance of the high dramatic style which casts a light on the difference in times without revealing it completely. For all its mannerisms, I know no historical drama that is more real and genuine than *Richard II*. It is utterly Elizabethan, and not at all late-fourteenth-century, but even so Shakespeare, with only his knowledge from Holinshed, came closer than any chronicler to the core of the historical character of the last Plantagenet.

Tragedy may be anything but sheerly natural and realistic. Shaw shuns the romantic like the plague: it is his perfect right to do so, but by using familiarity and humor to fumigate his work of the romantic he also banishes the heroic. To dramatize the heroic virtues of Saint Joan of Arc no less a style than the stern forms of Greek tragedy or the individual genius of Shakespeare will do.[1] And that is also the reason why, before Shaw, no one else had any better success in dramatizing the Maid.

Once one has realized, on reading *Saint Joan,* that it is too closely akin to *Man and Superman* and the rest of Shaw to be a satisfactory dramatization of its noble subject, it comes as a great surprise on seeing it to discover that the play is not only an exciting but also an affecting and elevating experience. This is undoubtedly so, in part (to leave aside the skill of the actors), because of Shaw's vivid depiction: the excellent dialogue at the court before Joan's entrance, the conversation between Warwick and Cauchon, the Inquisitor (especially in O. B. Clarence's portrayal as a blushing, debonair graybeard in the London production). Still, the high points of the play are precisely those where the author merely presents certain essential elements of the action itself: the irresistible bravery with which Joan swept away the dauphin and the court, the simplicity of the words we know she really spoke. Shaw is at his best when he sticks closest to history. "Be you Bastard of Orleans?" This is the very phrase, Dunois testified in 1455, with which Joan first greeted him. Shaw formulated as faithfully as possible from the records of the hearings themselves all Joan's answers to the judges, among them the moving reply to the query whether she thought she was in a state of grace: "If I am not, may God bring me to it; if I am, may God keep me in it!"

---

1. I am, of course, not thinking of Joan in *Henry VI*.

It is my impression that the play achieves its deepest effect almost beyond Shaw's own activity, as if the great theme has merely passed through him to manifest itself directly in all its gripping truth and spotless purity. Even when, at the end of the extremely questionable Epilogue, the white beam of light falling on Joan sends a shudder through us, it is not Shaw's greatness that causes it, but the greatness of the saint whose servant he there was. But what more does he want than that? In the greatest ages of drama was it not best when the truth and greatness of the subject weighed more heavily than the limited abilities of the dramatist?

Related to this is the fact that such an important part of the performance's effect is a result of ordinary stage techniques. It is as though the heroic style that Shaw was not able to give to the play has to be created in despite of him, and is ensured by the basic scenic means used. This leads me to compare the performance given by the Vereenigd Tooneel [United Theater] troupe in the Netherlands with that of the company playing the piece in London, first in the Haymarket and now in the Regent Theatre.[2]

From the point of view of style, one would tend to say beforehand that the theories of Eduard Verkade here applied skillfully by Wijdeveld—a sober *mise en scène,* the historical illusion reduced to a vague impression of past forms, a sharply tempered realism—are far preferable to the trappings of historical realism which are usually still sworn by in England, though in the Netherlands they have for years been looked upon as outdated and antiquated. Nevertheless, after having seen both performances I have begun to have some doubts, and Charles Ricketts's version lingers in my memory as much more forceful and impressive than Wijdeveld's. But that, it will be said, is precisely the mistake: the external trappings should not appeal so directly. Are they, then, no more than an indispensable husk, not to say a necessary evil? If that is so, there is something wrong with the theater. Now, that is certainly the case, but these notes do not pretend to provide fundamental solutions for such probing dramatic issues. Let us restrict ourselves to weighing the merits of the two types of staging in this particular case.

The advantage of a historical staging—provided it is designed as

2. February 1925.

excellently as Ricketts's—seems to me to be that the shortcomings of
the play, and in particular the lack of style, are obscured to some
extent. A certain unity of acting, costuming, and *décor* develops, held
together by a common degree of realism, or what can be taken for
realism. This is true of the scene at court and of those in the tent, the
cathedral, and the trial-hall, though not of the one in the castle at
Vaucouleurs and the one beside the river. The more direct the appeal
of the architecture or nature needs to be, the more all the objections to
stage realism press their validity: in the London production the scene
on the Loire is terrible, but the settings of gaily figured tapestries in the
tent and at court go well with the costumes of the actors. In the
Verkade production, on the other hand, there is a certain lack of
harmony between the play, the costumes, and the *décors.* If the play
had had Shakespeare's exalted style, which it is much in need of, a
soberness in the setting would have been the prescribed thing, since
every excessive effect would only damage and detract from the drama
itself. But soberness clashes with the spirit of Shaw, and Ricketts's gay
coloring has a salutary effect: without being discordant, it subdues that
Shavian spirit a bit, distracts from it somewhat.

I have no illusions that I shall ever see the fifteenth century—or any
other age—in the theater as I see it in my mind's eye, and as it is
suggested to me by the slightest historical document, whether in word
or in image. But I must admit that I have never seen more convincing
historical staging than this work of Ricketts's. I have in mind in particular the first court entry and the tent scene. Not that I should like to
defend the costuming throughout the play. Plate-iron armor, though it
may be more accurate historically than the hinted-at mail used by
Verkade, is too shiny and tinny, and hence always unacceptable on
stage. Verkade's costuming is also quasi-historical (though only defec-
tively so: all three of his prelates are post-Trent personages), yet by
comparison to him what a fine harmony in variety Ricketts offers: the
Heures de Chantilly come to life. Heraldic figures are used lavishly, but
with how much care and consideration! I am constantly struck by the
English eye for all the possibilities of the color red. We Dutch with our
gray tradition must remember, before we turn up our nose at all this,
that the period that for us begins with Jozef Israels started with the
Pre-Raphaelites in England. Actually, the only colors we know, except

for all the nuances of gray, are a great deal of green and some blue, and vistas and clouds rather than figures. The English eye, however, has been trained by an unbroken succession of masters who have tested all their aesthetic senses on the human figure clad in every shade and on its movement in gaily colored processions. I know that this decorative tendency in England gives birth to monsters every day—and yet when I see Ricketts following in the footsteps of William Morris and Rossetti and Ford Madox Brown I do not dare condemn.

It is risky to attempt to view art and its value as quite distinct from nationality. Is it not noteworthy that in the British production the two English characters, Warwick and the Chaplain, are by far the best? Or perhaps the Chaplain, whom Shaw has made too much of a caricature, is really no better than Cauchon, but Warwick is unsurpassed in his appearance as well as in other things. The care that was taken for historical accuracy is best illustrated by the fact that even his facial type has clearly been copied from the gilded bronze likeness on the earl's tomb at Warwick. Happy England, which has never known a French Revolution. For Pierre Cauchon's countenance one must be content with a seventeenth-century drawing of his tombstone, long since destroyed, at Lisieux.

The very fact that, in spite of myself, the element of historical accuracy has played a greater role in my evaluation of the performance than I had suspected, I should like to consider as evidence for the correctness of my theory that the powerful effect of the play stems from the historical theme itself. There is another argument for that point of view. Sybil Thorndike has the reputation of being England's finest tragedienne; I hope I do Nel Stants no injustice by calling her a rising young player. Nonetheless, the Dutch actress's Joan was much more to my satisfaction than her more famous English colleague's, because Nel Stants could be young, spontaneous, natural, boyish—she had the same gay, laughing face Joan's contemporaries describe. In Sybil Thorndike I was put off by an excess of dramatic art—a rapturous note in her voice and gestures, a touch of high tragedy that served as a disturbing rather than a contributing factor. I have been told that in America the choice was deliberately made to train a naïve country-girl for the part. That smacks of the film. But it does serve to confirm the fact that this drama is so subject to the gravitational pull of history that the usual dramatic requirements are distorted.

It has been remarked that though any number of writers have attempted a literary adaptation of the history of Joan of Arc, it was always without success. The work of art depicting her for all the ages to come does not exist. It will not be *Saint Joan,* no more than it is *Die Jungfrau von Orleans,* and very definitely not François Porché's *La vièrge au grand coeur,* which ran in Paris (perhaps partly as a protest against *Saint Joan*) for a while, till Shaw came, was seen, and conquered, even there.

What are the great writings one reads about Joan of Arc and her life? Michelet first of all. Then one may prefer Anatole France, the skeptic (or rather the unbeliever), or Monsignor Touchet, who devoted years of labor to bringing about Joan's canonization, or Gabriel Hanotaux, who attempted to bridge the gap between rationalists and Catholics. But it is in the books that attempt to give an accurate account of the history that the reader—including the general reader—goes searching for the Maid of Orléans. Is this not some sort of indication? Should it not be assumed that there is something in the very subject that resists literary treatment, and particularly dramatization? There are subjects, such as Troy, which find their highest expression in the epic, others that flourish only in the drama. There are also some whose character lies most intimately and indissolubly contained in the historical form itself, some in which the most sublime emotions of the tragic—the fellow suffering and the catharsis—are bound to the historical account as such. Grant Clio precedence over Melpomene now and then through the ages.

II

THE FIGURE OF JOAN OF ARC

We have reproached Shaw that his play is too much lacking in the qualities of tragic poetry to be commensurate with the sublimity of the subject, that it is too modernly prosaic to be able to take the dramatic flight that is needed—prosaic not only in form, but also in conception. The buskin is treacherous footwear; it is much more dangerous for the best of men than skis for the beginner.

And yet, I do not know whether Shaw, whom I imagine to be the most deliberate writer there is, could have given his view the poetic passion it lacks, if he had wanted to. It is, at any rate, certain that he did not want to. For it is precisely poetry, so he argues in his Preface, which has made so much mischief in regard to an accurate understanding of the figure of John of Arc. A twopenny-halfpenny romanticism picturing the heroine above all as a beautiful girl whose followers were all in love with her has hopelessly distorted the image of Joan. There is no other misconception that Shaw rounds on so angrily, and so justly, as this sort of cheap romanticism. But romantic sentiment is not the same thing as poetic sublimity, and it is an open question whether he has not thrown out the baby of tragedy with the bath of romanticism.

And Shaw, in his attack on the romantic view, is, as usual, exaggerating. He would like to reason away every touch of feminine charm in Joan, at whatever price. "Not one of Joan's comrades, in village, court, or camp . . ." says Shaw, "ever claimed that she was pretty." This is not true. Jean d'Aulon, the head of her military household, called her "a beautiful and well-formed girl," and Perceval de Boulainvilliers thought her "of satisfying grace." Perhaps a few details on her appearance are appropriate here. (I repeat that this article is intended as nothing more than a series of marginal notes.)

Over against the contemporaries just mentioned, Shaw can appeal to the Lombard monk who, quite some time later, briefly described her outward appearance. He spoke of her as "short of build and with a boorish countenance." But most of his evidence is of little value. Various historians have felt uneasy with the view that Joan was short of stature. Vallet de Viriville attempted to prove the opposite. Hanotaux described her as "large and strong," thus following Quicherat, who translated the *haulte et puissante* of the extremely romanticized *Chronique de Lorraine* as *grande et forte*. Whatever her stature may have been, the Lombard monk was right about another detail: that Joan had dark hair. For so she is described in a contemporary chronicle from La Rochelle, and the fact is perhaps confirmed by a black hair embedded, apparently intentionally, in the seal of Joan's letter to the town of Riom.

One might say that there is a quite general tendency to visualize Joan as being fair-haired and preferably dressed in blue. That is the way Boutet de Monvel presents her in his fine, well-known picture book.

Both Sybil Thorndike and Nel Stants portray her as fair-haired. And I imagine that a survey, "Do you visualize Joan of Arc as fair or dark?" would confirm their choice by a large majority. Is this a romantic notion? Ariosto paid homage to the ideal of the fair heroine. I can imagine the antiromantic Shaw expostulating with the players to avoid every element of romantic charm in the figure. No sacrifice might be made to the ideal of fairness, and even less to contemporary fashion; as the sources specify in detail, Joan's hair should be cropped close above the ears and her temples shaven, in keeping with the fifteenth-century style. But the actors point out to Shaw that his power as an author does not reach *that* far, and go their own way.

I do not know whether Shaw's passion in supporting his desire to see a portrait of Joan in the helmeted female bust in the church of Saint-Maurice in Orléans does not, in the last analysis, betray a certain chivalric sense. His argument "If this woman be not Joan, who is she?" and his challenge to prove the negative strike one as romantic in their utter groundlessness. We have no well-substantiated authentic image of the Maid. Certainly not in the thumbnail sketch with which the greffier of the Parliament of Paris, Clément de Fauquembergue, adorned the margin of his register. (And to imagine that it would have been possible for Jan van Eyck to visit her in prison at Arras in the autumn of 1430 and draw her!)

Among the few details preserved regarding her outward appearance, the most valuable is perhaps the phrase describing her voice. At Selles-sur-Cher, in June 1429, the brothers De Laval heard her address the ecclesiastics standing in front of the church "in a very womanly voice" as she sat on the fiery black horse she had just broken. De Boulainvilliers, too, was struck by her charming, feminine voice.

To understand her personality one would like to have something of a picture of her appearance, and though one does not need to visualize her as beautiful in the usual sense of the word, a harmony in her appearance is essential. Let us attempt to combine into a consistent picture the few scanty data preserved by her contemporaries, who were little interested in personal descriptions.

She talks little. She eats and drinks sparingly. (It is still De Boulainvilliers who is speaking, in June 1429.) She delights in beautiful horses and armor, she greatly admires armed and noble men. She avoids contact and converse with the many. "She sheds tears freely; her expression is cheerful" *(abundantia lacrimarum manat, hilarem gerit vultum)*. This strange combination of strength and lightheartedness with tearful emotion and an inclination toward silence provides what is perhaps the best approach to the essence of her being.

Shaw, it seems to me, has seen the basic contours of that essence lucidly, and has portrayed them clearly. I shall not paraphrase his portrayal here; everyone has it at his disposal in the play and the Preface, and I cannot do it better justice.

"In His strength I will dare, and dare, and dare, until I die." In these words, perhaps the most moving in the play, Shaw presents the essence of Joan's personality. Actually she had given herself a name that summarizes her whole personality when·she heard her voices call her *la fille au grand coeur. Coeur,* in this context, should be translated as "courage," and yet such a translation would not be complete, because all the other meanings of "heart" are also there as undertones. Her courage, and her confidence—these are the most immediate elements of her nature, and the ones that give the most tangible explanation of her success. A greatness that manifests itself in a superior, irresistible, and infectious bravery. What reason could there be to doubt Bertrand de Poulengy and Jean de Metz, who took her from Vaucouleurs to Chinon, when they testify that they felt incapable of resisting her will? The very fact that they took her there proves it. Anatole France is skeptical toward the numerous testimonies in the rehabilitation trial of men who declared that they had never felt any carnal desire for her. Shaw says they were too much afraid of her to fall in love with her. One might also say that her utterly guileless concentration on one goal emanated an awe that expressed itself in a great sense of shame. A stilling of the desires in her presence is on a par with the abstention from swearing and profanity which (as the sources thoroughly document) she brought about. Whoever cannot accept the fact that an exalted personality can exert an influence on his surroundings which makes the unusual the rule will never be able to understand Joan of Arc.

The incomparably high mettle of her courage no one doubts. But there are those who question whether, aside from the great impetus emanating from her courage, her insight and military talent also played a predominant role in the deeds accomplished under her guidance: the raising of the siege of Orléans and the expedition to Reims. This is one of the most difficult problems posed by the history of Joan of Arc, and it is out of the question to go into sufficient detail on the point here. As early as the rehabilitation trial, Jean Luillier, a burgher of Orléans, gave an evasive answer to the question whether the siege was raised by means of the Maid more than the strength of the warriors. The conviction that Joan applied a natural strategic and tactical talent in deliberate calculation is based chiefly on the testimony of a comrade-in-arms, the Duke of Alençon. He praises her as being "in war . . . very expert, whether to carry a lance, to assemble an army, to order a battle, or to dispose artillery." Shaw, like Hanotaux (and Quicherat before him), tends to assume these very real talents in her. Anatole France, on the other hand, is closer to the Catholic historians on the point, though for completely different reasons. In the Catholic view the attribution of extraordinary military skill would imply a certain diminution of the supernatural nature of her mission. For France it would not tally with his thesis that Joan had been a pawn in the hands of calculating persons.

In modern military science it would certainly be unbelievable for such strategic skill to exist in a simple girl from the country. But in the uncomplicated situation of her day military talent was still largely a matter of penetrating common sense, and once one assumes the genius of her personality there seems no reason to consider impossible the presence of such a talent in Joan of Arc.

The combination of common sense and natural straightforwardness with heroic enthusiasm gave her personality the utterly unique cast that appeals immediately to everyone. At first glance she saw everything in its true form, free of any veneer of convention. Hence the ready wit of her answers, for instance, the one to the dean of the theological faculty of Poitiers, who had asked what tongue her angel spoke. "A better than yours," she said, for Brother Seguin spoke the Limousin dialect.[3]

It is worthy of attention that Joan's conceptual world lies completely outside the conventions of her time. Anyone who knows how strongly

3. Salomon Reinach attempts to take away the point of the answer, arguing that Joan cannot have meant such an impertinence, but he does not convince me. *"Observations sur le texte du procès de condamnation de Jeanne d'Arc," Revue Historique,* CXLVIII (1925), 200-23, see p. 208.

the romanticism of chivalry dominated the culture of the fifteenth century will be amazed at the fact. She knew only the *deeds* of chivalry: pleasure in horses and arms, courage and fidelity; chivalry's gaudy concepts were alien to her. Her simple spirit did not feed on the fantasy of chivalric orders and festivities and oaths; it was not directed toward the obligatory ideal of liberating Jerusalem, but toward the one close at hand, that of liberating France. All the higher culture of her century was miles removed from her. There was no contact between her and the fashionable chivalric concepts. It is significant that even after her death literary fancy actually could find no place for her in the colorful tableau of chivalric glory. What could have been done with her? She was too real.

Also the elaborate concepts of religious life of her day were, in their details, actually alien to her. It is only when one compares Joan of Arc with other saints of the time, for instance, Saint Colette, that it becomes apparent that she lacks almost every element of mysticism, every developed sentiment of spiritual ecstasy. We find her participating in only one of the fifteenth century's many pious movements: the adoration of the name of Jesus, which she placed on her standard and had put at the head of her letters. But that is all. There is nothing to indicate that her mind was occupied by the great religious concepts of her day, the vividly colored and violently experienced awareness of the Sufferings of Our Lord, much less the shrill phantasmagoria of Death. She had no time and no place for them.

No one will ever know just how clear to Joan of Arc the forms of her conceptual world were. That they were very simple, and very forceful and direct, is obvious. And here we come to the question of the significance of her "voices."

The history of Joan of Arc—and this is another of the precious things about her—forces us to make a strict reckoning of our own convictions. The non-Catholic can understand and enjoy the story of Saint Francis or of Saint Catherine of Siena with an admiration for the Church of the Middle Ages which, though it is inevitably roused by an unprejudiced study of history, can go much deeper than purely historical and aesthetic appreciation. The story of Joan of Arc forces one to confess at once whether or not one believes in the category of sainthood in the strict Catholic sense. The person who cannot believe that the blessed

souls of certain persons once known as Catherine and Margaret manifested themselves to Joan in the substance does better not to force
himself to do so. The miracle does not have to stand or fall with that.

Shaw, it seems to me, has done a service by opposing violently the
idea that labeling Joan's voices a morbid symptom is enough to define
their significance. But in doing so he is less orignial than he thinks.
Quicherat, though more of a rationalist than Shaw, refused to look
upon Joan as a sick person. Indeed, if every inspiration that comes to
one with such commanding urgency that it is heard as a voice is to be
condemned out of hand by the learned qualification of a morbid symptom, a hallucination, who would not rather stand with Joan of Arc and
Socrates on the side of the mad than with the faculty of the Sorbonne
on that of the sane? We know that an anomaly only becomes a sickness
when it has a disturbing effect on the purpose of the organism. And
Joan's voices may have had a very disturbing influence on her lower
purpose of enjoying life and growing old, but it is not on such things
that we should like to base our conclusion. No matter how clear the
psychiatric report might be, historical judgment would retain the right
not to view the voices in the first place as *ces troubles . . . hallucinations
perpétuelles,* as Anatole France does, but to find in them the sign of a
mind occupied completely by high impulses. History has more to do
with her courage and its significance than with the physiological deter-
mination of her visions.

There is another special argument that should keep us from viewing
Joan's case too much in the pathological sphere. The gentlemen at
Rouen in 1431 did their very best to lure Joan's thoughts onto the
slippery terrain of demonology with their questions about whether
Saint Michael was naked, what parts of the bodies of the saints she had
embraced, and so forth. They succeeded not once. If there was anything really diseased in her mind, they would certainly have discovered
it. A fifteenth-century inquisitor was just as skilled as a present-day
Freudian in bringing the dregs of the soul into the open. Did Joan refer
even once to the devil?

Also with regard to the form in which Joan conceived of her celestial
advisers, Saint Michael, Saint Catherine, and Saint Margaret, it would
seem to me that Shaw has gone squarely to the core of the matter. The
form is bound to the conceptual world in which she lived. It was just as

natural and logical for her to visualize the voices as saints and angels as
it is for a modern man to borrow his terms from the concepts of
physics. When Shaw has Joan say to the Archbishop, "even if they [my
voices] are only the echoes of my own commonsense," he can appeal to
the hearing of March 15: "Asked how she knew it was the language of
angels: replies she believed it very soon; and had the will to believe."

On the question of how Joan's mind defined and explained the
concepts associated with her inspirations, I should like to go a bit
further than Shaw. The writers about Joan of Arc whom I have read
(only a few of the countless total) present it as established fact that she
associated her heavenly commands with the figures of the archangel
Michael, Saint Catherine, and Saint Margaret even at the beginning of
her mission. Is that so certain? She made the association in 1431, at the
trial, when she was asked to describe her visions in detail. But the
witnesses in the trial of rehabilitation who had heard her speak of her
voices in 1429, during her glory, do not as a rule know anything of the
two saints and the archangel. It is precisely in this and because of this
that they seem highly reliable. If they had merely recited what everyone knew in 1456, and what everyone wanted to hear, they would
undoubtedly have mentioned Saint Michael, Saint Catherine, and Saint
Margaret. It was just as natural for a person of the fifteenth century to
associate a notion with a saint as for our contemporaries to use the
words "mentality" and "intuition." But what do these witnesses have to
say? Joan's heavenly counsel was quite without visual form, a sheer
daimonion about which she talked with great diffidence and reticence.
She speaks only of *son conseil* ["her counsel"]. When Christopher de
Harcourt asked her in the presence of the dauphin whether she would
"explain the manner of your counsel when it speaks to you" *(modum
vestri consilii)*, she blushed and replied Yes, but what she then said
contains no reference to the three holy figures. And when Jean d'Aulon,
one of those who were closest to her, asked her who her counsel was,
she answered only: "There are three of them; one is constantly with
me, the second comes and goes, and the third is the one whom the
other two consult." From this it is not even clear that two of the three
were female.[4]

4. According to Catherine de la Rochelle's testimony in Jules Quicherat, *Procès de*

It seems plausible to me that it was only fairly late, perhaps even only during her trial, that Joan linked her inspirations to the figures she knew best and cherished most among the saints. Even during the hearings she was very little inclined to go into detail about her visions. Asked about the great light accompanying them, she said: *passez oultre* ["pass to another question"].

Everything Joan declared regarding the spiritual state in which she heard her voices is of the utmost simplicity. It was a state of great elation, in which she would always like to be. She was filled with a feeling of knowing much more than she might or would or could express. "There is more in the books of the Lord than in yours," she said to the churchmen who examined her at Poitiers. All visionary terminology of the usual sort is utterly alien to her.

Significant is the complete skepticism she displayed toward the visions of Catherine de la Rochelle, who was able to gain access to the king as her competitor. Catherine maintained that she was visited every night by a white lady. So Joan asked to sleep with her for a night, watched until midnight and saw nothing, and then slept. When morning came she asked if the lady in white had come. Yes, while you were asleep, you could not be wakened. Then Joan slept by day and stayed awake, often asking Catherine: Will she not come? And Catherine would answer: Yes, soon!

Catherine de la Rochelle's inspirations were of a different sort from Joan's: she went through the towns with royal heralds and trumpets to summon whosoever had gold or silver or hidden treasure. That was needed to pay Joan's soldiers. Or she would go to the Duke of Burgundy to make peace with him. But Joan advised her to go back to her husband to take care of the household and her children. And there would be no peace "except at the point of the lance."

Joan of Arc was also not a true ecstatic in that she was sometimes uncertain and doubtful. Not only of her calling but also of her fate. When she went to battle she was not at all confident that she would not be slain. Her hesitation before the battle of Montépilloy led to a defeat. Her awareness that God loved certain other living persons more than

condamnation et réhabilitation de Jeanne d'Arc, dite la Pucelle, five volumes (Paris, 1841-49), I, 295, and in Pierre Champion, *Procès de condamnation de Jeanne d'Arc,* two volumes (Paris, 1921), I, 244, Joan spoke of her two advisers as "the counselors of the spring," but the testimony is unreliable.

her (which she testified to at the trial, without clarifying it further) is a touching thing.

Her most human traits tend only to make her greatness more vivid. Alongside her purity, soberness, and simplicity I should not want to miss in her portrait the liking for costly clothing which is only seemingly in contrast with those qualities. "And wore very noble, well-furred habits of gold cloth and silk. . . ." She wore red by preference. An order to pay thirteen old gold crowns for two sumptuous garments made for her at Orléans in June 1429, at Charles d'Orléans's expense, has been preserved, together with the receipt.

The picture of a historical figure does not form itself in the mind on the basis of psychological definitions. It arises seemingly without any consciously logical function, like a view of something one could not see before, or could see only vaguely. It is built up out of the arbitrary and more or less circumstantial data that tradition has preserved for us. The conviction that our picture must be accurate (or let us merely say, of value) and that the tradition is reliable develops out of the feeling, usually very difficult to describe, that though the various data are disconnected in themselves, they harmonize, they fit together. The picture of Joan of Arc emerges from the sources with an unusually high degree of homogeneity and conviction. Even among scholars of quite divergent world-views, the differences in their conception of Joan of Arc are relatively small. It is as if her personality suggested itself to everyone who testified regarding her with an immediacy that forced them merely to tell the truth in all its simplicity, unobscured by the patterns of chivalric or religious forms which usually determined their expression. To our minds all the actions and words handed down regarding Joan fit together. "The sign I have from God is to raise the siege of Orléans." "The soldiers will do battle, and God will give the victory." She carried the standard, in order not to have to kill anyone. When the women of Bourges came with rosaries for her to touch, Joan said, with a laugh toward her hostess: "Touch them yourselves. They will be quite as good with your touch as with mine." She did not like to share a bedroom with old women, and wanted only young maidens around her. Every evening at sundown she had the church bell rung for half an hour. At the peak of her happiness, shortly before the coronation at Reims, when she could not yet know that the tide was turning, came the talk on the way from Crépy-en-Valois, on August 11, 1429, while she rode between the archbishop of Reims and the Bastard of Orléans, and the populace greeted the king with glad cries of *Noël.* In the trial of rehabilitation Dunois gave testimony regarding it, testimony that was perhaps somewhat refashioned in his memory and has unfortunately been preserved only in Latin. "These are a good people!" says Joan. "I have seen none elsewhere who have shown so much joy at the coming of our noble king." And then: "Would God I might be happy enough when I shall finish my days to be buried in this soil." At which the Archbishop asked her: "Joan, in what place hope you to die?" She answered: "Wherever it may please God, I am sure neither of the time nor the place. I know no more of it than yourself. But I would it were pleasing to God, my Creator, that I might now retire, laying arms aside, and that I might serve my father and my mother, guarding their sheep[5] with my sister and my brothers, who would be greatly rejoiced to see me. . . ."

For the person who would like to take exception to the testimonies in the rehabilitation trial of 1456 as too favorable to Joan, who was then already seen in the light of a re-evaluation, the trial of 1431 presents quite the same image of unimpeachable purity. According to Brother Isambard de la Pierre and Brother Martin Ladvenu, the executioner had declared that her heart had resisted every effort to be burned. One does not have to believe it. But there is something else that is just as great a miracle, and of a more tenuous variety: all those biased persons of 1431, her judges with their dry hearts and their still pens, were not able to tarnish the gold of her words. Let me give only one example out of many. Asked what words she used to summon the help of her voices, she replied: "Very tender God, in honor of Thy holy passion, I pray Thee, if Thou lovest me, that Thou wilt reveal to me how I ought to answer these churchmen. I know well, as to this habit, the commandment why I took it, but I know not in what manner I ought to leave it off. Be pleased therefore to teach me. . . ."

In the testimonies of the rehabilitation trial the recollections are often fragments, rather irrelevant details reproduced by the memory with the thoughtlessness of a film image, and precisely because of that

---

5. As Shaw also mentions, Joan was definitely not a shepherdess, and stressed the fact, though she had helped to care for the livestock. But the age could not conceive of a maid from the country as anything but a shepherdess, and the onus of the characterization I leave to Dunois.

inspiring confidence. There is the talk about the carp, which Shaw makes use of, and d'Estivet's curses. There is her answer to the question whether she had ever been on the spot when Englishmen were slain: "In God's name, of course! How softly you speak!" In 1456 Thomas de Courcelles himself could recall of the sermon to Joan given by Guillaume Erard in the churchyard of Saint-Quen only the words "the pride of this woman." He could remember but one single image of Joan's abjuration: Cauchon in conversation with some others. He stopped in the middle of a sentence, but De Courcelles no longer knew what was said. Thomas de Courcelles, in 1456 one of the lights of the Church and the University, displayed a very poor memory at the rehabilitation trial.

The picture of Joan of Arc is clear and sharply defined, but even so we cannot rigidly categorize it. Anyone who attempts to reduce it to the terms of scientific psychology will himself no doubt feel that he is violating it. That is fundamentally the case for every picture of a historical personality, but it is the more obvious the further the personality deviates from the usual norms of character and action. "The great man is unknowable," Hanotaux says rightly, and Shaw: "the superior being, being immeasurable is unbearable . . ." For us the person of Joan of Arc, perhaps more purely than any other figure in history, lies quite utterly within the sphere of the heroic. We can seek in vain for the term summarizing her essence. "Heroine" is not satisfactory. "Genius" even less. "Saint," whether or not one understands it completely in the technical, ecclesiastical sense, is far and away the best.

III

THE OPINION OF HER AGE

"At no single moment of her existence," says Anatole France, "was Joan known in any way but through fables, and if she set the masses in movement it was a result of the clamor of the countless legends that sprang up wherever she went, and sped on ahead of her." The first part of this statement is undoubtedly true; the second contains a serious mistake in logic. Her effect explained as a *result* of the countless legends? but then what explains the immediate emergence of those legends themselves? Wonder-workers were nothing unusual in the fifteenth century, and many of them made a fair amount of clamor, but not one aroused the amazement, the enthusiasm, and the terror that Joan of Arc immediately brought about. Nothing is more significant in this respect than the English ordinances attempting to counteract the mass desertion to the island and the refusal to be called to the colors.[6]

The way Joan of Arc's fame developed we know best from notices in Antonio Morosini's fifteenth-century chronicle, which first attracted attention in 1895. This Venetian kept a sort of diary of the news that came to Venice regarding remarkable events of the day. He recorded the news in whatever form he was able to obtain it, and so also inserted a number of letters that Pancrazio Giustiniani, a Venetian merchant at Bruges, sent to his father, Marco, in 1429 and 1430, and also letters from another Venetian in Avignon. These letters are remarkable not so much for their factual accuracy in details as for their illustration of how, in the mind of a "neutral," the image of Joan took form from day to day of her career. Giustiniani, an Italian and a merchant living in Burgundian territory, cannot be suspected of an immoderate tendency toward ready belief in the miracle of the Maid. His reports regarding Joan begin with a passing mention at the end of a detailed account of the raising of the siege of Orléans, written around the middle of May 1429: "In the past fortnight there has been much talk about all sort of prophecies found at Paris, and other things which all together promise the dauphin great prosperity. . . . Many people made the most priceless jokes in the world about them, particularly those of a girl, a shepherdess[7] from Lorraine." Merchants in Burgundy had written him about the matter. He knows the rough outlines of her activities at Chinon. One of the persons writing him about her is reported to have said, "it is making me crazy." It all seems unbelievable, and yet. . . . In his next reference, dated July 9,[8] there is only a trace of doubt left: "These are most wondrous things if they be true, and it seems to me that they are so. . . . I believe that God's power is great. . . ." Then he finds support: in his later letters, dated November 20, 1429, and January 4, 1430, he apparently knows Jean de Gerson's cautious but understanding opinion re-

---

6. G. Lefèvre Pontalis, *"La panique anglaise en mai 1429," Le Moyen Age,* VII (1894), 81–95.

7. See note 5 above.

8. In between is a brief summary of a letter dated June 4.

garding Joan (to which I shall return below) and subscribed to it: "Believe what you will of it; it is said that the Maid does all these things and a thousand wonders more, which if they be true, are done by the Lord. And it is a great wonder in our days." His last word about her he wrote on November 24, 1430: *La poncela* has been sent to the king of England at Rouen;[9] John of Luxembourg has received ten thousand crowns for her. "What will follow for her is unknown, but it is feared that they will let her die, and truly these are strange and great things."

If in Morosini's tidings we have a report of Joan's activities in a crude form, a literarily colored image also developed, even in the first months. While some people who saw her simply jotted down their impressions of the Maid, as did the brothers De Laval in a letter to their mother, others make the wondrous affair a test of their style and wit, much as a modern journalist does with athletic heroes or musicians. One of the latter was Perceval de Boulainvilliers, counselor and chamberlain of Charles VII, in a Latin letter to Filippo Maria Visconti dated June 21, 1429. Another was an unknown writer, thought to be Alain Chartier, in a similar letter to an unknown prince, a month later. Now, one might expect that the form in which such authors molded Joan's image would be inspired by the chivalric concepts that so sharply dominated the minds of the day. But that was not the case. They embroidered a humanistic and hagiographic pattern with elaborate miraculous details for purposes of adornment, and quite a bit of rhetoric, so that these most original and primary sources must, remarkably enough, be considered among the least reliable.

Two of the finest and most sensible intellects of France, whose thoughts on lofty subjects had met on another terrain long before, both devoted their last work, written shortly before their deaths, to Joan's activities. Jean de Gerson wrote his *Considerations on the Fact of the Maid* on May 14, 1429, and died two months later. Christine de Pisan, spending the days of her old age in seclusion, wrote on July 31, 1429, her *ditié* of sixty-one stanzas, the last poem known from her, a bit flat and dull, but charged with an absolute faith in the mission of the Maid. Gerson, the cautious psychologist who had earlier written a long tract on how to distinguish between true and false visions, and who feared

---

9. Giustiniani was anticipating events: Joan was not yet in Rouen.

nothing as much as that all sorts of crude and cheap superstitions would gain the upper hand, wrote with a certain reserve. He is filled with sympathy for this affair that has excited all the world. The chief arguments moving him to place confidence in the divinity of Joan's mission actually fit perfectly in Shaw's picture. The very fact that her call has been able to move the king's counselors and the commanders to attack has a great deal of weight for Gerson, and rightly so. He also counts as a sign for the genuineness of Joan's mission the fact that, despite the divine order, she and the commanders who follow her do not abandon the ways of human caution. He feels, as it were, the masterly, inspired reasonability of her idea. Even if there is much in it that is natural, he goes on to say, it can still be a miracle, for also in the ancient miracles testified to by the Scriptures, those of Deborah and Judith, "something natural was always intermingled. ... And," Gerson carefully warns, "after the first miracle everything does not always go as people expect. Hence, even if the Maid should be disappointed in all her and our expectations—far be it from me to wish it—one may not conclude that everything that has happened has been wrought by an evil spirit, or at any rate not by God."

Where there was no sincere love for France such as Gerson's at stake, the conclusion of an ecclesiastical arbiter proved to be more hesitant. There was, for instance, that of Hendrik van Gorkum, rector of a Latin school at Cologne. This same Hendrik van Gorkum is referred to by Hugo Grotius in the Introduction to *De iure belli ac pacis* as one of his predecessors, on the basis of a tract *De iusto bello.*[10] But when in June 1429 he set side by side *Propositiones* for and against the Maid it never entered his mind that hers, too, might be referred to as a just war. His earnest objection to the genuineness of Joan's calling is that now, in the time of grace, it does not seem very probable that a spiritual mission for the advancement of a purely secular matter like the French cause against England would emanate from God. If everything was in order as regards Joan's calling, then she must be unusually holy. But that such a saintly creature should dress as a worldly war-

---

10. The *Kirchenlexikon*, V, 1707, mistakenly states that this tract has not been published. It is the seventh piece in *Tractatus consultatorii venerandi magistri Henrici de Gorychum* (Cologne, 1503); the Royal Library at The Hague possesses a copy of this rare work.

rior—how inappropriate! Judith and Esther had not done so. All of which was argued with utter logic and matter-of-factness by the good Dutchman Master Hendrik van Gorkum.

Did the archbisop of Reims, Regnault de Chartres, honestly believe even for a moment in Joan's calling? For him, the advocate of a peace by means of a *rapprochement* with the Duke of Burgundy, everything she wished to accomplish after the coronation at Reims was inopportune. As soon as she was taken prisoner by the Burgundians at Compiègne on May 23, 1430, he dropped her. He did not deny her straight out, but what he did do was worse: he cast the first stone. It was her own fault, and the reward she deserved, he wrote in a letter to the inhabitants of Reims.[11] She was unwilling to listen to advice, but did everything her own way. God had suffered the capture of the Maid because of her pride and the rich raiment she had worn, and because she had not followed His commands but her own will.

From this bit of information Shaw, in his fifth scene, worked out the figure of the Archbishop in a portrayal that is pretty much in keeping with the historical tradition. Joan's irrepressible assurance interpreted as pride and obstinacy: that was perhaps the most tragic thing in her history. Her own followers could not endure that lofty courage.

Or was it really, as Shaw would have it, crushed between the Church and the established Law that Joan met her doom as the masterly and insufferable herald of a new freedom for the individual and a new power for society? Shaw would like us to consider her trial as nothing more than the necessary defense of her age against the unknown and immeasurable danger that would destroy that age.

Undoubtedly the most exciting and most original aspect of Shaw's work is his relative rehabilitation of Joan's judges. If this dramatic argument were used for any other subject, for Caesar or even Napoleon, we might yield readily to such a view of the matter without being bothered by historical scruples. No longer to consider the trial as an infernal design to destroy Joan, but as a well-meant, regrettable mistake—it seems so logical, so understandable, so satisfactory, so historical. The countless people throughout the world who will carry with them for years to come the image of Joan of Arc as Shaw has imprinted

11. Extant only in extract.

it in them will all have made this correction of their earlier view: Pierre Cauchon was not a bribed and dishonest judge, but a decent and relatively honorable man who spared no effort to save the Maid.

Nonetheless, I believe that in this case many people who are as a rule not interested first of all in the historical course of events, but in the imaginative powers of the artist, will ask whether Shaw's view is correct.

Several points can be granted him without further ado. The proceedings of the 1431 trial of condemnation are in many respects more reliable than those of the rehabilitiation trial of 1456. Indeed, as Shaw remarks with a jeer, the judges at Rouen, who after long preparations spent more than three months on her trial proper, took an extremely serious view of their task when compared with the hasty procedures we can remember from the World War. Is this at the same time proof that they were unbiased?

Shaw traces the opinion that Cauchon served the English cause and the trial took place under pressure to a sin of romanticism. Joan was spotless, says romantic sentiment, hence her judges must have been rascals. Shaw rightly condemns such a trivial antithesis. But what if even the most serious historical research cannot lead to any conclusion but a disqualification of the judges? True, the pressure that was exerted is frequently exaggerated. It has been claimed, without grounds, that the proceedings were forged. The trial was conducted properly. Nonetheless, while he recognizes all this, Pierre Champion, more at home than anyone else in the France of the fifteenth century, refers to it as "a masterpiece of partiality under the appearance of the most regular of procedures"; it remains "odious" to him, as it was before him to Hanotaux, to Quicherat, and to a thousand other historians.

Reading through the proceedings of the trial, one does obtain an impression of relative gentleness, of a serious desire to spare Joan and to save her. But Shaw, basing his opinion on this impression, has merely become the dupe of a machination of the judges themselves. The detail and moderation of the trial had as their basis the political intent of making Joan's condemnation as unimpeachable as possible. Even the unusually large number of judges, far from proving a serious and scrupulous fairness, is suspect. They mark the trial as a political affair, a deliberate *cause célèbre.* Cauchon said even before the trial began

"that it was intended to give her a fine trial. ..." During the deliberations of the judges as to whether torture should or should not be
applied, one responded in the negative, for "it might bring disrepute
upon a trial thus far so well conducted. ..." All the expressions of
gentle admonition and sympathy with her hardened disposition can also
be explained as feigned gentleness. Shaw was perhaps not aware that
the words used on transferring a condemned person from the ecclesiastical court to the secular arm, "with the request to deal with her
tenderly," were nothing more than a customary formula that no one
expected to lead to anything but the bonfire.

As far as the bishop of Beauvais is concerned, Shaw could appeal to
the sources for more than one point in his picture of Cauchon. The
English accused him of being prejudiced in favor of Joan, and he
answered: "You lie: by law I must seek the redemption of the body and
the soul of this Joan. ..." The general accusation, both in comtempo-
rary chronicles and in the testimonies of the rehabilitatioñ trial, that
hatred and political intrigue had been the reasons for the acts of 1431
are not sufficient to brand Cauchon as an unjust judge, though there is
a great deal that is damning against him. Even his antecedents in the
service of England and Burgundy do not prove that he violated his duty
at Rouen. Nonetheless, among the testimonies in 1456 there is one that
it is very difficult to reject as groundless, and which is almost enough to
condemn Cauchon and invalidate Shaw's view. It was made in almost
identical terms by Brother Isambard de la Pierre and Brother Martin
Ladvenu. When the judges had gone to see for themselves that Joan,
after her abjuration, had put on man's dress again, and as a result were
forced to adjudge her an obstinate and relapsed heretic, the bishop of
Beauvais, on leaving the prisoner, was heard to address Warwick
among a number of Englishmen. "With laughter on his lips he said in a
clear voice: 'Farewell, farewell, it is done! Have good cheer!' or similar
words."

If it is hard to maintain the historicity of a well-meaning Cauchon, if
many of the judges were his creatures, if a few of them did raise their
voices against him, none of that indicates, on the other hand, that the
whole trial was sheer wickedness and conscious bias. Though she was
asked cunning questions that she could not answer, though the reasoning was formalistic and one-sided, the crucial issue—whether Joan had

been able to develop her amazing power owing to divine help or demonic—was a very serious one, one that, inspected on its own merits, would have been completely dubious for any other court of that day. It is perfectly understandable that ecclesiastical judges who did not share in the enthusiasm for the cause of Charles VII catalogued Joan among a host of overwrought persons who set the world in turmoil. "If it should ever come so far that the people in their rashness would rather listen to soothsayers than to the shepherds and teachers of the Church, religion will be doomed. . . ." These words out of a letter from the University of Paris to the pope, the emperor, and the college of cardinals will be recognized as the basis for Shaw's sentences put in the mouth of Cauchon in Scene IV. It was a logical syllogism when her judges reasoned: a revelation from God always leads to obedience; Joan ran away from her parents and wears man's dress, both of which are evidence of disobedience; hence her revelation is not from God. Dogmatically it was quite correct that one might not believe in visions and inspirations "just as strongly" as one "believed that Christ was crucified. . . ." If only Joan had said "it seems to me" instead of "I know for certain," there was no man who would condemn her, Master Jehan Lohier, who was favorably inclined toward her, said to Guillaume Manchon. Visions such as hers are possible with God, Master Jehan Basset considered during the deliberations, but she did not support them with a miracle or with a proof from the Scriptures, hence they should not be believed. Again it was completely logical according to the formal rules of the faith.

Given the conceptual system of the day, an impartial modern judge would be able to endorse completely the conclusions of the 1431 deliberations. The judges reached the same decision a judge who did not believe in the cause of Joan could arrive at even today. Her visions were declared to be "certain fictions, conceived humanly or the work of the Evil One. . . ." She had "not had sufficient signs to believe therein and to know them. . . ." Jehan Beaupère, master of theology, who was inclined to consider the phenomena "to be not supernatural, but traceable, in part, to physical causes, and in part to imagination and human invention . . . ," was not so very far from explaining them as morbid symptoms. The chief distinction between the judges of 1431 and some psychologists of today is that, while the judges needed several months, the psychologists would probably have been ready with their statement within half an hour at the outside.

The method of the judges of 1431 was utterly scholarly. They are usually reviled in the historical studies (even in Champion's) because of the weight they attached to the innocent children's games of Joan's youth at Domremy, beside the spring and under the beech tree called the Fairy Tree, which they danced around and hung wreaths upon. But they are unjustly accused of cunning and antipathy in this respect. It *was* an important point for them. If it became clear from Joan's statements that there was a link between the appearance of her "voices" and the pagan customs centered around the tree, the diabolical character of her visions would be as good as proved. Whence the urge to know whether Saint Catherine and Saint Margaret had ever talked with her *beneath that tree.*

Finally there is the question of Joan's view of the Church and her refusal to submit without reserve to the judgment of the Church Militant. Again and again the judges asked her if she would leave the decision on the nature of her deeds to the Church. They attempted to explain to her the difference between the Church Triumphant and the Church Militant. But she did not understand. "I refer them to Our Lord who sent me, to Our Lady, and to all the blessed saints of Paradise," she says. "And she thought it was all one, Our Lord and the Church, and that these difficulties should not be made for her, and asked why we made difficulties when it was all one." According to the auditor of the Rota (a court of the Roman Curia who around 1454, in connection with her rehabilitation, made a close study of the twelve articles drawn from her confessions, she had sometimes understood that her judges were the Church and sometimes merely that the Church was the building where she was not allowed to go to hear mass. To the question whether she would submit, her answer in the hearings is once recorded as only to the Church on high, and later that she would submit to the Church Militant, "provided it does not command anything impossible. ..." The ecclesiastical court of 1431 was, indeed, from its point of view on very firm ground when it counted such an attitude heavily against her. There had to be a limit to *sancta simplicitas.*

It is not in the objective value of their decision that the infamy of the judges of Rouen lies. They could justify the decision, looked upon as a matter in itself, to the feeling of their time and to their own consciences. The most august learned body of the day, the University of Paris, had done more than anyone else to help prepare the verdict, to elicit it, and to cloak it with its authority. The University of Paris should bear the burden of memory more than the judges at Rouen. Let us hope that the rector who guided the solemn assembly of the university on April 29, 1431—Pieter of Gouda, a canon of Utrecht, born at Leiden—was an insignificant chairman. The university judged logically, bitterly, and harshly; it judged from a distance, according to the facts, and did not see its victim.

Among those who did see her, the judges at Rouen, there was more than one who became somewhat aware of her greatness and her purity and was inclined toward a more favorable judgment. But the majority could see in her only "stubborn malevolence and hardness of the heart," "a sly mind tending toward evil and devoid of the grace of the Holy Ghost," without virtue and humility as they understood them. To them it was all pride and disobedience. They thought that in her they were punishing the sin of Lucifer himself.

Can the Rouen sentence rightly be looked upon as the reaction of the Church Militant to the spirit of individual religious opinion which was to shake that Church to its foundations less than a century later? In other words, is there any historical justification for Shaw's witty toying with the word "Protestantism"?

I do not believe so. The concept of Protestantism is a composite concept. It assumes much more than merely Joan's naïve obstinacy against the Church Militant in her direct obsession with the glory of the Church Triumphant. The term Protestantism makes sense only with regard to persons who, after having tested the whole medieval Catholic concept of the Church, deliberately rejected it. If she had not become implicated in an ecclesiastical trial, the weak point in Joan's faith would never have become public. She does not testify against the Church of her own free will, but an ecclesiastical court forces her, on formalistic grounds, to a consistency that seems heretical. True Protestantism can only lie on the yonder side of the whole system of Scholastic theology; Joan's ignorant faith falls completely on this side of it—or outside it. Her spirit has nothing in common with those of Huss and Wycliffe. In her saintly simplicity she is just as Catholic as the (legendary) old woman who carried the bundle of faggots for Huss. Protestantism presupposes humanism, intellectual development, a modern spirit; in her faith Joan of Arc was in the full sense of the word a primitive. It would be regrettable if the non-Catholic world allowed Shaw's authority to lure it into denying the Catholic Church the glory of its most touching saint.

So much for Warwick's discovery: "I should call it Protestantism if I had to find a name for it. ..." To a certain extent the same thing applies to Cauchon's countermove "Nationalism." But there Shaw is not alone. Many French authors before him have celebrated in Joan of Arc the birth of French patriotism. In a certain sense rightly so. The great love of France as a whole, concentrated on the king, became a conscious thing during (and because of) the protracted war against England. Long before Joan that patriotism had had its heroes and its martyrs, for example, the ship's captain from Abbeville, Ringois, who was thrown into the sea at Dover in 1360 because the demand that he swear loyalty to the king of England rebounded upon his "I am French." Eustace Deschamps had testified to it in many a poem thirty years before Alain Chartier interpreted that patriotic love. But Shaw means something more than mere love of country. The transformation that he would like to attribute to Joan is the assertion of national monarchy as opposed to feudal particularism, and that not only in France but also in England. *Tua res agitur,* Warwick believes. Now, this is completely incorrect. The national monarchy, both in France and in England, was from the very outset aware of its antithetical position toward feudalism, its superior task, and its superior right. In England the monarchy had had the upper hand in the conflict ever since the Conqueror, and repeatedly it was only as a result of crises and slumps that the aristocracy won ground temporarily. In France the monarchy was triumphing over the lords slowly but surely. The conflict had begun long before the fifteenth century—as early as with Louis VII and Philip Augustus in the twelfth. The elements of the modern state came into being in France in the thirteenth century under Saint Louis and Philip the Fair. In the fifteenth century Louis XI, in his struggle with Burgundy and the League of Public Weal, gained the ascendancy in what was merely a last dangerous crisis, and completed a structure it had taken centuries to build. Joan of Arc brought a new patriotic spirit, but not a new concept of the state. Her patriotic love, like her faith, was primitive, rather prefeudal than modern. To her—and not only to her—the cause of France was "the quarrel of the king of France." They are the king's faction, his loyal followers; he is their liege and France is his heritage, which an intruder unjustly contests. Joan's patriotism is built up out of utterly primitive notions. In this, too, she is sublime simplicity and sheer courage. As a result of those lofty qualities her conception of love and sacrifice could have a seminal influence on the modern notion of the state, but she did not create it. Shaw's "Nationalism" placed in Cauchon's mouth is nothing more than a brilliant touch of his wit.

Joan of Arc as the subject of a historical hypothesis, as Shaw would have it, an exponent of certain ways of thinking—there is something annoying in it. In her irreducible uniqueness she can be understood only by means of a sense of sympathetic admiration. She does not lend herself to being used to clarify currents and concepts of her day. Her own personality attracts all the attention as soon as one touches on her history. She is one of the few figures in history who cannot be anything but protagonists, who are never subordinate, always an end and never a means. And this—if I may end these marginal notes with a word of personal apology—is also the reason why there is hardly a reference to her in the work that I wrote some years ago on life in the fifteenth century in France and the Netherlands. It has been charged to me as an error. But it was a considered, deliberate omission. I knew that Joan of Arc would have torn the book I visualized in my mind completely out of balance. What kept me from introducing her in it was a sense of harmony—that and a vast and reverent humility.

IX/Mr. Shaw and "The Maid"

Coming back to the strictly literary or dramatic aspect of *Saint Joan,*
recognising its effervescent cleverness, its effectiveness for its purpose,
its measure of intellectual force, one asks oneself whether this is really
the best that modern drama can do with the Middle Ages. It could not
easily find a better story: could it not reach something nearer the
verisimilitude which Mr. Shaw confesses he has sacrificed for his satirical (or didactic) purposes? "I have taken care to let the mediaeval
atmosphere blow through my play freely," he writes, after alleging that
"there is not a breath of mediaeval atmosphere in Shakespeare's histories." This after confessing to have made many characters in *Saint Joan*
talk in twentieth-century fashion in order to make them intelligible to a
modern audience!

Let us grant that Mr. Shaw has given us a real breath of medieval
atmosphere by making the change of wind on the Loire a miracle
accruing upon Jeanne's announcement that she will go and pray to St.
Catherine for it. That, it must be admitted, is something beyond Shakespeare. And what, one wonders, would Shakespeare have thought of it!

As it happens, though Mr. Shaw will not bring himself to face the
problem, the one English history play, apart from *Henry IV,* which we
have adequate reason for believing to be of Shakespeare's writing, is
King John; and that is but a careful rewriting of a previous piece. But
the difference here between Shakespeare and Mr. Shaw is that the

Reprinted from *Mr. Shaw and "The Maid"* (London, 1925), X, 91-100. Chapters untitled
in book.

former would never have pretended to be recovering the atmosphere of
the Middle Ages; while Mr. Shaw, professing to be doing so, is in the
main a great deal further from doing it. Constance is about as true for
the thirteenth century as for the sixteenth: Mr. Shaw's blend of Jeanne
and Marie Bashkirtseff and George Eliot is true for neither the fifteenth
nor the twentieth.

Shakespeare made or remade or adapted plays for an Elizabethan
audience which had, broadly speaking, no ideas whatever about historical perspective. The twentieth century has historical-documentary re-
sources compared with which Shakespeare's were as those of an elementary schoolbook of our day; and he no more dreamt of finding an
old Celtic atmosphere for *Lear* or *Macbeth* than of making an Athenian
one for the *Dream.* Cannot the twentieth century, then, really achieve
for the stage what Mr. Shaw professes to have sought—a re-creation of
the turbulent past as it can be seen or divined to have been, with its
blind beliefs, its brutalities, its tumultuous energy, its splendours and its
squalors, its intellectual darkness and its aesthetic lights?

Far be it from the critic to dictate to the artist as such. He who
would read Mr. Shaw at his best should turn to the section of the
preface to *Saint Joan* in which he retaliates on those who adjured him
to improve the play by shortening it on accepted blue-pencil principles.
The wielders of that instrument, Mr. Shaw points out, would after
disembowelling his play have wasted hours in building elaborate scen-
ery, with real water in the Loire and a real bridge across it, and a sham
fight for the possession of it, led by Joan on a real horse. Then they
would have had a coronation scene and procession at Rheims, eclipsing
all previous efforts; Joan would be burned on the stage "as Mr. Mathe-
son Lang always is in *The Wandering Jew*"; and the intervals necessi-
tated by these constructions, to the great profit of the refreshment bar,
would have made the play longer than ever. Yes; better Mr. Shaw's
three-ply heroine than a mediaeval pageant, with real river and real fire
and real horses.

But is there no alternative? The mere student of history, musing over
its immense stores of recorded reality, can by means of elementary
"dramatic imagination" conjure up scenes and dialogues a little nearer
verisimilitude than Mr. Shaw's; and would swiftly blue-pencil many of
the latter. The presentment of the bullheaded chaplain who bellows for

the burning of the witch, and, having seen it, returns bellowing in remorse, will really not stand for the fifteenth century. In the sixteenth, men and women still looked on heretic-burning, it may have been with tears of compassion, but without bellowing hysteria. And why not, when we remember, as Mr. Shaw might have been expected to do, how many myriads, in much later times, gaped eagerly at hangings? We have a story of remorse in regard to Jeanne's martyrdom; but it is of a quite credible kind, and the personage is quite different. Mr. Shaw's chaplain is vivacious but bogus, like his Joan, his Charles, his Archbishop, his Bishop, his Inquisitor. It is a delightful anti-climax to find that, after the quite contrary argument in the preface, his most serious didactic effort in the play is to convince us that the burning of a person at the stake is to be avoided because it is a horrible spectacle; but that conviction does not lend historic verisimilitude to his chaplain.

So one still feels that a really imaginative dramatist, well nourished on history, might make for us a dramatic vision of the Middle Ages in terms of his knowledge, modelling himself, on the whole, rather on the undidactic and impersonal and missionless Shakespeare than on the missionary and didactic and—shall we say?—un-Shakespearean Mr. Shaw. So oriented, the dramatist would spare us farce and comedy, because mediaeval farce and comedy, to be true, would have to be very primitive; while mediaeval tragedy is just as tragical as any other. The best tragic stories, barring the Greek and Roman, come to us thence. Of such are the stories of Macbeth, Lear, Othello, Hamlet, and Romeo and Juliet. And the truly tragic dramatist, staging Charles VII, the uncrowned and unstrung King who knew that the Treaty of Troyes, made by his mother, excluded him from kingship, and wondered whether he were really the son of his mad father, and feared divine judgment for the assassination of Jean of Burgundy, might give us something nearer to *Hamlet* than to Dickens.[1] At least Shakespeare might, *redivivus.*

1. "N' étair nulle part sûr, nulle part fort; craignoit toujours morir par le glaive par jugement de Dieu, parce que present fut en la mort du duc Johan. Ne s'osait loger sur un plancher, ni passer un pont de bois à cheval, tant fût bon." ("He was nowhere sure, nowhere strong; feared always to die by the sword, by judgment of God, because he had been present at the death of Duke Jean. Did not dare to stand on a plank, nor cross a wooden bridge on horseback, however sound it might be.") Testimony of Georges Chastelain, cited by Vallet de Viriville, ed. of *Chronique de la Pucelle*, p. 325.

However that may be, we shall not get the ideal mediaeval tragedy from Mr. Shaw. The latter explains to us that he has exaggerated the qualities of Cauchon and the Inquisitor "because only by doing so can I maintain my drama on the level of high tragedy." Seeing that in the same paragraph we learn from him that the fact of the murder of Joan being a judicial and pious murder "at once brings an element of comedy into the tragedy," it is unnecessary to spend argument in support of the verdict that Mr. Shaw is not destined to yield us any high tragedy.

And why? Because, I take it, great tragedy founds above all things on the sense of moral reality. Comic reality, indeed, has its plain place in the order of things, and the sense of humour is vital to philosophic and moral sanity. But while anybody can appreciate the fact that the French tiler of the fifteenth century could actually give points to the bricklayer of today in the art and craft of "ca' canny," the sense of reality takes in larger relations. Mr. Shaw might have put a "ca' canny" tiler into *Saint Joan* without departing from documentary evidence, though some readers might have ignorantly accused him of unwarrantably imposing the twentieth century on the fifteenth. But his sense of the comic is no pilot to the plane of tragedy. He has at best made his Joan's martyrdom pathetic. How could it be otherwise when he avowedly sees comedy in the concept of judicial murder, just after arguing that it is that element that solely constitutes the horror of the stake? The dramatist to whom a thing is *at once* comic and tragic, and to whom the horror of the earthquake is non-significant, is visibly not a tragedian, whatever else he may be.

The epilogue confirms the verdict. "As to the epilogue," he breezily writes, "I could hardly be expected to stultify myself by implying that Joan's history in the world ended unahppily with her execution, instead of beginning there. It was necessary by hook or crook to show the canonised Joan as well as the incinerated one; for many a woman has got herself burnt by carelessly whisking a muslin skirt into the drawing-room fireplace; but getting canonised is a different matter, and a more important one. So I am afraid the epilogue must stand." Quite so: for Mr. Shaw there is no tragedy at all: not even the small tragedy of the old father dying of a broken heart. Both for himself and for the audience to whom he so successfully and so skilfully ministers laughter, he must have a comedy-ending, though the element of hysteria in him dictates strokes of *that* order. Finally, his play is but propaganda. I am not sentimental enough to see in the process the tragedy of an artist; but some might.

Deep, truly, are the differences between Shakespeare's methods and Mr. Shaw's. The Elizabethan Master had no thought of suggesting that the history of Antony and Cleopatra, or Coriolanus, or Macbeth, or Lear, began with the functioning of his play as an exponent of the fatality of character. He probably never felt that getting canonised is an important matter. He certainly never dreamt that after three hundred years we should be discussing *Hamlet.* Yet so it is; while it may plausibly be doubted whether posterity three hundred—or thirty— years hence will be discussing *Saint Joan.* The didactic aim, in art, is notoriously susceptible of self-frustration.

Still, let us shun fanaticism. Great tragedies are not to be produced by merely trying to write like Shakespeare, whether in prose or verse; and the ministry of the comic, however fantastic, is real in its own concrete way. And though fine dramatic verse is (other things equal) curiously antiseptic, even that mastery will not yield great tragedy without the sense for reality in life. Strangely enough, it is the chief master of imagined reality who has written that we are such stuff as dreams are made of, and that our little life is rounded with a sleep. The canonisation of Joan would not have shaken him. He wrote for another kind of believer than Mr. Shaw's. The fact remains that Mr. Shaw's audience is large, and thinks it has the sense of reality, whether or not it believes that Joan is alive somewhere to enjoy her own mundane prestige, or Shakespeare his.

Drama, it may be, is economically destined to become un-Shake-spearean, not only as to verse but as to spirit. Mr. Shaw has devoted a good deal of practical, and even some theoretic, attention to economics, though he does not seem to bring it into connection with the phenomena of canonisation in particular or of Catholicism in general. He certainly comprehends the economics of the stage, to the extent of "saving the theater manager a salary and a suit of armour" by lumping Dunois and D'Alençon into one. And if, by some such social evolution as finally turned the public drama of ancient Rome wholly to panto-mime, we are destined to see the drama of the stage expelled by that of the picture-palace, as the sparrow crowds out the song-bird, it is temporarily comforting to have such drama as his *Saint Joan* (passing for "all that *need* be known about her") staving off the decline and fall for a little. It is really very good fun; and not many plays are that. Even the preface as a whole is fairly good fun for the critic, if fun is all he wants. "A sober essay on the bare facts" is the author's account of it.

X/Shaw, Robertson and "The Maid"

It is itself a worn-out proverb, that no philosophy is ever refuted, but every philosophy becomes outworn. The fact that Mr. Bernard Shaw's currency is steadily declining in value, as more and more of it appears in circulation, and the probability that in ten or fifteen years it will no longer be accepted at all, do not constitute sufficient evidence that it is bad money. The more intelligent among those persons who have lost interest in anything that Mr. Shaw says, ought to be glad of some proof that their feelings are justified. Mr. Robertson has provided for such people a very valuable document. There are still many people so devoted as to stop their ears to any criticism of Mr. Shaw whatever, and, on the other hand, a growing number who are too fatigued by him to want to think about the matter at all. But no one should be too tired of the subject to read Mr. Robertson's small book. In 'St. Joan' Mr. Shaw has unluckily chosen a subject in which Mr. Robertson has interest and of which he has knowledge. Mr. Shaw's subject is also one in which Facts matter. Mr. Robertson likes Facts, and deploys his facts with a grim northern wit which operates with the effect of a steam roller.

Mr. Robertson's book is so brief, and his arguments so compact, that it would be a pity to attempt to summarise or select; everyone who is interested in the truth will read the book. Mr. Robertson is a Rationalist, with a genuine respect and admiration for Sainte Jeanne; but his book is of equal value to people who approach the problem from an

Criterion, IV (April, 1926), 389-90.

orthodox Christian standpoint. For what issues most clearly from a reading of Mr. Robertson's book is Mr. Shaw's utter inability to devote himself wholeheartedly to *any* cause. To Mr. Shaw, truth and falsehood (we speak without prejudice) do not seem to have the same meaning as to ordinary people. Hence the danger, with his 'St. Joan', of his deluding the numberless crowd of sentimentally religious people who are incapable of following any argument to a conclusion. Such people will be misled until they can be made to understand that the potent ju-ju of the Life Force is a gross superstition; and that (in particular) Mr. Shaw's 'St. Joan' is one of the most superstitious of the effigies which have been erected to that remarkable woman.

✍ CHARLES SAROLEA

XI/Has Mr. Shaw Understood Joan of Arc?

There has been in recent years an extraordinary growth of the cult of Saint Joan of Arc in Anglo-Saxon countries. When Anatole France, the greatest master of French speech, applied the methods of the higher criticism to the life of Joan of Arc and attempted to take her down from the pedestal to which the admiration and gratitude of her countrymen had raised her, a distinguished Scottish writer, Andrew Lang, constituted himself the champion of the maid. About the same time as Lang, on the other side of the Atlantic, Mark Twain wrote a remarkable book in which he tried with loving minuteness to reproduce the style and spirit of the old French chronicles. It is notable that in America the cult of Joan has extended to the common people. During the war I was repeatedly asked to lecture on the French saint to the American troops in France, and I was commissioned by the American Y.M.C.A. to write a special biography for the benefit of American soldiers. I found that the "Sammies" were mainly interested in one French hero—Napoleon, and in one French heroine—St. Joan of Arc; truly a quaint combination!

Recently the ever-increasing band of worshippers of Joan of Arc has been joined by a most surprising recruit, Mr. George Bernard Shaw. The Arch Iconoclast, the Mephistophelean philosopher is adoring what one would have expected him to burn. And such is the spell which is exercised by the Maid that Shaw has approached his subject almost in a spirit of reverence. Many poets before him have been attracted to Joan

English Review, XLII (August, 1926), 175–82.

of Arc. It cannot be said that any of them, from Chapelain to Voltaire, and from Shakespeare to Schiller, has been particularly successful in his poetic impersonations. The question before us is whether Mr. Bernard Shaw has been luckier than his predecessors? Has he succeeded where they conspicuously failed? I do not think that he has. No doubt, from a theatrical point of view, his play has been a wonderful and a deserved triumph. An almost unanimous chorus of praise hailed it in Paris as well as in London. But I am afraid that the literary critic cannot be quite as unqualified in his praise as the dramatic, and I believe that the sober historian is likely to be even less enthusiastic. Indeed, no student of medieval history who has taken the trouble to study the facts will be inclined to admit that Mr. Shaw has given us the real maid. I feel sure that there is no more relation between the historical Joan of Arc and his theatrical heroine than there is between the historical Macbeth and Shakespeare's.

The Joan of Arc of Mr. Shaw is not a medieval drama. It is neither a miracle play nor a mystery play. It is at best what the old dramatists called a "morality play." Or rather, it is a modern problem play. The illiterate peasant girl of eighteen who could not read or write, and who always maintained towards religion the simple, unquestioning attitude of the humble believer, is transformed into a latter-day advanced thinker, a herald of revolt, shaking the foundations of medieval society. The pious mystic who is so pre-eminently Catholic that she is unintelligible except in a Catholic setting, the obedient child of Mother Church who, even while she was engaged on the liberation of France, was planning a crusade against the Hussite heretics, is made into a heretic and into a Protestant. Could the travesty of history be carried further? Has Mr. Shaw ever imagined a character which looks more dangerously like a freak of fantasy?

Mr. Shaw reproves every one of his predecessors because they failed to catch the spirit of the times. He justly remarks that you cannot understand Saint Joan of Arc unless you also try to understand the atmosphere in which she lived, and the conditions in which she had her being. The remark is perfectly apposite, but I would submit that Mr. Shaw himself is extraordinarily ignorant of the medieval atmosphere and conditions. Indeed, he betrays that deeper kind of ignorance of the writer who does not even know that he does not know. He is a glaring illustration of the truth that no amount of genius or wit can take the place of accurate and scientific knowledge.

Mr. Shaw's main thesis is that the trial of Joan of Arc was a religious trial and not a political trial. Now it is perfectly true that in the history of Joan the religious issue is bound up with the political, as was inevitable in a state of society where there was constant fusion and confusion of the temporal and spiritual powers, and where the Canon law of the Church was constantly mixed up with the civil law of the State. But this close connection of the medieval Church and State does not prevent the fact that in the case of Joan of Arc the paramount issue was political, and that it is the political passions and prejudices alone which can make us understand the trial and condemnation. The Maid of Orleans was not a teacher or a preacher, like her contemporary John Huss, with whom Mr. Shaw compares her and who suffered a similar martyrdom. She never pried into the mysteries of faith. She did not question nor defy either the dogma of the Catholic religion or the authority of the Catholic Church. Her activity was purely political and military. She simply proclaimed that she had received from on high a mission to liberate France from the yoke of the foreign invader. Since she thus became the self-appointed leader of a political party and the champion of a political cause, her opponents were bound in self-defence to challenge her mission. And they took the only possible means to get rid of a dangerous enemy. They used religion as a pretext. It was inevitable that they should do so, at a time when France was undergoing the most terrible ordeal of all her chequered history, when political passion was burning at fever heat, and when all the horrors of civil war were being added to the cruelties of a foreign war.

I quite understand the position which Mr. Shaw chooses to take up. Like many a modern Socialist and democrat, he is really an aristocrat. He has the pride of intellect. He has a Nietzschean contempt for the opinions of the herd. And he believes that in one essential respect the herd are radically wrong about the trial of Joan of Arc. The vulgar always have a tendency to transform the great dramas and tragedies of history into commonplace melodramas, where consummate villains are always engaged in a conspiracy against helpless victims. The vulgar therefore quite naturally assume that Joan of Arc was at the mercy of wicked men like Bishop Cauchon, and that she never got a fair trial.

In justice to Mr. Shaw, I believe that he is right in his protest that the Maid of Orleans got as fair a trial as could be expected considering the errancy of human nature, and the circumstances of the times. Indeed, before Mr. Shaw, I tried to prove in a little book on Joan of Arc that posterity has been grossly unfair to the worthy politicians and theologians of the Rouen tribunal. But I submit to Mr. Shaw that his interpretation of the trial as being mainly a religious trial is entirely inconsistent—whereas my interpretation of the trial as mainly political is entirely consistent with a belief in the honesty and sincerity of the judges. Once we admit that the judges were just ordinary political partisans, that they were subjected to all the passions of political parties and that they believed in the justice of their cause, we are driven to the conslusion that the Tribunal of Rouen was bound in duty and conscience to condemn the maid. Indeed, I do not see that there was any alternative for them. Let us consider the position in which they were placed and the atmosphere of a terrible civil war. The judges could not reasonably deny the supernatural character of Joan's mission. They could not understand or explain her any more than we can, when we test her by ordinary human standards. They were therefore driven to assume a supernatural interposition. The only question was whether that supernatural intervention did come from God Almighty, or whether it came from the Infernal Powers. The judges could not possibly believe in a Divine interposition, because if they had they would have had to admit that God was on the side of the English and Burgundian enemy. Quite obviously, if the fruits of the glorious victory of Agincourt were not to be thrown away, if the English King was to justify his claim to the French throne, if the Duke of Burgundy was to assert his sacred obligation to avenge the horrible murder of his father, perpetrated by the supporters of Joan of Arc, then the peasant girl in man's clothing must be an emissary of the Evil One. She must be a witch in league with Satan. And the duty of the secular as well as of the ecclesiastical power was to deal with her in the only way in which medieval law dealt with witches—namely, by burning her at the stake.

Holding, then, that Joan's trial was primarily a political and not a religious trial, I further hold that this political trial must be conceived as being essentially a moving epic and tragedy of patriotism. Prompted by his temperamental disposition to dispute all commonly received opinions, and systematically to defend the paradoxical, rather than the common-sense view, Mr. Shaw would make us believe that Joan was not the patriotic heroine which she is supposed to be. It is true that in the opinion of the French people of every class, of every party and persuasion, pity for, and love of, her country was the compelling motive behind her activities. But, forsooth, the French people are a benighted people, and they cannot be trusted to understand their own history. Therefore we must assume that they are entirely wrong, and that they impute to Joan sentiments which were entirely foreign to medieval society. Medieval society, so Mr. Shaw tells us, was international and cosmopolitan. Nationalism and patriotism are new-fangled, artificial, and recent notions. They are a wicked invention of the modern capitalist bourgeois State, which invention is intended to plunge the people into quarrels with an imaginary foreign enemy, in order to divide their attention from their real domestic enemies and from the the beneficent class war.

With all respect to Mr. Shaw, here again he betrays his strange ignorance of the elementary realities of medieval history. The fact is that the "principle of nationality" and national passions played as important a part in the Middle Ages as in our present enlightened age. It is quite true that in religious matters medieval society was international and universal. On the other hand, in political matters the Middle Ages were intensely national and even parochial. Every kind of patriotism, even from the municipal patriotism of the City State, was familiar to them. Has it not occurred to Mr. Shaw that the wars between France and England and between England and Scotland were national wars? Has it not occurred to him that even universities, which from their very name ought to have been universal, were run on nationalist lines, and that, strangely enough, they were organized, not in faculties, but in separate "nations." of which separate divisions we still have a survival in the present curious organization of Glasgow University? Has it not occurred to him that in Flanders, across the northern border of France, the battle of languages and of nationalities had been raging for centuries, that Flanders was divided into Flemings and Frenchies, and that on one occasion in the terrible Matins of Bruges the Frenchies had been cruelly massacred? Has it not occurred to him that in every city of Italy there was a national or Guelph party, and an international Ghibel-

line or German party? Has it never occurred to him that even John
Huss was almost as much a Bohemian patriot as a heretic, and that it
was his action, as Rector of the University of Prague, to enforce the
supremacy of the Bohemian "nation" over the German "nation," which
decided 5,000 German students to leave Bohemia in bitter indignation,
and to found a new university at Leipsic? Has it not occurred to Mr.
Shaw that even allegiance to the Pope, which ought to have been
decided on purely religious grounds, was, in fact, determined by national considerations? When the great schism of the Papacy came the
various sections of Europe took sides for or against the respective Popes
and anti-Popes, not on the merits of the individual candidates, but for
political and national reasons. Frenchmen were Clementists because
Pope Clement had his residence at Avignon. Scotsmen were on the
same side because the Scots were the allies of the French. On the
contrary, the English were for the Pope of Rome, and supported Pope
Urban because they were the enemies both of the French and of the
Scotch.

Considering that Mr. Shaw goes out of his way to revolutionize all
the accepted views about Joan, it is somewhat astonishing and disap-
pointing that he should not have denounced one commonplace view
and advanced one paradox which personally I am prepared to argue,
and which is a paradox only in appearance. I submit to him that he has
missed a great opportunity. For 400 years millions of French people
have been convinced, and they are still convinced, that England was
mainly and, indeed, solely responsible for the tragedy of Rouen. They
have never forgiven the English for burning Joan any more than the
Germans have forgiven the French for burning the Castle of Heidel-
berg. I am sorry that it has not occurred to Mr. Shaw to challenge that
opinion in the interest of historical truth, in the interest of England,
and of international goodwill. The probability is that as an Irishman he
would not have liked to hold a special brief for England. But if he had
had the courage of his convictions, and if he had followed the logic of
his argument that Joan of Arc received a fair trial, and that it is unjust
to accuse the judges of Joan of Arc of unfairness and cruelty, he would
have further argued that it is even more unjust to accuse the English
people of a guilt which ought to be imputed to others. Even if we are to
admit that the condemnation of Joan of Arc was a judicial error and a

judicial crime, it was not an English crime, it was primarily a French crime.

The soldier who made Joan a prisoner was a French soldier. The officer who sold Joan for a few pieces of silver was a French officer. The Duke of Burgundy, who delivered over Joan to the tribunal was a French prince. Bishop Cauchon, who was the most bitter of Joan's prosecutors, was a French bishop. The University of Paris, which rebuked the ecclesiastical judges for their lukewarmness and slowness in prosecuting Joan, was a French university, the highest spiritual and judicial court in the French kindgom.

I have tried to prove that in all fundamentals Mr. Shaw is hopelessly wrong, and that he does not give us in "Joan of Arc" a historical character, but an imaginary one. I believe that my arguments are unanswerable, and I defy Mr. Shaw to answer them. It is highly probable that, if he does answer them, I shall have the worst of the argument in an intrinsically good cause. But all his genius and ingenuity will not prevail against the sober facts of history.

I have a suspicion that in his lucid intervals Mr. Shaw himself realizes that he is wrong. In a very interesting letter which I received from him some time ago he admits with characteristic candour that he does not claim to understand Joan of Arc.

"I do not profess to understand Joan of Arc: and neither will you, unless you are growing rasher with advancing years, instead of more cautious. Lots of writers have tried to explain her, and to account for her, to dramatize her, to glorify her, vilify her, and diagnose her; and she has beaten them all, the series of defeats culminating in the frightful 'gaffe' perpetrated by Anatole France. I have been more wary. I took the only documents that are of the smallest value; the report of the process, and that of the rehabilitation. I simply arranged what I found there, for the stage, relying on Joan to pull me through, which she did.

"I then amused myself by reading as much as I could stand of Joan literature. It is crusted with inventions, for the most part quite unconscious. The writers give one fact rather doubtfully as a fact, and then proceed to give as additional and unquestionable facts half-a-dozen ideas of their own which happen to have become associated with that fact in their minds through their historical and religious training. If you read a lot of this stuff before writing your article you are a lost man. Read the trial and nothing else, and you will see that it turned, with insistent laborious explicitness, on the Protestant point. When Joan said 'God must come first,' that is, before the Church, there was nothing for it but to burn her or canonize Wycliff and Huss. What else is there in the case worth writing ten lines about? Of talking round it there is no end; but what a waste of time!

"Of course, I shall read whatever you write with interest, and you can hardly suppose that after forty years of controversy I am turning thin-skinned. But I warn you that I have no theory about Joan, and understand her no more than I understand myself. Necessarily I take a certain view of the facts, and it will be very interesting if you can give another view of them, but none of us *know.* Anatole France may be dismissed as simply wrong, because he invented several pseudo-facts and refused to recognize the most glaring real fact (Joan's force and ability); but nobody who sticks to the fact, and is not the slave of theories about woman's sphere of a sectarian faith, can be convicted of error. So beware of my simplicity. I have deliberately abstained from learning in this matter so that I might the easier get into Joan's skin, and not into that of her historians; and as I have evidently got her alive somehow, you will have some trouble in persuading the world that I went the wrong way to work."

Mr. Shaw's admission is highly significant. It is a striking illustration of his sterling intellectual honesty. But the admission and confession entirely miss the point of the controversy. My main point is not only that he does not understand the Maid of Orleans. Nor is it only that he does not explain her. Rather it is that he distorts her personality, and that he misrepresents her mission. I must leave it to the critical reader to decide whether I have succeeded in proving my argument.

EDITH J. R. ISAACS

XII/Argumentative Martyrs

One of the essential differences between a saint and a law-maker is that a saint, for whom there is no might but righteousness, beyond and apart from self, attains his ends by faith in a superior spirit that works through him, and not through a power delegated to him by his inferiors. The saints are closer to the arts than the law-makers; their aloofness seems to forbid the average painter, sculptor, playwright—especially the playwright—from trying to do a part of their job for them, perhaps because the average man is willing to grant the saints their privilege of martyrdom, but the humblest sees himself as a potential improvement on any law-maker.

Even Saint Joan and Thomas à Becket, two very argumentative martyrs in the hands of two very argumentative dramatists, G. B. Shaw and T. S. Eliot, manage to keep their sainthood—and their theatricality—in command over their interpreters, at a time when dictators, economists, politicians and the lesser household tyrants are failing ignobly to assert themselves. The theatre today is so full of preachers, orators, advocates, that there is hardly room on the stage for the actor. It is a fashion and will pass, as soon as enough playwrights have had to listen to the exhortations, sermons, epilogues and orations of their fellows. But it might not be such a bad idea (now that the teachers of the land—which, of course and by precedence, includes the artists— are being firmly invited to subscribe to several new forms of oath) to

Originally titled "Saints and Law-Makers," as part of a Broadway in review column. *Theatre Arts Monthly,* May, 1936, pp. 333-34, 337-38. Retitled by the editor.

102

add one oath more, to which every playwright must subscribe before his play can be produced: 'I promise to write a play (that is, a work for the theatre to be performed by actors), a whole play, and *nothing but a play.*'

Saint Joan believed in the Voices that spoke through her, that were not the peasant girl of Domremy but Saint Catherine, Saint Margaret and Saint Michael. Except for the short months of her defeat, imprisonment and death, she made others believe in those Voices for the length of her young life and for centuries after her death. Such a saint, such an historic figure, such a dramatic personality, is a 'natural' on any stage that has faith in its rightness for the task, and that can make an audience believe in Joan and fight her battles by her side.

The character of the Maid offers a wealth of opportunity to the actor, and Shaw has contributed his richest gifts of enthusiasm and imagination to the chronicle of Saint Joan, so that it stands as one of his major achievements; yet there can be no doubt that the presentation of the play to an audience accustomed to buying plays as news carried a heavy risk today. *Saint Joan* is already known to the New York stage through one of the Theater Guild's notable productions twelve years ago. Moreover, Shaw himself is no longer the popular intellectual hero that he was when he wrote *Saint Joan*. Again, the play is over-long, and in half a dozen places is deeply involved in the sound of its own scintillant words; nor will Shaw permit his plays to be whittled down to the measure of normal audience attention. The gibes at England and the English—which are the major element in the play's humor—are just contemporary enough to be old-fashioned and not yet illuminated by time's perspective.

An actress-manager who trusted the theatre less than Katharine Cornell does, and who still wanted to produce *Saint Joan*, might easily have focused her faith on her own undoubted talents, have chosen a designer and a director who would point up the values in Shaw's play as a star vehicle for an actress, and have surrounded herself with players little enough to make her seem big by contrast. But the theatre has now come to know that that is not the way Katharine Cornell works. If the play is too long for ordinary attention, the individual speeches too big for the average actor to handle, the play's theme too magnificent for our own mental habit, she will, with Guthrie Mc-

Clintic's cooperation and his skill as director, not scale it down, but scale it up still more. She will choose a designer—Jo Mielziner—who instead of detracting from the vibrant color and pattern of the period will add a slight, very slight, edge of elegance to the setting, the costumes, the light, which will remove the play at once from hurried, immediate reality, and take it up into the world of poetry and painting where we have become accustomed to sit and look and listen.

She will engage actors like Arthur Byron who, by the range and mellowness of their voices and the sustained continuity of their projection, can compel attention for even such a long, difficult, philosophical speech as that of the inquisitor, Brother John Lemaître, at Joan's trial, one of the finest theatre speeches in all modern drama, without the fullness of which the play would never make quite explicit the depth of the conflict between the Maid and the established order represented by the Church and the Feudal system. She will give time and point to scenes in which she has no part, like the religious-political discussion between Peter Cauchon, the Bishop of Beauvais; Richard de Beauchamp, Earl of Warwick; and Master John de Stogumber—and put actors like Eduardo Ciannelli and George Coulouris so on their mettle that they play better than they have ever played before. She will give Maurice Evans, playing the Dauphin, such scope in the creation of the strange and difficult role that you will accept his unaccounted Cockney accent without objection, because it belongs to a characterization that is free and creative, and that expresses so well the weak and muddled spirit of the king and the temporal kingdom for which Joan fought, thinking she was fighting heaven's fight. At the moment of Joan's triumph, pushing forward to the ramparts of Orléans, and at the moment of her greatest tribulation, when the tide of the trial is finally overwhelming her, instead of turning the scenes inward upon herself in a star's way, she will open them up widely enough to include young players like Kent Smith (as Dunois, the Bastard of Orléans) and John Cromwell (as Martin Ladvenu), so that they spontaneously turn back to her an enriched opportunity.

In *Saint Joan* Shaw has aimed to retrieve both a martyr and her judges from the legends in which their humanity was interred. The play is a study of a girl who sees clearly because she is never blinded by fear or prejudice, who becomes a prey to society because 'fear will drive men to any extreme: and the fear inspired by a superior being is a mystery which cannot be reasoned away.'

The qualities that mark Katharine Cornell's conception of the part of Saint Joan are all in Shaw's portrait: the joyous, simple faith in the voices and her humble dedication to their service; her blatant pride before men, the vanity that makes her love her youth's clothes and her uniform, the boyishness that demands an equal association with soldiers and their commanders. Out of these elements Katharine Cornell builds up her Joan from the inspired village girl who comes to the castle at Vaucouleurs, asking for a guard to take her to the King, through the leadership of the King's forces and the hour of triumph, to the tragic final day of trial as a sorcerer and heretic. Through the scene of the trial—one of the season's memorable hours—she weaves all these elements of character like counterpoint against the fears, the bitterness and revenge, the narrowness of her opponents, lifting the scene up and up so that when she is finally led forth to the burning in the public square you are there with her, and at the same time she is still there with you in the hall of the castle, the scene of the trial, where Joan remains alive in spirit to this day.

XIII/*Saint Joan:* A Marxist View

Shaw wanted a world without struggle, a world in which he could feel at home. His attack upon Darwin for importing capitalist morality into nature is a barrier against consciousness both of the struggle for existence in nature and of the class struggle in society. He does not examine in what respects Darwinism gives an accurate account of the struggle for existence, and in what respects it is falsified by the ideology which the bourgeoisie employs in its class struggle against the workers; he says, in effect, "Let us think, not of these things, but of the working of the Holy Ghost." His enemy in Darwinism is its lack of religion.

As a result, his conception of creative evolution, which is intended to inspire society to free itself from the deadening power of capitalism, becomes indistinguishable from the disguises of capitalism. Shaw was aware of this danger, but he underestimated it. In a section of the preface to *Back to Methuselah* entitled "The Danger of Reaction," he warns against running back to our old superstitions.

> It must therefore be said very precisely and clearly that the bankruptcy of Darwinism does not mean that Nobodaddy was Somebodaddy with 'body, parts, and passions' after all; that the world was made in the year 4004 B.C.; that damnation means an eternity of blazing brimstone. . . .

And so on through the rest of the dogmas of orthodox Christianity. He concludes:

> If dwindling sects like the Church of England, the Church of Rome, the

Reprinted from *George Bernard Shaw: "A Good Man Fallen Among Fabians"* (New York, 1950), 158–66.

Greek Church, and the rest, persist in trying to cramp the human mind within the limits of these grotesque perversions of natural truths and poetic metaphors, then they must be ruthlessly banished from the schools to free the soul that is hidden in every dogma. The real Class War will be a war of intellectual classes; and its conquest will be the souls of the children.

Shaw not only makes the mistake of thinking that the real class war is a war of ideas only; he also mistakes the issues in the war of ideas. In this war, the main weapon of reaction in the 20th century has not been the old orthodox Christian theology of fire and brimstone, but an irrationalism whose gods are no longer recognizable as such. They are stripped of theology till there remains nothing but an *élan vital,* or are given an apparently real form in the Faustian urge of Spenglerian culture, in blood and soil and race, in the fictitious unity of a "nation" which is elevated above the real nation of class struggle (to say nothing of such later developments as existentialism and all the revivals of Comte's Republic of the West—without even the republicanism). Because they do not provoke the disbelief which rejects the literal dogmas of hell and brimstone, they are far more effective than the orthodox Christian theology which Shaw singles out for attack in fulfilling the purpose of reaction.

Shaw did not realize the necessity of fighting these disguises of reaction and eradicating their influence on his own ideas. Like any Tory, he upholds against Darwinist materialism the "scientific fact of the Holy Ghost." And just as he tries to reconcile religion and science, so also in the Postscript written to *Back to Methuselah* in 1944, when the play appeared in the World's Classics, he tries to find a middle way for humanity between "a Marxist world in which the millennium will be guaranteed by a new Catholicism in which the proletarians of all lands are to unite," and "an idolatry of imaginary Carlylean heroes and bogus Nietzschean supermen."

The resulting confusion of ideas is particularly apparent in the preface to *Saint Joan.* Shaw repeats in different words what he had written about *Candida* in the preface to the *Pleasant Plays:* that it was a "modern pre-Raphaelite play," an expression of the new understanding of the Middle Ages; "religion was alive again," a sense of membership of the community whose corporate life expressed humanity's Godhead. In a similar sense, Shaw now says:

I write in full view of the Middle Ages, which may be said to have been rediscovered in the middle of the nineteenth century after an eclipse of about four hundred and fifty years. The Renascence of antique literature and art in the sixteenth century, and the lusty growth of Capitalism, between them buried the Middle Ages; and their resurrection is a second Renascence.

And he adds: "I have taken care to let the medieval atmosphere blow through my play freely."

In the religious spirit of the Middle Ages Shaw finds that vision of truth which the theologians of to-day have lost through misunderstanding their own theology, and the scientists through misunderstanding their own science. Scientists and theologians alike are guilty of the heresy that "theology and science are two different and opposite impulses, rivals for human allegiance;" whereas the real subject of both is the working of the Holy Ghost. Theologians maintain that the visions which appeared to Joan were objectively real; scientists declare them to have been merely hallucinations. But because "modern science is making short work of the hallucinations without regard to the vital importance of the things they symbolize," the danger is in the blindness of modern science to the truth in the content of the symbols rather than in the assertion by religion of their objective reality. For the scientists sin against the Holy Ghost: they are blind to the religious truth, which the theologians recognize even while they distort it, of man's divinity; and in that truth is the only hope of civilization.

At the time of *Candida*, Shaw presented the revival of the religious sense as finding its fulfilment in the quickening of Christian Socialism; but in the preface to *Saint Joan* the religious consciousness has become an end in itself. There is no longer a mention of socialism, not even Christian. Society is to be regenerated by men casting off the self-centred individualism of the age of reason and of capitalism and by their feeling within themselves the working of the Holy Ghost. And as in *The Quintessence of Ibsenism* and *The Perfect Wagnerite* Shaw's refusal to face the practical issues of his theory of anarchism as the liberation of man's Godhead led him to compromise with capitalism, so now he will not define his theory of the Holy Ghost in terms of action, but compromises with the Catholic Church.

In the earlier works he was afraid of the State; and when his theory

of anarchism confronted him with the question whether the will of
humanity must accept the existing form of capitalist State as necessary
and permanent, he sought refuge in a trick of words: the State must be
recognized, not as the State, but as a committee of citizens, "mostly
fools." In the preface to *Saint Joan* he says that "the Holy Ghost . . .
flashes with unerring aim upon the individual;" but what if the Holy
Ghost inspires the individual to defy the Church and the State? Shaw's
confortable answer is that "thought, when really free, must by its own
law take the path that leads to The Church's bosom." The Holy Ghost
must be patient; all things work for good. Shaw continues:

> I have before me the letter of a Catholic priest. "In your play," he writes,
> "I see the dramatic presentation of the conflict of the Regal, sacerdotal, and
> Prophetical powers, in which Joan was crushed. To me it is not the victory
> of any one of them over the others that will bring peace and the Reign of
> the Saints in the Kingdom of God, but their fruitful interaction in a costly
> but noble state of tension." The Pope himself could not put it better; nor
> can I. We must accept the tension, and maintain it nobly without letting
> ourselves be tempted to relieve it by burning the thread.

Those words were written, by a man professing himself a communist,
six years after the Socialist Revolution. That Revolution had already
burned the thread.

Such is the intellectual background to *Saint Joan;* yet the play rises
above it. For when Shaw begins to imagine dramatic situations, and his
characters begin to speak and act and come into conflict with one
another, his idealism, though it affects and restricts his dramatic vision,
no longer dominates as it does in his more abstract thinking.

The movement of the play in its first three scenes creates the sense of
the surge of a popular rising, with Joan at its head, winning over the
waverers and carrying them along with it, sweeping aside all those who
say that France can never be liberated, infecting the court and the king
with its own enthusiasm, inspiring the army, and making straight for
the enemy's guns in the confidence of victory.

Each of the scenes works up to a burst of irresistible onward movement. As the first scene closes, Joan dashes out in wild excitement,
followed by Poulengey—the time of waiting is over, and action has
begun. At the close of the second scene, the king and all the knights
draw their swords, shouting "To Orleans!" At the close of the third, the

contrary wind that has kept the rafts moored to the banks suddenly changes. Joan and Dunois dash out to lead the attack, and the Page "capers out after them, mad with excitement."

This is not mysticism, but a real movement of liberation; this is the real sense of life, which Shaw's Fabianism and idealism perverted into the mysticism of the Holy Ghost.

The weakness is that Joan herself does not come from the movement; she creates it by her personal qualities, and the people follow. Her identity with them is in her ways of speech, her country accent, and blunt manner rather than in their common passion for the freedom of France. She, rather than the movement she represents, overcomes the hesitations of the doubters, and she does so by bewildering an opponent like Baudricourt with that quickness of retort characteristic of the earlier Shavian heroes, whom she closely resembles. Thereby the conflict loses the greatness of its subject, and the action falls from the level of the people's struggle for freedom to such trivial comedy as the Steward rushing in at the end of the first scene to say that "the hens are laying like mad."

The individualism which makes Joan's personality the impulse of the movement she leads also confuses the theme of the play. Despite the individualism, dominant in the first three scenes is the advance of the people; it is dominant also in the fourth scene, where the Earl of Warwick and Cauchon, Bishop of Beauvais, ally themselves to crush this national, Protestant movement which threatens equally the power of the feudal aristocracy and of the Church. It is still strong in the fifth scene, in the ambulatory of Rheims Cathedral, after the coronation of the King, when Joan wants to press the attack and liberate Paris, but the King, the Church and the General commanding the army want to play for safety; Joan replies that they are timid because they are still fighting in the old way, trusting to knights who are thinking only about chivalry and ransoms, instead of to common folk.

> Remember the day your knights and captains refused to follow me to attack the English at Orleans! You locked the gates to keep me in; and it was the townsfolk and the common people that followed me, and forced the gate, and shewed you the way to fight in earnest.

When they all turn on her and warn her that she is alone, she answers:

> I will go out now to the common people, and let the love in their eyes comfort me for the hate in yours. You will all be glad to see me burnt; but if I go through the fire I shall go through it to their hearts for ever and ever. And so, God be with me!

And the moving impression of this speech is made articulate when, in answer to Dunois' words that he must leave Joan to her doom if she gets caught, her faithful follower La Hire replies:

> Then you had better chain me up; for I could follow her to hell when the spirit rises in her like that.

But in this scene there is divided emotion. For the conflict is not so much between Joan, the leader of the common people, and the rulers of Church and State, but rather between the lonely, inspired saint and those who mistrust or hate the strangeness and reckless passion of such holiness. Joan seems to stand, not among the people, but alone with the sound of the bells, in which she hears the voices of her saints. As Joan's loneliness deepens, so does the mysticism; and as the people kneel to kiss the feet of their saint, the onward impetus of their movement ceases, and France becomes an abstraction.

In the trial, their movement is forgotten. Joan is not accused as leader of the people. There is only one passing reference to Protestantism, none of the people's national movement. Warwick, as the representative of the English State rather than of feudal aristocracy, strives to speed Joan's sentence, but the trial itself is presented as a fair examination of a heretic by an ecclesiastical court which, in strange and sudden contrast to the corrupt worldliness of the Church as represented by the Archbishop, is sincerely anxious to save the heretic's soul; and her heresy is that she believes in her voices. The first part of the play succeeds in creating the impression of the people in every country rising against reactionary feudalism; but the trial scene dramatizes rather that "costly tension" which must be "nobly maintained" between "Regal, sacerdotal, and Prophetical powers" of which Shaw spoke in the preface. Joan is sentenced, the preface states, by "normally innocent people in the energy of their righteousness;" and the Inquisitor recognizes the innocence of Joan herself. Her death is the tragedy inherent in the very nature of society; man's liberation can only come, as *The Quintessence of Ibsenism* said, by the individual's repudiation of all duty except that to his own inner voice; yet the thread must not be burned which holds Church, State and individual in a noble tension. The contradiction must be borne, though it involves the death of the innocent.

Thus at the climax of the play Shaw eliminates from the action what has been its mainspring—the movement of the people; and he ennobles the enemies of the people with that impartiality and justice with which bourgeois idealism always endows the State. It is here that the influence of the reactionary ideas in the preface is most apparent. The force which is the positive content underlying Shaw's conception of creative evolution, the struggle of the people to make their own lives, is suppressed, and the leader of that struggle becomes a figure in a mystic tragedy; and since one of the antagonists, the people, suddenly passes out of existence and the other antagonist, feudal authority, is suddenly spiritualized, the tragedy is no tragedy.

But again Shaw's artistic vision rises above his mysticism. After Joan has been led away to be burned, the Inquisitor says to the Bishop of Beauvais:

> I am accustomed to the fire: it is soon over. But it is a terrible thing to see a young and innocent creature crushed between these mighty forces, the Church and the Law.

They follow Joan out. Then comes one of the most dramatic moments in all Shaw's work.

The Earl of Warwick—the real author of Joan's death; for as the action has shown from the start, it is his deliberate policy, not the costly tension between Regal, sacerdotal, and Prophetical powers, which has brought her to the stake—is left alone on the empty stage, while from the courtyard outside "the glow and flicker of fire can now be seen reddening the May daylight."

> *Warwick looks round. Finding himself alone, he calls for attendance.*
> *Warwick* Hallo: some attendance here! *(Silence)* Hallo, there! *(Silence).*
> Hallo! Brian, you young blackguard, where are you? *(Silence).* Guard! *(Silence).* They have all gone to see the burning: even that child.

There is a sense of growing uneasiness, a menace, in the emptiness of the stage. Warwick's words "even that child" show even in him a consciousness of the atrocity that is being committed; and as his calls for attendance echo without answer, the silence seems to be the gathering of the forces that will bring him to account.

The silence is broken by someone frantically howling and sobbing.
Warwick What in the devil's name—?
The Chaplain staggers in from the courtyard like a demented creature, his face streaming with tears, making the piteous sounds that Warwick has heard. He stumbles to the prisoner's stool, and throws himself upon it with heartrending sobs.

This is the first voice from the silence.

The Chaplain rushes wildly out, shrieking; and Brother Martin follows him. The Earl of Warwick, turning at the door, finds himself alone with the black figure of the Executioner. As the two of them stand face to face, after the threatening silence and the Chaplain's heartbroken sobs, the Executioner seems to confront Warwick as Joan's avenger. She is again the leader of the people; and though she is dead, the movement which she led has but begun.

This moment, not the appearance of the gentleman in Captain Brassbound's top hat with the canonization order from the Vatican, is the true epilogue, which shows that there can be no final defeat of the people.

In the Epilogue which Shaw actually wrote he cancels this moment. Joan becomes again the lonely saint, which has been Shaw's favourite daydream. All the characters kneel to recite their litany to her, while the halo brightens round her head, as if the force that moves society were not in themselves, but in a heaven above them. Ironically, when heaven threatens to open and its saints to descend, they one and all make excuses to hurry away; but the religious feeling lingers, and Joan's last words are filled with it. The poetry with which Shaw wishes to heighten the scene is a cry from the past.

But in his full power as dramatist, Shaw knows that the movement of society comes from its conflict, and he looks towards the future.

~ JOHN MASON BROWN

XIV/The Prophet and the Maid

Statements beyond challenge are as rare as virtue untested. In spite of this, it would seem safe to say that "Saint Joan" is not only Shaw's greatest play but one of the greatest plays to have come out of the modern theatre. Yet as I write these words I realize their rashness. I recall how even "Hamlet," a tragedy the world has been dull enough to accept as a masterpiece, was once dismissed by T. S. Eliot as being "most certainly an artistic failure."

It is this same Olympian Mr. Eliot, however, who at this moment gives me courage. In his recent "Poetry and Drama" he has admitted that his "Murder in the Cathedral" may have been written "slightly under the influence of 'Saint Joan.'" Such a statement from such a source, though not expressed in the ordinary terms of praise, is no doubt meant to be taken as praise from Sir Hubert. I know it makes me feel the safer from attack when I assert that most people (notice I say "most") have a special and rightful admiration for Shaw's drama about the Maid who heard voices.

"Saint Joan" may not have been Shaw's own favorite among his works. In her "Thirty Years with G.B.S." Blanche Patch reports it was not. She reveals that in Frank Harris's copy of "Heartbreak House" Shaw wrote, "Rightly spotted by the infallible eye of Frank Harris as My Best Play." Nonetheless, to the majority of Shavians, regardless of how high is their esteem for other plays by him, "Saint Joan" is his masterpiece.

Saturday Review of Literature, XXXXIV (October 27, 1951), 27–29.

Shaw was sixty-seven when he finished it in 1923, and Joan had been made a saint only three years before. Her posthumous fate had not been without its ironies. As Shaw reminds us, she had been burned for heresy, witchcraft, and sorcery in 1431; rehabilitated after a fashion in 1456; designated Venerable in 1904; declared Blessed in 1908; and finally canonized in 1920.

There was everything about Joan as a subject to interest Shaw, and everything about her to release his mightiest gifts once his interest had been won. Yet apparently he resisted Joan as a theme and would have continued to do so had not Charlotte Shaw employed strategy to get her husband started on a play she wanted him to write. Being a good wife, in other words a woman blessed with Maggie Shand's knowledge, she did not argue with Shaw or let him feel that she was influencing him. Instead, she left books about the Maid and her trial around the house in places where he was certain to see them, pick them up, and read them in his moments of idleness. He fell for the bait and, once having fallen, became absorbed in Joan.

When "Saint Joan" first appeared there were many even among the most stalwart of Shaw's followers who were surprised by the reverence of the play which the notoriously irreverent GBS had written. They had long since admitted his brilliance. They had recognized his audacity. They had prized his originality. And they had laughed at his jokes. But they had grown so accustomed to identifying him as a professional iconoclast and jester that they had lost sight of his seriousness. Remembering his wit, they had forgotten his eloquence. They had closed their eyes to the fact that his spirit was as sizable as his mind. Above all, they had failed to recall, or, worse still, misunderstood, "Androcles and the Lion" and the noble simplicity of the scene in which the Roman soldier asks the Christian woman who is about to face martyrdom in the arena, "What is God?" and she answers, "When we know that, Captain, we shall be gods ourselves."

A man who in Shaw's manner could refuse his Government's offer of the Order of Merit by saying he had already conferred it upon himself was bound to be suspected by the humorless of immodesty. When it came to "Saint Joan," however, he was far more modest than he had any right or cause to be. Hesketh Pearson reports that Shaw said to Sybil Thorndike, the first actress to play the part in England, "I have told the story exactly as it happened. It is the easiest play I have ever had to write. All I've done is to put down the facts, to arrange Joan for the stage. The trial scene is merely a report of the actual trial. I have used Joan's very words: thus she spoke, thus she behaved."

Count this among the least reliable of Shavian utterances. In "Saint Joan" Shaw matters at every turn and with the turn of almost every phrase. What makes the play magnificent is not that he retells the familiar story but that this story comes to life in a new and memorable way as the issues involved and the problems raised by Joan provoke his eloquence, appeal to his mysticism, stir his imagination, and ignite his thinking.

Though a Protestant himself, Shaw refuses to use Joan's trial and burning as a means of attacking the Catholic Church. With all the fairness of his incredibly fair mind he insists she was given a very careful and conscientious trial by men who were anxious to save her. To understand her fate, he points out, one must understand not only her character and claims but the mind and beliefs of the Middle Ages. Joan's paradox, he maintains, was that though a professed and most pious Catholic she was in fact one of the first Protestant martyrs. In a feudal period when nobles were jealous of their prerogatives, she imperiled these prerogatives by being an early exponent of nationalism and championing the powers of her king. That a country girl in her teens presumed to tell military leaders what they should do was bound to antagonize the Brass Hats to whom she gave orders. Moreover, she was an individualist who invited religious disfavor by claiming that she could speak directly to God through her visions and voices "without the intercession of the Church.

Beyond and above these causes for Joan's unpopularity with her contemporaries there were, as Shaw demonstrates, other and more disconcerting reasons for her undoing. Because she was exceptional her contemporaries could not tolerate her, and because she was their moral superior they burned her. Indeed, the point of Shaw's play is summarized by two ageless questions asked in the Epilogue. The first is Cauchon's "Must then a Christ perish in torment in every age to save those that have no imagination?" The second is Joan's "O God that madest this beautiful earth, when will it be ready to receive Thy saints? How long, O Lord, how long?"

The dimensions of the tragedy (the poetry of its prose, the unfettering simplicity of its construction, its tenderness, its intellectual power, indeed its grandeur) are unmistakable throughout. No scene in the modern theatre is more touching as an affirmation of faith than the one by the banks of the Loire when the wind changes. None is more charged with the electricity of ideas than the discussion by Cauchon, Warwick, and De Stogumber of the religious and political problems raised by the Maid. No on-stage trial is more stirring than Joan's and no single speech mightier in its language than the one addressed to the court by the Inquisitor. As for the Epilogue, it is hard to see why it was subject to furious attacks when the play was originally produced. It is the needed summary of what has gone before and is essential to our understanding both of Shaw's meaning and of Joan's posthumous fate and ultimate canonization.

Any production of "Saint Joan" is bound to be as dependent upon the actress playing Joan as "Hamlet" is upon the actor who plays the Prince. The present production, as directed by Margaret Webster, has its genuine merits. It moves swiftly. It is set and costumed in an acceptable enough style. And in Kendall Clark's sensitive Brother Martin, the fire of Robert Pastene's Dunois, the sinister brilliance of Andrew Cruickshank's Warwick, and the complete and hilarious excellence of John Buckmaster's Dauphin, it achieves distinction. But most decidedly something is lacking. The full fervor of the text is not communicated. In such a scene, for example, as the lovely one by the Loire the mere mechanics of the production fail to create the sense of the miraculous. Then, too, the Inquisitor's great plea for tolerance (a plea never more needed than today) is tamely read by Frederick Rolf. But, to my way of thinking, the production's major disappointment comes in Uta Hagen's Joan.

Although Miss Hagen has on many occasions demonstrated how fine a performer she is, Joan eludes her. She has her good scenes, reads intelligently, and is properly earthy and unsentimental. At her best, however, she is no more than competent, and at her worst plainly inadequate. The final requisite for Joan is that inner radiance which is in the text and which flamed in Katharine Cornell's performance. This is missing, and the absence of this simple, shimmering spirituality is a major loss.

Several actresses have played Joan, and many more will. But the Joan of all Joans I should like to have heard—and seen—was the one Margaret Webster once told me was the best she ever saw. It was Bernard Shaw himself; Shaw when he read the part to Sybil Thorndike's company in which Miss Webster was an understudy. Apparently as one listened to his marvelously flexible and musical voice, his beard and age, his sex and dress were all forgotten, and the spirit of the real Joan, his Joan, came magically to life.

Doubtless Shaw read his Joan as well as he had written her because both he and she, by his own insistence, were geniuses. A genius, says he in his superb preface to the play, "is a person who, seeing farther and probing deeper than other people, has a different set of ethical values from theirs, and has energy enough to give effect to this extra vision and its valuations in whatever manner best suits his or her specific talents." No wonder, therefore, the old Prophet understood the young Maid so well, or that from his understanding he was able to write a play the greatness of which cannot be obscured even in a production that fails to do justice to its splendors.

XV/Joan as Unhappy Trotzkyist

It is hard to see what future can be built out of cinders. Shaw's anti-traditionalism comes out amusingly in his impatience even with "old familiar faces". "It is frightful for the citizen", he exclaims, "as the years pass by him, to see his own contemporaries so exactly reproduced by the younger generation, that the companions of thirty years ago have their counterparts in every city crowd ... All hope of advance dies in his bosom as he watches them." This frightful experience is certainly not my own, nor, I think, most people's: far from it. G.B.S.'s historical plays, even at their best, strike us a little as Christmas panto-mimes; of these inventions it is, to a great extent, true—what is only intermittently true of his contemporary plays—that the characters are "gramophones". Or rather, while they are living enough, they live from no independent life—the navel-string connecting them with their au-thor is not cut: in Caesar there is nothing of the Pagan sense of Fate, with St. Joan none of the intimate presence of the Supernatural, with Adam and Eve no feeling of the dawn of a world. *Caesar and Cleopatra* contains some of Shaw's noblest writing—attached to a dull historical charade, which might have been written purposely for Hollywood. Shaw's ignorance of the past would have mattered little if he had been a simple emotional being—after all, who cares whether Shakespeare's historical plays are "true to period"? But Shaw was as different from natural men as if he had been one of Yeats' "holy centaurs of the hills". The result of despising the Flesh is not that it makes a man spiritual but

Reprinted from *Three Great Irishmen: Shaw, Yeats, Joyce* (New York, 1952), 29-36.

that it makes him mechanical—imaginatively *dead;* and a concentration on the mechanics of life is also, as Bergson showed, germane to the
comic vision. G. B. S., who hated travel, had no more conception of an
ancient Roman or a 14th Century French girl than he had of a 20th
Century German or Russian. It is hard to forgive him his bouquets to
Hitler; feeling, no doubt, that one Wagnerian must understand another,
he could apparently forgive the *Führer's* second musical enthusiasm—
The Merry Widow. And his film-star-like trip to Moscow—the story of
the visit to Comrade Stalin, when the great man said severely, "But you
beat children in England", and the plucky Lady Astor, rising like a
tornado to the defence, "rocked the Kremlin to its foundations"—all
this is merely irritating in its Social Column frivolity. In that world of
ice-cold fanaticism—of terror raised to a consummate science—a world
in which it might be said "Greater love than this hath no man, that he
should inform the police of every word spoken in his hearing, no matter
by whom"—a world in which tolerance, civilised discussion, all the free
play of the mind, are unknown and proscribed: against that background
moves a jocular old Irish gentleman—fêted, beaming and joking—seeing nothing at all—catching no murmur fainter than the "amplifiers" or
deeper than the rustle of the snow—the perfect pedagogue-on-vaca-
tion, the complete Mark Twain innocent abroad. Broadbent, thou art
avenged!

But the mention of Broadbent reminds me of the one play of Shaw's
which really has atmosphere—almost indeed the only one: namely,
John Bull's Other Island. The very topicality of that play makes it more
real than some of his more ambitiously "imaginative" efforts. The
Laughter Scene has a quality which we do not meet again in Bernard
Shaw until *Heartbreak House*—something Dantesque, almost surrealis-
tic. Even the remarks of Peter Keegan to the grasshopper ring less false
than Shaw's poeticisms in general do; because the phraseology is that of
actual Irish colloquial speech.

It is not quite the same with Shaw's other saintly character—St.
Joan; G. B. S. had not *seen* her, as he might have seen the village saints
and originals of his native country—he had only seen the excellent
Dame Sybil Thorndike. In the play that bears her name, we find the
following piece of dialogue between the peasant-maid and the Dauphin:

CHARLES: ... If you are going to say "Son of St. Louis: gird on the sword of your ancestors, and lead us to victory" you may spare your breath to cool your porridge; for I cannot do it. I am not built that way: and there is an end of it.

JOAN *(trenchant and masterful):* Blethers! We are all like that to begin with. I shall put courage into thee.

CHARLES: But I don't want to have courage put into me. I want to sleep in a comfortable bed, and not live in continual terror of being killed or wounded. Put courage into the others, and let them have their bellyful of fighting; but let me alone.

JOAN: It's no use, Charlie; thou must face what God puts on thee. If thou fail to make thyself king, thoult be a beggar: what else art fit for? Come! Let me see thee sitting on the throne. I have looked forward to that.

It is not differently—or not very differently—that Dick Whittington's cat apostrophises the future Lord Mayor in the pantomime. And the play continues in this vein—half comedy, half debate—almost right up to the unpleasant, very jarring, incident of Joan being taken and burned to ashes. We like this heroine—she is indeed nothing mystical, like Péguy's Jeanne, but a plucky intelligent girl with no nonsense—and yet there is little in her or in the world we are being shown to make such a horrible climax convincing. It is as if we were presented with Nancy Astor, cracking jokes with Stalin, and Koestler's Arlova, the girl-secretary of *Darkness at Noon* who was liquidated, as one and the same character. If we did not happen to know the story beforehand, we should look on the burning as merely a bad artistic fault; and because we *do* know the story, the argument and persiflage ring a little hollow—as a bright bit of dialogue at a dinner-table might fall flat for a looker-on who knew the food was poisoned. Suppose that Shaw had rewritten *Othello* with the philosophical Iago for hero (and Iago was made to be a Shavian character). It might in some ways be as good a play—certainly a very interesting one—but the strangling of Desdemona would strike us as simply an extraordinary lapse of taste; the Aristotelian pity and terror would not form any great part of our emotions. After the first production of *Saint Joan*, there was a great deal of discussion among the critics as to the propriety of the Epilogue; but without the Epilogue, I think, the abruptness of the play's ending would strike us much more forcibly. Its purpose is, in fact, to restore the easy argumentative note which the intrusion of the brutal historical facts has a little disturbed. Yet nothing could be a more shocking anti-climax than this Epilogue in a true tragedy.

And yet there is real poignancy in *Saint Joan,* in spite of the rather brittle dialogue; not the tragedy of Joan of Arc—it needs an effort to remember that the play is about her—but the nostalgia of George Bernard Shaw. The hero who is laughed at, tolerated, petted, cannot conceal a certain envy for the heroine who is taken seriously and killed. Shaw knew only too well that had he been a fighting revolutionary, in many European countries, he might have suffered a martyrdom no less repulsive than Joan's; and the fashionable crowds who had delighted in his wit would not have raised a finger in his defence. I am not a communist, but Shaw was; and in spite of the pains he took to justify it, there is something necessarily a little ironical about the communist who dies a millionaire. Whatever one's politics, one cannot but be glad that the modern Socrates declined the hemlock; for martyrs are two a penny, and a great playwright is a prodigious exception. But we are touched that for once he laid off his slightly metallic self-assurance, and wondered—when he wrote *Saint Joan*—if after all he had made the better choice.

Full credit, of course, must be given to Shaw—and has been given him—for his sympathetic and "understanding" portrayal of the Inquisition—probably the most sympathetic one that exists in any literature (for Dostoievski's Inquisitor is not offered as more than a fantasy). Historically, it is doubtful whether the scheming Cauchon and his assistants were really nice men; but we can let that pass. That Shaw could so represent them is proof, at least, of how his mind had out-grown the rather crude secularism of his youth. In his preface he draws a devastating satirical contrast between the 14th Century and the 20th—much to the latter's disadvantage! And yet one is left at the end, of course, with the uncomfortable sense that there is "something more behind it". Did not Shaw's conversion to the Middle Ages keep exact pace, one asks, with the decay of libertarian faith in the world at large—that despairing readiness to welcome despotism in all its forms which has been so distressing a feature of the last half-century? Is it not a sign of the metamorphosis of a Fabian into a totalitarianist? One has something of the feeling one had on seeing an attractive and persuasive Soviet film-version of the life of Ivan the Terrible. Shaw's heart, of course, is with Joan; but he regards her in the end almost as his Inquisitor does—a charming child indeed, but a bit too much of a good thing in the present world. Her last prayer, in the Epilogue, is weak and sentimental: O God that madest this beautiful earth, when will it be ready to receive Thy Saints? Her enemies, who had quitted the stage too hurriedly, would surely all have sighed "Amen". The moral to be drawn from that is that *until* the earth is ready for the reception of saints, it will be the painful duty of the practical men and the guardians of order to keep such foreign bodies out. Shaw may mock, but he really sees no alternative; for you cannot have people ruled for their good without an efficient police. To some of us the growing power of police-states is as appalling a menace as ever was the anarchy of capitalism; but one remembers that G. B. S. wrote a whole tract (his Preface to *The Simpleton of the Unexpected Isles*) to justify "liquidations" and to hold up the Inquisition as a model. Joan is a "sport"—almost a spirit—an anticipation of the super-humanity which, in Shaw's biological vision, is to replace man in an unforeseeable future. She is an unhappy Trotzkyist—whose place, unfortunately, is before the Stalinist firing-squads.

I have dealt with *Saint Joan* at disproportionate length because it is perhaps Shaw's most important play, whether or not it is his best. (The difficulty of classing Shaw's plays lies in the fact that his finest works—*Candida, Pygmalion, Saint Joan*—tantalise us the most by their inadequacies, and only comparative trifles like *Androcles* send us away quite satisfied.) It deals with great themes, and deals with them well—whereas *Back to Methuselah* deals with the great themes rather abstractly and superficially. It is not perhaps (like Ibsen's *Ghosts*) a true tragedy, but it is a highly fascinating drama of ideas; for Shaw's admirable knack of "seeing both sides"—never shown to better advantage than in the Trial Scene—is in fact the comedic genius and not the tragic one. Moreover the portrait of the heroine, whatever else it is, is extremely sensitive. Shaw handles Joan with a teasing fondness, which reveals him as the old enchanter and cavalier he really was—an attractive side of his personality which we are also shown in his correspondence with Ellen Terry. G. B. S. could always draw a charming female when he wanted to, even if his males are over-afflicted with the curse of garrulity. Sometimes of course he did not want to, but deliberately sacrificed his heroines' charm to their intelligence: I think, however, that he did this less than is usually supposed. His success with female characters has been recognized by French critics (otherwise little appreciative of Shaw's work) more often than by English ones. It is too often asserted, even still, that Shaw's plays are only "disguised tracts", and his women mere "suffragettes"; but in fact the plays (all except the early *Widowers' Houses* and *Mrs. Warren's Profession*) are poor and incoherent considered as propaganda, and the heroines are often quite disconcertingly wily and feline. In all Shaw's major plays I can call to mind no revolutionists, except the scarcely-very-attractive brigands of *Man and Superman* and the housebreaker in *Misalliance;* for the eugenical-minded Tanner has certainly never even smelt a trade-union office. G. B. S. was not really a problem-playwright at all—either a good one like Ibsen or a bad one like Brieux; his true affinities were with the Anglo-Irish playwrights of the 17th and 18th Centuries—only that his world was a woman's world and not, like theirs, a man's, so that in the comparison he seems both more realistic than his predecessors and more prim. His art in fact bears much the same relation to the great Scandinavian realists as that of the Restoration dramatists to the Elizabethans; but he had the advantage that realism and the feminine wit are essentially more fitted to comedy, as romance and gallantry are the proper themes for tragedy.

~ E. J. WEST

XVI/ *Saint Joan:* A Modern Classic Reconsidered

One of the worst occupational diseases of scholarship is the habit of repeating oneself, or, to use a bad metaphor, of persistently riding a hobby-horse long after the paint has lost its garish freshness and the mechanism has developed crankiness. Having in the dim and distant days of secondary school become an unconscious Shavo-maniac and having since developed into an unconscionable one, I have perhaps too loudly and too long bewailed the absence of a volume on Shaw which should confine itself wholly to a consideration of his plays *as plays, presented in the theatre.* In the absence of such a complete evaluation, I hailed in print with welcome one of the few books published after Shaw's death which contributed in any measurable way to a proper appreciation of the major playwright of our time. This book was Desmond MacCarthy's *Shaw,* a compilation of his reviews of such plays of Shaw as he had witnessed in production from the early days of the Vedrenne-Barker management at the Court Theatre up through the century until Shaw's death in November of 1950. From the beginning, this critic was notably swift and accurate in gauging the values of the Shavian plays and in steering clear of the muddle-headedness which afflicted most of the first reviewers of Shaw in performance. Of the first English production of *Saint Joan,* that starring Sybil Thorndike, in April of 1924, MacCarthy wrote two notices, one concerned with "The Theme," the other with the play as a whole.

In the first he shrewdly perceived that the "many and splendid

Quarterly Journal of Speech, XL (October, 1954), 249–59.

merits" of the play would actually disturb critics and audiences, for immense seriousness was wedded to the extreme of entertainment, great "intellectual energy to a maximum of pathos and sympathy." Its great length, he thought, was compensated for by its depth: "I am by no means sure that I have got, or that I am going to get, to the bottom of it." In a memorable phrase he noted: "We are lifted on waves of emotion to be dashed on thought." But the main difficulty for the spectator, MacCarthy warned, "may distrust religious emotion, dislike exceedingly many of its manifestations (as, indeed, I do myself), but he must know what kind of a feeling it is and how it can draw and drag at the heart; otherwise he will neither apprehend the whole, nor feel the force of its most dramatic moments." I am sure I have not yet, despite much study and an actual production, apprehended the whole of the play, but I should like to comment upon a few of its most *dramatic* moments.

I especially distrust facile closet dicta upon any great plays. Among the many historians and scholars who when *Saint Joan* first appeared attacked Shaw on critical grounds other than aesthetic was one Professor Charles Sarolea; in an article questioning "Has Mr. Shaw Understood Joan of Arc?" he quoted, with a lack of humor unhappily characteristic of Shaw's critics, a letter from the playwright reading in part:

> I do not profess to understand Joan of Arc: and neither will you, unless you are growing rasher with advancing years, instead of more cautious. Lots of writers have tried to explain her, and to account for her, to dramatize her, to glorify her; and she has beaten them all, the series of defeats culminating in the frightful "gaffe" perpetrated by Anatole France. I have been more wary. I took the only documents that are of the smallest value: the report of the process, and that of the rehabilitation. I simply arranged what I found there, for the stage, relying on Joan to pull me through, which she did.

After commenting upon the quixotic whimsy of misinterpretation indulged in and frequently wallowed in by most of the writers about Joan, Shaw with lovely irony warned the Professor: "I have no theory about Joan, and understand her no more than I understand myself. Necessarily I take a certain view of the facts, and it will be very interesting if you can give another view of them, but none of us *know*. ... So beware of my simplicity. I have deliberately abstained from learning in this matter so that I might the easier get into Joan's skin, and not into that of her historians; and as I have evidently got her alive somehow, you will have some trouble in persuading the world that I went the wrong way to work."

Both the irony and the warning were wasted on Professor Sarolea, who in company with such academic fellows as Professors J. C. Blankenagel, J. H. Buckland, J. L. Cardazo, J. Kooistra, C. M. Newman, Arthur M. Ropes, and J. van Kan, rushed into print in learned periodicals from 1925 to 1927 eager to prove that Shaw did not understand the Maid nor history. Whether or not he had nevertheless "got her alive somehow," few of them seemed to know—or to care. The most industrious of the attackers, the rationalist Shakespeare disintegrator then famous or at least noted for his mathematical distribution of fractional parts of the Shakespeare canon among a score or more of Shakespeare's contemporaries, was J. M. Robertson, who paid Shaw the dubious compliment of devoting to the controversy in 1926 a whole book, *Mr. Shaw and "The Maid."* Specifically denying to Shaw any understanding of the Middle Ages or of any of the forces operative therein, Robertson showed the quality of his attack by apparent preliminary recognition of Shaw's merits. Attempting, I suspect, to be disarming, he unhappily disarmed himself by such condescending remarks as these:

> For my own part I found it, as a play, quite unexpectedly interesting and effective throughout, even in long scenes which to a reader might seem overwritten. That is owing to the specific illusion of the stage, which, when skilfully managed, inhibits a large part of the critical faculty, and operates emotion in a medium of pure receptiveness. The interest and the effectiveness were largely due, I think, to the almost invariably excellent acting; and I trust I do no injustice to the many accomplished artists in the cast if I infer that their collective success was in no small measure due to the expert drilling of Mr. Shaw. His ripened skill in stagecraft is obvious throughout, from the farcing of the first scene to the farcing of the close—alike the work of the most gifted master of stage farce in our day.

This short passage so bristles with snide nastiness and self-revealing critical incompetence that I find it difficult to interrupt myself to note that the rationalistic Robertsonian attack was hailed by the young Anglo-Catholic Thomas Stearns Eliot in his snobbishly-titled organ, *The Criterion,* as justly due both to "one of the most superstitious of the effigies that have been created to that remarkable woman" and to the "corpse" of Shaw. 1926, mind you! At least the pipe-smoking and

absent-minded Eliot of 1951 recanted by classifying Congreve and
Shaw as the "two greatest prose stylists in the drama," and he suggested that the speeches of the knights who dispose of Becket in
Murder in the Cathedral "may, for aught I know, have been slightly
under the influence of *Saint Joan.*"

But let us return to Robertson's remarks, since he was acknowledged
leader of the first onslaught against the play. Not implicitly, but explicitly, Robertson argued the case for the closet-critic, proclaiming his
broad-mindedness by admitting the interest and effectiveness in the
theatre even of "long scenes which to a reader might seem overwrit-
ten." This broad-mindedness he apologized for by claiming that much
of his critical faculty was *inhibited* by "the specific illusion of the
stage"—obviously an intruding force in the art of the drama, especially
"when skilfully managed." The theatre is also a bad place to encounter
drama because, forsooth, emotion therein operates, or rather the afore-
said "specific illusion of the stage . . . operates emotion in a medium of
pure receptiveness." The image, if such it is, is too clinical for me.
Robertson also seems to have felt that he was unfairly interested and
made to accept the play as effective because of "the almost invariably
excellent acting," obviously another intruding and inhibiting force,
made all the worse by the critic's suspicion that this acting was aided
and abetted by "the expert drilling of Mr. Shaw." This directorial
faculty is finally judged to be a part of the "ripened skill in stagecraft
. . . of the most gifted master of stage farce in our day." Not dramaturgy, not outright master-craftsmanship, just gifted farcing (the point
with cheap rhetoric emphasized by repetition of the damning word).
This is closet scholarship with a vengeance.

In 1930 The Institute of French Studies published, as obviously the
work of a candidate for an advanced degree, a bibliography entitled
*Jeanne d'Arc in Periodical Literature 1894-1929 with Special Refer-
ence to Bernard Shaw's "Saint Joan."* A rather confused title for a
scholarly work, since periodicals for only five of the years covered could
have "special reference" to Shaw's play. Religiously I have consulted
this unrewarding work; happily for me I have succeeded in tracing
down but few of its entries. But the passion for this kind of most
undramatic and untheatrical criticism persists; recently *The Shakespeare Quarterly* published an article, written before Shaw's death but

finally appearing as a pseudo-recognition of him after death, by the highly regarded F. S. Boas on "Joan of Arc in Shakespeare, Schiller, and Shaw." While Professor Boas was forced to admit that Schiller, in *Die Jungfrau von Orleans* "completely falsified history, both psychologically and factually," and that he did "not envy Schiller if he has to meet either Joan or the Muse of History in the Elysian Fields," the burden of his longish article was a defense of the dubious Shakespearean handling of Joan (let us at least grant it bifurcated) in the first part of *Henry VI,* as opposed to Shaw's treatment.

One sympathizes more and more with Shaw's desire that his plays be treated as plays, studies in the theatre, and kept out of the classroom (and, by implication, out of the purely scholarly closet). When Shaw protested against the use of his plays in the classroom, professedly he seemed to sense danger in the student encountering him under the wrong auspices, but surely his emphasis was upon the wrong auspices. In the masters, the scholars, lay the danger. In November of 1927 another publishing firm asked Shaw's publishers if they might have the author's permission to use the third scene of *Saint Joan* for a "book intended for the Middle Forms of secondary schools," and he replied: "NO. I lay my eternal curse on whomsoever shall now or any time hereafter make schoolbooks of my works, and make me hated, as Shakespeare is hated. My plays were not designed as instruments of torture. All the schools that lust after them get this answer, and will never get any other from   G. Bernard Shaw."

Unhappily, as I have had occasion to remark elsewhere in writing of the master ironist of our time, irony usually backfires. By 1928, candidates for a Higher School Certificate from the University of London were being assigned *Saint Joan* for "critical and detailed study," and I wager no candidate was advised, should he be unable to see the play presented, to confine his critical and detailed study to the play and to skip the preface, or at least to read it, as Shaw always advised readers to treat the prefaces, as an allied but separate economico-politico-religious treatise.

I am not denying the specific interest of the preface to this particular play. It starts arrestingly:

> Joan of Arc, a village girl from the Vosges, was born about 1412; burnt for

heresy, witchcraft, and sorcery in 1431; rehabilitated after a fashion in 1456; designated Venerable in 1904; declared Blessed in 1908; and finally canonized in 1920. She is the most notable Warrior Saint in the Christian calendar, and the queerest fish among the eccentric worthies of the Middle Ages. Though a professed and most pious Catholic, and the projector of a Crusade against the Husites, she was in fact one of the first Protestant martyrs. She was also one of the first apostles of Nationalism, and the first French practitioner of Napoleonic realism in warfare as distinguished from the sporting ransom-gambling chivalry of her time.

The preface proceeds for some forty pages of close and heady if exciting and entertaining reasoning and argument to develop the arresting ideas proposed in the opening sentences and then, unlike most of the prefaces, actually turns to a consideration of the play with the words:

> For the story of Joan I refer the reader to the play which follows. It contains all that need be known about her; but as it is for stage use I have had to condense into three and a half hours a series of events which in their historical happening were spread over four times as many months; for the theatre imposes unities of time and place from which Nature in her boundless wastefulness is free. Therefore the reader must not suppose that Joan really put Robert de Baudricourt in her pocket in fifteen minutes, nor that her ex-communication, recantation, relapse, and death at the stake were a matter of half an hour or so.

He did not claim historical accuracy for the figures of the play, but he suggested that his Joan was at least more like the original than the Joan of Mark Twain or Andrew Lang, "skirted to the ground, and with as many petticoats as Noah's wife in a toy ark, ... an attempt to combine Bayard with Esther Summerson from Bleak House into an unimpeachable American school teacher in armor." Ironic tongue in deadpan cheek, he gaily concluded that he really knew no more about Joan's circle "than Shakespear knew about Falconbridge and the Duke of Austria, or about Macbeth and Macduff." "In view of the things they did in history," he said, "and have to do again in the play, I can only invent appropriate characters for them in Shakespear's manner." He emphasized, however, that as a man of his own time he could see the Middle Ages in perspective and thus could more accurately than the Elizabethans portray the clash of great forces; and also could suggest that "the world is finally governed by forces expressing themselves in religions and laws which make epochs rather than by vulgarly ambitious individuals who make rows." Thus, he hoped, those who see *Saint Joan* performed, will not mistake the startling event it records for a mere personal accident. They will have before them not only the visible and human puppets, but "the Church, the Inquisition, the Feudal System, with divine inspiration always beating against their too inelastic limits; all more terrible in their dramatic force than any of the little mortal figures clanking about in plate armor or moving silently in the frocks and hoods of the order of St. Dominic."

Even in these brief quotations from the preface, one might become suspicious that the interest in the religions and the laws might overshadow that in the visible and human puppets, that in the little mortal figures. But he who sees the play performed will sense the terrible dramatic force conveyed in the embodiments of divine inspiration in Joan herself, with her amazing variety and multiple facets of personality (successively, writes Louis Kronenberger in his recent *The Thread of Laughter*," five very sympathetic things—a young girl, a dazzling conqueror, a heroine, a victim, and a martyr"); of the Church in the convincing and moving figure of Bishop Peter Cauchon, here probably for the first time shown not as a bullying villain but as a sincere and essentially humane being contrasted with the more conventionally minded and lip-servicing Archbishop of Rheims; of the Inquisition in the gentle and judicially fair if worldly-wise Lemaitre; of the Feudal System in the shrewd diplomat and cultured knight, Warwick. The spectator will also find embodiments of what we might call reluctant regality in the fully realized if grotesque character of the Dauphin Charles; of fanatical and ignorant nationalism in the original character of Chaplain de Stogumber (built up by Shaw simply on the base of a nameless cleric "who is known only by his having lost his temper and called Cauchon a traitor for accepting Joan's recantation"); of common humanity, responding to common humanity, in the simple English soldier who gave to the burning Joan a cross made of two sticks: "Well, she asked for it; and they were going to burn her. She had as good a right to a cross as they had; and they had dozens of them. It was her funeral, not theirs. Where was the harm in it?" Yes, the spectator will not be worried over the ideologies of puppets, but fascinated by the dramatic force, terrible or otherwise, of realized human figures whose ideologies are fascinating because of the warmth and vitality of their holders, not only of the figures I have mentioned but of a dozen or so more, down to the three briefly-appearing minor figures of the pages, each carefully differentiated, each a definite reflection of his environment and a comment upon the character of his master.

Deep-reaching and provocative as the ideas of the play are—and like Desmond MacCarthy I repeat, "I am by no means sure that I have got, or that I am going to get, to the bottom of it,"—it is in the first place the humanity and the credibility of the characters that make *Saint Joan* a great play; that make it to that fine critic John Gassner, as to many others, the "one genuine English tragedy" of our time, to Brooks Atkinson "one of the great plays in the English language," to George Jean Nathan "a rhapsodic symphony . . . wittily and beautifully composed." Shaw rightly defended his treatment of the Joan theme as tragic rather than melodramatic (as had been the treatment by Shakespeare, by Voltaire, by Schiller, by Mark Twain, by Andrew Lang) precisely because he made his characters human beings, not stage puppets, human beings driven by forces bigger than themselves and necessarily more articulate in expressing these forces than their historic originals could have been. Claiming that his play contained "no villains," he argued:

> The rascally bishop and the cruel inquisitor of Mark Twain and Andrew Lang are as dull as pickpockets; and they reduce Joan to the level of the even less interesting person whose pocket is picked. I have represented both of them as capable and eloquent exponents of the Church Militant and the Church Litigant, because only by doing so can I maintain my drama on the level of high tragedy and save it from becoming a mere police court sensation. . . . The tragedy of such murders [as that of Joan] is that they are not committed by murderers. They are judicial murders, pious murders; and this contradiction at once brings an element of comedy into the tragedy: the angels may weep at the murder, but the gods laugh at the murderers.

This passage is highly suggestive. For one thing it explains the necessity of the Epilogue, originally much deprecated, and now accepted but almost always made the subject of some apology by the critics; that ironic but deeply human and frequently moving Epilogue, with its tremendous litany of praise to Joan from Cauchon, Dunois, the Archbishop, Warwick, de Stogumber, the Inquisitor, the Soldier, the Executioner, and King Charles; and with its ironic echo of Joan's recantation in the Trial Scene, as the nine men express their horror at her proposed return to earth, and show her that only in her death can mankind accept her greatness, and leave her alone to sound out her last great cry that settles this play into the sorrowful perspective of tragedy: "O God that madest this beautiful earth, when will it be ready to receive Thy saints? How long, O Lord, how long?" (This Epilogue, remember, to Professor Robertson, as to many subsequent critics, is "farce." Well!)

And the simple power of this closing speech recalls Shaw's insistence upon the necessary eloquence of the major figures. Probably the most famous scene of Shavian dialogue is the Tent Scene in this play between Cauchon, Warwick, and de Stogumber, finer because basically more serious, more profound, and less obviously pyrotechnical even than the Don-Juan-in-Hell scene from *Man and Superman*. Probably the most famous and finest single Shavian speech is the Inquisitor's seven-minute disquisition on heresy in the Trial Scene, matched in power but not in length, if not surpassed in emotional quality, by Joan's speech of recantation in the same scene. Each of these, like all Shavian dialogue, is magnificently idiosyncratic and revelatory of the character of the speaker. Note in contrast to the artful rhetoric of the Inquisitor's speech the simple but moving eloquence of Joan's. But the play is permeated with eloquence. Critic after critic, even frequently critics not essentially favorable to Shaw, has echoed the tribute paid by his fellow-dramatist, the Italian Pirandello, when the latter attended the first production of the play by the New York Theatre Guild in 1923: "There is a truly great poet in Shaw [who] here, in *Saint Joan*, . . . comes into his own . . . with only a subordinate role left, as a demanded compensation, to irony and satire . . . *Saint Joan* is a work of poetry from beginning to end." With this praise, extravagant as it is, I would not essentially disagree. Not a work of verse, no, but a masterpiece of poetic prose, yes. Not from beginning to end—no audience could stand for three hours of playing-time the sustained rhetorical and poetic power of the Tent Scene and most of the Trial Scene or the end of the Epilogue. Contrast is necessary—of prose and poetic phrasing, of comedy and tragedy.

It is my belief that Shaw consistently and deliberately wrote tragicomedy, as he confirms in his comment upon this play: "this contradiction at once brings an element of comedy into the tragedy: the angels may weep at the murder, but the gods laugh at the murderers." Writ-

ing some time ago of "the true harmonies, the undisturbable and stable
compositions" of musical prose which so permeate Shaw's best plays, I
instanced the "tent scene in *Saint Joan* [and] that paean of litany,
wrongly much criticized as redundant or irrelevant, which is the epilogue to that play, that reverent litany of real religious faith which is no
more disturbed by its moments of humor than is the simple reverence
of *The Second Shepherds Play* disturbed by the simple horseplay with
the thieving Mak." With this opinion I still hold. Commenting upon the
shocked and alarmed reaction of the nine male litanists to Joan's half-
naïve, half-humorous suggestion that if all they say of her is true she
should return to earth, the late Alan Thompson wrote in his provocative book on irony in drama, *The Dry Mock:*

> After that tremendously moving litany to Joan, what a reversal! The ironic
> clash is extraordinary. The painful joke is a joke at our expense, a joke on us
> as human beings who can praise the great dead sonorously but scuttle away
> at the very thought of having to live with them and in the terrible contrast
> of their greatness to our littleness. Mankind can revere a saint in heaven but
> not on earth. Could any dramatist but Shaw have conceived this "cold
> douche of irony" at such a point, in such a play? And yet, how magnificent
> it is in the way it deflates us to humility and pity and richer understanding!
> ... Shaw's daring in writing the whole Epilogue, with its mingling of the
> sublime and the farcical, has often enough been noted. This ending justifies
> it and lifts us again, in a more complete sense than could otherwise be
> possible, to the height of tragedy.
>   Thus ... Shaw uses genuine and profound irony with grandeur and
> masterly power. ... Thus ... it became possible for him not only to see the
> joke in human fallibility but also to feel and communicate the pain of it.

Or, as Louis Kronenberger has recently put it: "The scene, enforcing
the great gulf between practicality and piety, between the real and the
ideal, makes its point in comic terms, but the point itself is tragic—and
harsh tragedy, not high—realistic, not heroic. Between the real and the
ideal there is not a clash, but a gulf." Remember MacCarthy's revealing
sentence I quoted in starting: "We are lifted on waves of emotion to be
dashed on thought." Shaw himself, so frequently represented, or mis-
represented, by his major critics as the exponent only of the play of
ideas, the creator of mouthpieces for his own fads and fancies, quite
rightly reproved Hesketh Pearson on the appearance of the latter's *Full
Length Portrait* in 1942:

> You are still a bit in the nineteenth century in respect of arranging religion,

politics, science, and art in braintight compartments, mostly incompatible and exclusive. They don't exist that way at all. There is no such thing as the religious man, the political man, the scientific man, the artistic man; in human nature they are all mixed up in different proportions, and that is how they are mixed up in my plays. In *Saint Joan* the Bishop, the Inquisitor, and the feudal baron are as religious as Joan without her peculiar delusions; and I have brought out the fact that she was a very dangerous woman as well as a saint.

Shaw's characters, then, possessed, he hoped, the complexity of human nature. Talking early in 1924 to his first and even more uncomprehending biographer, Archibald Henderson, he made more extended comment on Joan. He said he found Julia Marlowe's Joan in Percy MacKaye's dramatization of her story "very soft and very sweet," but "about as much like Joan as Joan's kitten was like Joan's charger. Nobody could possibly have burned Miss Marlowe: Job himself would have burned the real Joan." By making his Joan "pitiable [and] sentimental," Shaw complained, MacKaye like other writers made "her fate unintelligible" and "herself vapid and uninteresting." The indefatigable Henderson, always probing for mathematical explanations of the workings of the creative intellect, asked why so many humorists and satirists—he instanced Twain, Lang, and France—and hinted at Shaw—should be drawn to Joan, "heroic, saintly figure that she unquestionably is." Shaw's answer, while he admitted it was not reflected in the heroine of the other three, was a nice comment upon certain distinguishing characteristics of his Joan. "Because," he answered, "Joan, in her rough shrewd way, was a little in that line [the ironic] herself. All souls of that sort are in conflict with the official gravity in which so much mental and moral inferiority disguises itself as superiority. Joan knocked over the clerical, legal, and military panjandrums of her time like ninepins with her trenchant commonsense and mother wit; and though they had the satisfaction of burning her for making them ridiculous, they could not help raising up indignant champions for her by that same stroke." His own Joan consistently refers to common sense even while proclaiming her mystic belief in her Voices, and she practices irony on practically everyone she meets in the play from the blustery and stupid de Baudricourt of the first scene to the formal d'Estivet and the equally blustery and stupid de Courcelles of the Trial Scene. And it is worth noting that this self-conscious possession of

humor, which makes Shaw's Joan more endearing and more truly
sympathetic to audiences than other interpretations, while sharpened
by her creator's finely tempered wit, was still mother wit, for many of
Joan's sharpest sallies, especially to her judges at the trial, are almost
literal transcriptions of her comments as noted in the records published
by Quicherat in the 1840's.

But Shaw insisted always on Joan's tragedy, however much he under-
lined her common sense and irony; these qualities indeed contributed,
as he shows, to her inevitable dangerousness. When Henderson pursued
the question, "Would you mind telling me why *you* chose Joan of Arc
as a dramatic subject," Shaw almost impatiently answered:

> Why not? Joan is a first-class dramatic subject ready made. You have a
> heroic character, caught between "the fell incensèd points" of the Catholic
> Church and the Holy Roman Empire, between Feudalism and Nationalism,
> between Protestantism and Ecclesiasticism, and driven by her virtues and
> her innocence of the world to a tragic death which has secured her immor-
> tality. What more do you want for a tragedy as great as that of Prometheus?
> All the forces that bring about the catastrophe are on the grandest scale;
> and the individual soul on which they press is of the most indomitable force
> and temper. The amazing thing is that the chance has never been jumped at
> by any dramatic poet of the requisite caliber. The pseudo-Shakespearean
> Joan ends in mere jingo scurrility. Voltaire's mock-Homeric play is romantic
> flapdoodle. All the modern attempts known to me are second-rate opera
> books. I felt personally called on by Joan to do her dramatic justice; and I
> don't think I have botched the job.

Note that Shaw quite unselfconsciously referred to himself as dramatic
poet.

Some of the finest criticism of Shaw has been devoted to the analysis
in musical terms of his plays or scenes from his plays. Both academic
and theatre critics have frequently commented upon the almost sym-
phonic structure of the Trial Scene when properly played. That spar-
kling critic, the late James Agate, was inspired by Elizabeth Bergner's
playing of Joan in 1938 at Malvern and by his memories of Shaw's
tremendous knowledge of music to make the playful proposal:

> Why not turn Mr Shaw's St Joan into an opera? How Mozartian could be
> that trio for Warwick, Cauchon, and the Chaplain in Scene IV! Scene V
> contains a Verdi-ish sextet for Joan, Dunois, La Hire, Gilles de Rais, the
> Archbishop, and the Dauphin, all disposed about the steps of the cathedral.
> Why not a baritone and Rossini-like "Stogumber-here, Stogumber-there,"

followed by a bass aria on a familiar model, but this time on heresy? Joan's opportunities for *Una Voce*-ing are too obvious to need pointing out. Then how about a couple of Soldiers' Choruses, one French, t'other English? And for Wagnerish finale, a trio of Loire Maidens, a Warwick's Farewell, and a closing Scene with Joan bel-canto-ing at the stake surrounded by a Meyer-beer-ish chorus.

So much for comic relief. ... A few years ago, lecturing to the English Instutite on "Poetic Drama and the Well-Made Play," Arthur Mizener very persuasively argued that Shaw was the finest practitioner of *both* these forms in our time, because he possessed real imaginative grasp of dramatic and theatrical devices. One of his illustrations was Shaw's use of a conventional modern "curtain" at the end of the Tent Scene to attain "the maximum dramatic force." Mizener quoted the last speeches of that scene and analyzed them perceptively:

> WARWICK. (Rising) My Lord, we seem to be agreed.
> CAUCHON. (Rising also, but in protest) I will not imperil my soul. I will uphold the justice of the Church. I will strive to the utmost for this woman's salvation.
> WARWICK. I am sorry for the poor girl. I hate these severities. I will save her if I can.
> THE CHAPLAIN. (Implacably) I would burn her with my own hands.
> CAUCHON. (Blessing him) Sancta simplicitas!

And the curtain descends on the tableau. It is a magnificent though entirely conventional moment—perhaps I ought properly to say, *because* entirely conventional. Without stepping outside the habitual language of the theatre, it even gets most of the advantages of verse. Cauchon and Warwick each speak three declarative sentences which are parallel in structure and three-stressed. De Stogumber caps their exchange with one more such sentence and Cauchon rounds off the pattern with his comment, which—counting the necessary pause before it—is also three-stressed.

But what is far more important than the poetry of the language is the poetry of the action, the amazing variety of implication and irony within the visually simple pattern of movement. Warwick rises, suavely, a little wearily. Cauchon's answering movement is polite, too, but almost violent with controlled indignation; Warwick faces this indignation with the perfect self-possession of his own sophisticated sincerity And then de Stogumber erupts beside them with the uncontrolled and comically naïve violence of his conviction. Each movement, with its accompanying speech, is a comment on all the others, and the Bishop's gesture applies to all three of them. It is beautifully simple and clear, because it is a moment perfectly realized in terms of the theatre with which its audience is completely at ease.

That final moment of this scene, Mizener declared, "echoes in the imagination because the implications Shaw has embodied in it are so wonderfully varied and penetrating"; and he concluded:

> But it would be a bold man who would say how much of the irony is a thing that characters themselves are to be thought of as understanding and meaning and how much of it a thing that exists, as it were unbeknownst to them, between play and audience. It would be an even bolder man who would say how the interanimating meanings of this moment add up. It is as impossible to answer the question about "what Shaw means" in any serious way as it is to answer that question about any great poet.

I think it is impossible to question Mizener's last statement, provided it applies to the work of a really great dramatic poet, and in *Saint Joan* I think Shaw at his best is that. Referring specifically to his treatment of Cauchon, Warwick, and the Inquisitor in lending to them his own superb articulateness, he wrote in his Preface: "the writer of high tragedy and comedy, aiming at the innermost attainable truth, must needs flatter Cauchon nearly as much as the melodramatist vilifies him ... it is the business of the stage to make its figures more intelligible to themselves than they would be in real life, for by no other means can they be made intelligible to the audience. .... All I claim is that by this inevitable sacrifice of verisimilitude I have secured in the only possible way sufficient veracity to justify me in claiming that as far as I can gather from the available documentation, and from such powers of divination as I possess, the things I represent these three exponents of the drama as saying are the things they actually would have said if they had known what they were really doing. And beyond this neither drama nor history can go in my hands." Mizener's analysis of the end of the Tent Scene suggests how very far and how very deep drama and history went in Shaw's hands.

Critics have always complained of the length of the play. When the New York Theatre Guild put it into rehearsal before the London production got under way, they wired a complaint to the author that it was too long, as the audience would miss the last suburban trains. His answer is famous: "The old old story begin at eight or run later trains"; but he added, "await final revision of play." The Guild were working from his first proofs, which usually he revised, cutting much for the final printing. He later told Hesketh Pearson: "I had to cut it down to the bone. Even then some people seemed to think that three and a half hours of it made a fairly substantial bone." It is worth noting possibly that Rebecca West wished the Inquisitor's seven-minute speech had been made even longer.

Toward the conclusion of his Preface Shaw ironically considered "Some Well-Meant Proposals for the Improvement of the Play" offered by dramatic critics after the first production, these proposals being mainly "the excision of the epilogue and all the references to such undramatic and tedious matters as the Church, the feudal system, the inquisition, the theory of heresy and so forth." Remembering the Shakespearean "improvements" of Irving and Tree, he pointed out:

> The experienced knights of the blue pencil, having saved an hour and a half by disemboweling the play, would at once proceed to waste two hours in building elaborate scenery, having real water in the river Loire with a real bridge across it, and staging an obviously sham fight for the possession of it, with the victorious French led by Joan on a real horse. The coronation would eclipse all previous theatrical displays, shewing, first, the processing through the streets of Rheims, and then the service in the cathedral, with special music written for both. Joan would be burnt on the stage . . . on the principle that it does not matter in the least why a woman is burnt provided she is burnt, and people pay to see it done.

But the experienced knights of the blue pencil were professional critics, and to "a professional critic (I have been one myself)," wrote Shaw, "theatre-going is the curse of Adam. The play is the evil he is paid to endure in the sweat of his brow; and the sooner it is over, the better." He expressed some compassion for these critics and for "the fashionable people whose playgoing is a hypocrisy . . . when they assure me that my play, though a great play, must fail hopelessly, because it does not begin at a quarter to nine and end at eleven"; and he suggested:

> They can escape the first part of the play by their usual practice of arriving late. They can escape the epilogue by not waiting for it. And if the irreducible minimum thus attained is still too painful, they can stay away altogether. But I deprecate this extreme course, because it is good neither for my pocket nor for their own souls. Already a few of them, noticing that what matters is not the absolute length of time occupied by a play, but the speed with which that time passes, are discovering that the theatre, though purgatorial in its Aristotelian moments, is not necessarily always the dull place they have so often found it. What do its discomforts matter when the play makes us forget them?

When Shaw is being played simply, intelligently, and with the proper mingled gusto and reverence, the theatre is not a dull place. When we "are lifted on waves of emotion to be dashed on thought," it is an exciting, a moving, and a pleasant place to be. *Saint Joan* is inspiriting and inspiring; as Desmond MacCarthy wrote at the conclusion of the review of the first London production which I quoted from in starting:

> The extraordinary intellectual merit of this play is the force and fairness with which the case of [Joan's] opponents is put; the startling clarity with which each of them states it, and consequently our instantaneous recognition of its relation to the religious instinct. One of Mr. Shaw's most remarkable gifts has always been this rare generosity. It is odd, but he has never drawn a wicked character—plenty of characters who do wicked things, but not one wicked man. He has never believed in the devil, only in blindness, inertia, and stupidity; faults so widely spread it seems a failure of common sense to distinguish particular people by special abhorrence.
>
> The other extraordinary merit of the play is the intensity of its religious emotion and the grasp the dramatist shows of the human pathos of one who is filled with it, as well as showing his or her immunity from requiring anything like pity. It is probably, I think, the greatest of Shaw's plays.

This point of view was summed up a few years ago by a British radio commentator: "The shining glory of Saint Joan is that she is seen through the eyes of Saint Bernard."

With MacCarthy's judgment that the play is Shaw's greatest probably most critics have agreed. The few dissenters, Arthur Mizener, Eric Bentley, Mr. Shaw, and myself, for instance, would probably admit that in all aspects of the theatre, our own choice, *Heartbreak House,* has not been and will not be, so successful. So our choice is probably made on grounds of prejudice, compounded with a feeling almost of awe toward *Saint Joan.* The little heartbroken people of the twentieth century, the "aspiring, tormented, erratic vehicles," as Shaw once called them, in this Heartbreak House of a beautiful earth, may seem more our fellows; Joan as Shaw conceived her stuns us with her strength of character, her incredible balance and resilience, her sublime faith even in that last moment when her impatience extends almost to God: "O God, who madest this beautiful earth, when will it be ready to receive Thy saints? How long, O Lord, how long?" But note that that last speech questions only the time it takes Man to accept the signs of Godhead; it does not question either the beauty of the earth of the existence of the saints.

✍ T. C. WORSLEY

XVII/An Irish Joan

Several times in the last few months we have heard that most exhilarating sound in the theatre—bravos hailing a performance, and we heard it again last week for Miss Siobhan McKenna's Irish Joan in the Arts revival of Shaw's play. Deservedly, too, for Miss McKenna was by a long way the best Joan I remember. Passionate, sincere and poignant, she convinced in just the right way. She succeeded too (and here the production is extremely helpful) in tracing clearly the development in Joan. For Shaw's Joan is not, just because she is perfect, a static character. The rather absurd naif who, in the first scene, convinces Squire Robert has gone a long way externally, in her manner and her manners, by the time she reaches her cell at Rouen. She has learned to walk with kings and prelates and princes and the edges have been softened, though the fire by which she lives never dies. All this Miss McKenna seems to me to portray to perfection; and then her Irish lilt worked astonishing well for this purpose—it was enough to mark her off from the metropolitan dignitaries without drawing too much attention to itself. It works in another way too. It is easy to forget that the rhythm in which Shaw thought was Irish, and then to find his purple passages unconvincing: Joan's speech, for instance, at the end, where she prefers death to perpetual imprisonment, has been singled out as an example of his inability to rise to the emotional moment and his falling into a false poeticism whenever he attempts it. No one who heard Miss McKenna deliver this speech would ever, I think, hold this view again.

New Statesman and Nation, October 9, 1954, pp. 434-35.

Its rhythm is the rhythm of Irish rhetoric, and spoken so it is extremely effective.

At a time when Shaw is under that interdict of fashion which commits every great writer to a temporary oblivion of twenty years after his death, how does this masterpiece of his stand up? Remarkably well, in my view, solid and indestructible. Those who write down this play do so, I suggest, because they are incurable romantics, and to the incurable romantic Joan must be a heroine of some sort and her accusers and executioners villains of some sort. For the romantics Shaw's play ends before the epilogue, and they judge it on the degree of success with which Shaw moves our sympathies on Joan's behalf. Myself a half incurable romantic, I always find myself falling into the same heresy and dreading the epilogue which, when it comes, always convinces. For it is, of course, just to opposing the romantic view that Shaw dedicated his dramatic life.

That Shaw regarded his *Saint Joan* as a tragedy is undeniable: he talks of it as such in his preface to the play. But the term had its special Shavian significance; tragedy for him lay in the clash between two irreconcilable forces, each of which was justifiable in its own time and place. The problem then was to make Joan completely convincing without glamourising her, and to put over her accusers as normally innocent people doing their best with the best of intentions. In this he certainly had his work cut out, for to the average Protestant or rationalist Englishman the beliefs and behaviour of an orthodox Catholic seem faintly ridiculous, and the expression of those beliefs a series of cheap casuistries. Yet I should have thought it obvious that Shaw marvellously succeeded. A contributing factor to his dramatic genius was his ability to sympathise uncannily closely with types of intellect quite different from his own. Just as more emotive writers, novelists or playwrights can get under the skin of a variety of characters and express their feelings, so Shaw could get under the skin of other intellects and put their points of view as vividly and convincingly as he could put his own. Cauchon and the Inquisitor in this play are superbly understood and realised. Cauchon, by being played off against the worldly wise Warwick, asserts at once his intelligence and his superior sincerity. In the Arts production Mr. Oliver Burt understood this very well. His scenes with Warwick were quite excellent, though I think that a slightly insincere note is allowed to creep in during his scenes with Joan (perhaps because he uses exclusively head notes which give him at this point a rather parsonical air). Mr. Charles Lloyd Pack's Inquisitor, on the other hand, struck me as less right, simply because his appearance and manners are against Shaw's intention. Technically the whole part, and the famous long speech especially, was interestingly delivered. Mr. Lloyd Pack's limitations are the limitations of his appearance; it takes the edge off, if the Inquisitor's manner and bearing suggest anything but complete intellectual integrity and strength. He mustn't, of course, have anything of the bully about him, for he mustn't fall in with any of the *idées reçues* about the Inquisition's wickedness. But Mr. Lloyd Pack in his appearance goes to the opposite extreme. The personages in this play— Joan no less than the rest—are not people or even types: they embody in themselves whole social or intellectual systems, and the actor playing the Inquisitor, for instance, must by his demeanour and appearance predispose us towards what he stands for so that when he launches out on his defence we accept not only his honesty but the necessity of his office. Shaw made in his preface this claim for his play:

> Those who see it performed will not mistake the startling events it records for a mere personal accident. They will have before them not only the visible and human puppets, but the Church, the Inquisition, the Feudal System, with divine inspiration always beating against their too inelastic limits: all more terrible in their dramatic force than any of the little mortal figures clanking about in plate armour or moving silently in the frocks and hoods of the order of St. Dominic.

I don't think it can be denied that he makes the claim good. Naturally there are tiresome Shavianisms in it which no longer stand up, if they ever did. The English Chaplain is as bad a comedy interpolation as any of Shakespeare's and will need in the future as strategical a handling as do the Shakespearean clowns. On the other hand the Dauphin is a perfectly legitimate comedy figure, and if well and tactfully played as he was here by Mr. Kenneth Williams, he more than earns his place. And what superb theatre, as always, Shaw supplied! I would instance especially the duel between Cauchon and Warwick (Mr. Douglas Wilmer was an excellent Warwick), the scene on the Loire where the wind changes and—a smaller moment of the kind which at once reveals the master dramatist—that little reversal after the trial scene when the Inquisitor pronounces the word "Innocent." Mr. John Fernald's production made the most of the small stage at the Arts and brought the play splendidly alive.

~~~ Louis L. Martz

XVIII/The Saint as Tragic Hero

Saints and martyrs have frequently been regarded as impossible subjects for true tragedy. The reasons have been forcibly summed up by
Butcher in his standard commentary on Aristotle's *Poetics*. One trouble
is, he says, that Goodness "is apt to be immobile and uncombative. In
refusing to strike back it brings the action to a standstill." This is
exactly the objection sometimes made to Eliot's presentation of Becket,
who is certainly immobile and, in a sense, uncombative:

> We are not here to triumph by fighting, by strategem, or by resistance,
> Not to fight with beasts as men. We have fought the beast
> And have conquered. We have only to conquer
> Now, by suffering.

But even in the case of more combative saints, such as Joan of Arc,
Butcher would see a serious difficulty: "Impersonal ardour in the cause
of right," he says, does not have "the same dramatic fascination as the
spectacle of human weakness or passion doing battle with the fate it
has brought upon itself." And in short, the chief difficulty is that "the
death of the martyr presents to us not the defeat, but the victory of the
individual; the issue of a conflict in which the individual is ranged on
the same side as the higher powers, and the sense of suffering consequently lost in that of moral triumph."[1] This, I suppose, is what I. A.

Originally titled "The Saint as Tragic Hero: *Saint Joan* and *Murder in the Cathedral*,"
reprinted from Cleanth Brooks, ed., *Tragic Themes in Western Literature* (New Haven,
1955).

1. S. H. Butcher, *Aristotle's Theory of Poetry and Fine Art, with a Critical Text and
Translation of the Poetics* (4th ed., London; Macmillan & Co., Ltd., 1932), pp. 310–12.

Richards also means when he declares that "The least touch of any theology which has a compensating Heaven to offer the tragic hero is fatal"[2]—fatal, that is, to the tragic effect. But we remember:

> Good night, sweet prince,
> And flights of angels sing thee to thy rest.

And we remember the transfiguration of Oedipus at Colonus. Hamlet and Oedipus, we might argue, are in the end on the side of the higher powers. I do not know what we should call Oedipus at Colonus, if he is not a kind of saint, and there is something almost saintly in Hamlet's acute sensitivity to evil. Butcher concedes that Aristotle does not take account of this exceptional type of tragedy "which exhibits the antagonism between a pure will and a disjointed world."[3] We are drawn, then, into some discussion of the nature of tragedy, into some discussion of the plight of tragedy today, and into some discussion, also, of another excellent kind of writing, sometimes called tragic, in which the modern world has achieved a peculiar eminence.

Let us begin with this other kind, for it lacks the touch of any theology. I am thinking of the kind represented by Hemingway's *A Farewell to Arms.* I am thinking particularly of the attitude represented by the dying words of Hemingway's heroine: " 'I'm going to die,' she said; then waited and said, 'I hate it' . . . Then a little later, 'I'm not a bit afraid. It's just a dirty trick.' " This scene is as painful and pitiful as all that earlier misery in the same novel, during the rainy retreat from Caporetto, at the beginning of which Hemingway's hero sums up the central impact of the book, in words that are often quoted: "I was always embarrassed by the words sacred, glorious, and sacrifice and the expression in vain." And he proceeds to emphasize his embarrassment in words that echo a biblical cadence, faintly, and ironically: "We had heard them, sometimes standing in the rain almost out of earshot, so that only the shouted words came through, and had read them, on proclamations that were slapped up by billposters over other proclamations, now for a long time, and I had seen nothing sacred, and the things that were glorious had no glory and the sacrifices were like the

2. I. A. Richards, *Principles of Literary Criticism* (New York, Harcourt, Brace & World, Inc., 1948), p. 246.
3. Butcher, p. 325.

stockyards at Chicago if nothing was done with the meat except to bury it."[4]

The tragedies of Oedipus, Phèdre, Samson, or Hamlet certainly include something like this sense of shattered illusions, this painful recognition of man's fragility, and this pitiful recognition of the inadequacy of human love—but along with, in the same moment with, equally powerful affirmations of the validity of these terms sacred, glorious, sacrifice, and the expression in vain. Tragedy seems simultaneously to doubt and to believe in such expressions: tragedy seems never to know what Wallace Stevens calls "an affirmation free from doubt"— and yet it always seems to contain at least the ghost of an affirmation. Oedipus the King and Samson Agonistes, blind and erring, still sacrifice themselves "gloriously," as Milton puts it. Racine's drama of Phèdre affirms the validity of the Law of Reason, even as the heroine dissolves herself in passion. And Hamlet sees mankind, simultaneously, as the most angelical and the most vicious of earthly creatures; like the Chorus of *Murder in the Cathedral,* Hamlet "knows and does not know."

This sense of a double vision at work in tragedy is somewhat akin to I. A. Richards' famous variation on Aristotle, where Richards finds the essence of tragedy to reside in a "balanced poise." In the "full tragic experience," Richards declares, "ther is no suppression. The mind does not shy away from transcendental matters, when he declares that the mind, in tragedy, "stands uncomforted, unintimidated, alone and self-reliant." This, it seems, will not quite square with Richards' ultimate account of tragedy as "perhaps the most general, all-accepting, all-ordering experience known."[5]

A clearer account, at least a more dogmatic account, of this double vision of tragedy has been set forth by Joyce in his *Portrait of the Artist.* "Aristotle has not defined pity and terror," says Stephen Dedalus, "I have." "Pity is the feeling which arrests the mind in the presence of whatsoever is grave and constant in human sufferings and unites it with the human sufferer. Terror is the feeling which arrests the mind in the presence of whatsoever is grave and constant in human sufferings and

4. Ernest Hemingway, *A Farewell to Arms* (New York: Charles Scribner's Sons, 1929), pp. 353–54, 196.
5. Richards, pp. 246–8.

unites it with the secret cause."[6] Tragedy, then, seems to demand both the human sufferer and the secret cause: that is to say, the doubt, the pain, the pity of the human sufferer; and the affirmation, the awe, the terror of the secret cause. It is an affirmation even though the cause is destructive in its immediate effects: for this cause seems to affirm the existence of some universal order of things.

From this standpoint we can estimate the enormous problem that faces the modern writer in his quest for tragedy. With Ibsen, for example, this power of double vision is in some difficulty. In *Ghosts* or in *Rosmersholm* the element of affirmation is almost overwhelmed by the horror and the suffering that come from the operation of the secret cause—here represented by the family heritage—the dead husband, the dead wife. The affirmation is present, however, in the salvation of an individual's integrity. Ibsen's *Ghosts,* which has the rain pouring down outside for most of the play, nevertheless ends with a view of bright sunshine on the glaciers: symbolizing, perhaps, the clear self-realization which the heroine has achieved. But it is not a very long step before we exit—left—from these shattered drawing rooms into the rain of Ernest Hemingway, where we have the human sufferers, "alone and self-reliant," without a touch of any secret cause. We are in the world of pity which Santayana has beautifully described in a passage of his *Realms of Being,* where he speaks of the "unreasoning sentiment" he might feel in seeing a "blind old beggar" in a Spanish town: "pity simply, the pity of existence, suffusing, arresting, rendering visionary the spectacle of the moment and spreading blindly outwards, like a light in the dark, towards objects which it does not avail to render distinguishable."

It seems a perfect account of the central and powerful effect achieved in many of the best efforts of the modern stage, or movie, or novel, works of pity, where pity dissolves the scene, resolves it into the dew that Hamlet considers but transcends. Thus *A Farewell to Arms* is enveloped in symbolic rain; in *The Naked and the Dead* humanity is lost in the dim Pacific jungle; and the haze of madness gradually dissolves the realistic setting of *A Streetcar Named Desire* or *Death of a*

---

6. James Joyce, *A Portrait of the Artist as a Young Man* (New York: B. W. Huebsch, 1916), p. 239.

Salesman. In the end, Willy Loman has to plant his garden in the dark. "The pity of existence ... spreading blindly outwards ... towards objects which it does not avail to render distinguishable."

The problem of the tragic writer in our day appears to be: how to control this threatened dissolution, how to combine this "unreasoning sentiment" with something like the different vision that Santayana goes on to suggest: "Suppose now that I turn through the town gates and suddenly see a broad valley spread out before me with the purple sierra in the distance beyond. This expanse, this vastness, fills my intuition; also, perhaps, some sense of the deeper breath which I draw as if my breast expanded in sympathy with the rounded heavens."[7] Thus we often find that the modern writer who seeks a tragic effect will attempt, by some device, such as Ibsen's family heritage or his view of the glacier, to give us the experience of a secret cause underlying his work of pity—to give it broader dimensions, sharper form, to render the ultimate objects distinguishable, to prevent it from spreading blindly outwards. We can see this plainly in O'Neill's *Mourning Becomes Electra,* where O'Neill, by borrowing from Aeschylus the ancient idea of a family curse, is able to give his drama a firm, stark outline, and to endow his heroine with something like a tragic dignity. The only trouble is that this Freudian version of a family curse is not secret enough: it tends to announce itself hysterically, all over the place: "I'm the last Mannon. I've got to punish myself!" In the end we feel that this family curse has been shipped in from Greece and has never quite settled down in New England.

Eliot has described much the same difficulty which appears in his play *The Family Reunion,* where he too, even more boldly than O'Neill, has tried to borrow the Furies from Aeschylus. Eliot deploys his Furies, quite impolitely, in the middle of Ibsen's drawing room. As we might expect, they were not welcome: "We put them on the stage, and they looked like uninvited guests who had strayed in from a fancy-dress ball. We concealed them behind gauze, and they suggested a still out of a Walt Disney film. We made them dimmer, and they looked like shrubbery just outside the window. I have seen other expedients tried":

7. George Santayana, *Realms of Being* (New York: Charles Scribner's Sons, 1942), pp. 147-49.

Eliot adds, "I have seen them signalling from across the garden, or swarming onto the stage like a football team, and they are never right. They never succeed in being either Greek goddesses or modern spooks. But their failure," he concludes, "is merely a symptom of the failure to adjust the ancient with the modern."[8] Or, we might say, a failure to adjust the ancient Aeschylean symbol of a secret cause with the modern human sufferer.

How, then, can it be done? It is in their approach to this problem that *Saint Joan* and *Murder in the Cathedral* reveal their peculiar power, in an approach that seems to have been made possible by this fact: that both Shaw and Eliot feel they cannot depend upon their audience to accept their saintly heroes as divinely inspired. The dramaturgy of both plays is based upon a deliberate manipulation of the elements of religious skepticism or uncertainty in the audience.

As Eliot's play moves toward the somber conclusion of its first half, the Four Tempters cry out in the temptation of self-pity ("It's just a dirty trick"):

> Man's life is a cheat and a disappointment . . .
> All things become less real, man passes
> From unreality to unreality.
> This man [Becket] is obstinate, blind, intent
> On self-destruction,
> Passing from deception to deception,
> From grandeur to grandeur to final illusion . . .

And a page later the Chorus too cries out from the world of Ernest Hemingway, with also, perhaps, a slight reminiscence of the millrace in *Rosmersholm:*

> We have seen the young man mutilated,
> The torn girl trembling by the mill-stream.
> And meanwhile we have gone on living,
> Living and partly living,
> Picking together the pieces,
> Gathering faggots at nightfall,
> Building a partial shelter,
> For sleeping, and eating and drinking and laughter.

8. T. S. Eliot, *Poetry and Drama* (Cambridge, Mass.: Harvard University Press, 1951), p. 37.

And then, at the very close of Part I, Becket sums up the whole attitude when he turns sharply to address the audience:

> I know
> What yet remains to show you of my history
> Will seem to most of you at best futility,
> Senseless self-slaughter of a lunatic,
> Arrogant passion of a fanatic.
> I know that history at all times draws
> The strangest consequence from remotest cause.

It is exactly the challenge that Shaw has thrown at his readers in the Preface to *Saint Joan:* "For us to set up our condition as a standard of sanity, and declare Joan mad because she never condescended to it, is to prove that we are not only lost but irredeemable."

Eliot and Shaw, then, seem to be assuming that the least touch of theology in their plays will serve—to raise a question. And so the saint may become a figure well adapted to arouse something very close to a tragic experience: for here the words sacred, glorious, sacrifice, and the expression in vain may become once again easily appropriate; while at the same time the uncertainty of the audience's attitude—and to some extent the dramatist's own—may enable him to deal also with the painful and pitiful aspects of experience that form the other side of the tragic tension.

But this conflict, this double vision, is not, in these plays, primarily contained within the figure of the saint as tragic hero: Joan and Becket do not here represent humanity in the way of Hamlet, or King Oedipus—by focusing within themselves the full tragic tension. They are much more like Oedipus at Colonus, who, although a pitiful beggar in appearance, speaks now through the power of a superhuman insight. Most of his mind lies beyond suffering: he feels that he has found the secret cause, and under the impulse of that cause he moves onward magnificently to his death and transfiguration. The sense of human suffering in *Oedipus at Colonus* is conveyed chiefly in retrospect, or in the sympathetic outcries of the Chorus, the weeping of the rejected Polynices, and the anguish of the two daughters whom Oedipus must leave behind.

To see these plays as in any sense tragic it seems that we must abandon the concept of a play built upon an ideal Aristotelian hero, and look instead for a tragic experience that arises from the interaction between a hero who represents the secret cause, and the other characters, who represent the human sufferers. The point is brought out, ironically, by the Archbishop, near the end of Shaw's play, when he warns Joan against the sin of pride, saying, "the old Greek tragedy is rising among us. It is the chastisement of hubris." Joan replies with her usual bluntness, asking, "How can you say that I am disobedient when I always obey my voices, because they come from God." But when the Archbishop insists that "all the voices that come to you are the echoes of your own wilfulness," when he declares angrily, "You stand alone: absolutely alone, trusting to your own conceit, your own ignorance, your own headstrong presumption, your own impiety," we are reminded of Creon berating Oedipus at Colonus, and we are reminded too of Oedipus' long declaration of innocence when Joan turns away, "her eyes skyward," saying, "I have better friends and better counsel than yours."

There is nothing complex about the character of Shaw's Joan; it is the whole fabric of the play that creates something like a tragic tension. For whatever he may say in his preface, Shaw the dramatist, through his huge cast of varied human types, probes the whole range of belief and disbelief in Joan's voices. "They come from your imagination," says the feeble de Baudricourt in the opening scene. "Of course," says Joan, "that is how the messages of God come to us." Cauchon believes the girl to be "inspired, but diabolically inspired." "Many saints have said as much as Joan," Ladvenu suggests. Dunois, her only friend, senses some aura of divinity about her, but becomes extremely uneasy when she talks about her voices. "I should think," he says, "you were a bit cracked if I hadn't noticed that you give me very sensible reasons for what you do, though I hear you telling others you are only obeying Madame Saint Catherine." "Well," she replies, "I have to find reasons for you, because you do not believe in my voices. But the voices come first; and I find the reasons after: whatever you may choose to believe." *Whatever you may choose to believe:* there is the point, and as the figure of Joan flashes onward through the play, with only one lapse in confidence—her brief recantation—Shaw keeps his play hovering among choices in a highly modern state of uncertainty: we know and do not know: until at the close Shaw seems to send us over on the side of affirmation. We agree, at least, with the words of the French captain in the opening scene: "There is something about her. . . . Something. . . . I think the girl herself is a bit of a miracle."

She is, as Eliot would say, "a white light still and moving," the simple *cause* of every other word and action in the play; and her absolute simplicity of vision cuts raspingly through all the malign or well-intentioned errors of the world, until in its wrath the world rises up in the form of all its assembled institutions and declares by the voice of all its assembled doctors that this girl is—as Shaw says—*insufferable*.[9]

Thus Joan's apparent resemblance to the Aristotelian hero: her extreme self-confidence, her brashness, her appearance of rash impetuosity—all this becomes in the end a piece of Shavian irony, for her only real error in the play is the one point where her superb self-confidence breaks down in the panic of recantation. And so the hubris is not Joan's but Everyman's. The characters who accuse Joan of pride and error are in those accusations convicting themselves of the pride of self-righteousness and the errors of human certitude. It is true that the suffering that results from this pride and error remains in Shaw's play rather theoretical and remote: and yet we feel it in some degree: in the pallor and anguish of Joan as she resists the temptation to doubt her voices, in the rather unconvincing screams of Stogumber at the close, and, much more effectively, in the quiet, controlled sympathy of Ladvenu. It would seem, then, that some degree of tragedy resides in this failure of Everyman to recognize absolute Reality, the secret cause, when it appears in the flesh. Must then, cries Cauchon in the Epilogue, "Must then a Christ perish in torment in every age to save those that have no imagination?" It is the same symbolism that Eliot has evoked in the beginning of his play, where the·Chorus asks: "Shall the Son of Man be born again in the litter of scorn?"

We need not be too greatly concerned with Shaw's bland assertions that he is letting us in on the truth about the Middle Ages, telling us in the play all we need to know about Joan. Books and articles have appeared—a whole cloudburst of them—devoted to proving that Shaw's methods of historical research in his play and in his preface are open to serious question. But Shaw gave that game away long ago when

---

9. See the amusing anecdote recorded by Archibald Henderson, *Bernard Shaw, Playboy and Prophet* (New York: Appleton-Century-Crofts, 1932), pp. 693-95.

he announced: "I deal with all periods; but I never study any period but the present, which I have not yet mastered and never shall";[10] or when he said, with regard to Cleopatra's cure for Caesar's baldness, that his methods of scholarship, as compared with Gilbert Murray's, consisted in "pure divination."[11] The Preface to *Saint Joan* lays down a long barrage of historicity, which in the end is revealed as a remarkable piece of Shavio-Swiftian hoaxing: for in the last few pages of that long preface he adds, incidentally, that his use of the "available documentation" has been accompanied by "such powers of divination as I possess"; he concedes that for some figures in his play he has invented "appropriate characters" "in Shakespear's manner"; and that, fundamentally, his play is built upon what he calls "the inevitable flatteries of tragedy." That is, there is no historical basis for his highly favorable characterizations of Cauchon and the Inquisitor, upon which the power and point of the trial scene are founded.

I do not mean to say, however, that our sense of history is irrelevant to an appreciation of Shaw's play. There is a point to be made by considering such a book as J. M. Robertson's *Mr. Shaw and "The Maid,"* which complains bitterly, upon historical grounds, against Shaw's "instinct to put things both ways."[12] This is a book, incidentally, which Eliot has praised very highly because it points out that in this kind of subject "Facts matter," and that "to Mr. Shaw, truth and falsehood . . . do not seem to have the same meaning as to ordinary people."[13] But the point lies rather in the tribute that such remarks pay to the effectiveness of Shaw's realistic dramaturgy.

Shaw is writing, as he and Ibsen had to write, within the conventions of the modern realistic theater—conventions which Eliot escaped in *Murder in the Cathedral* because he was writing this play for performance at the Canterbury Festival. But in his later plays, composed for the theater proper, Eliot has also been forced to, at least he has chosen to, write within these stern conventions.

Now in the realistic theater, as Francis Fergusson has suggested, the artist seems to be under the obligation to pretend that he is not an

---

10. Shaw, Preface to *The Sanity of Art* (New York: B. R. Tucker, 1908), p. 5.
11. See Shaw's notes appended to *Caesar and Cleopatra: Nine Plays*, p. 471.
12. J. M. Robertson, *Mr. Shaw and "The Maid"* (London: Cobden-Sanderson, 1926), p. 85.
13. T. S. Eliot, *Criterion*, 4 (April 1926), p. 390.

artist at all, but is simply interested in pursuing the truth "in some pseudo-scientific sense."[14] Thus we find the relation of art to life so often driven home on the modern stage by such deep symbolic actions as removing the cubes from ice trays or cooking an omelette for dinner. Shaw knows that on his stage facts matter—or at least the appearance of facts—and in this need for a dramatic realism lies the basic justification for Shaw's elaborately argued presentation of Joan as a Protestant and Nationalist martyr killed by the combined institutional forces of feudalism and the Church. Through these historical theories, developed within the body of the play, Joan is presented as the agent of a transformation in the actual world; the theories have enough plausibility for dramatic purposes, and perhaps a bit more; this, together with Shaw's adaptation of the records of Joan's trial, gives him all the "facts" that he needs to make his point in the modern theater.

Some of Joan's most Shavian remarks are in fact her own words as set down in the long records of her trial: as, for example, where her questioner asks whether Michael does not appear to her as a naked man. "Do you think God cannot afford clothes for him?" answers Joan, in the play and in the records. Shaw has made a skillful selection of these answers, using, apparently, the English translation of the documents edited by Douglas Murray;[15] and he has set these answers together with speeches of his own modeled upon their tone and manner. In this way he has been able to bring within the limits of the realistic theater the very voice that rings throughout these trial records, the voice of the lone girl fencing with, stabbing at, baffling, and defeating the crowd of some sixty learned men: a voice that is not speaking within the range of the other voices that assail her. Thus we hear her in the following speech adapted from half-a-dozen places in the records:

"I have said again and again that I will tell you all that concerns this trial. But I cannot tell you the whole truth: God does not allow the whole truth to

14. Francis Fergusson, *The Idea of a Theater* (Princeton: Princeton University Press, 1949), p. 147.
15. *Jeanne D'Arc, Maid of Orleans, Deliverer of France; Being the Story of her Life, her Achievements, her Death, as attested on Oath and Set forth in the Original Documents,* ed. by T. Douglas Murray (New York: McClure, Phillips, 1902; published in England the same year). See p. 42: "Do you think God has wherewithal to clothe him?" This contains a translation of the official Latin documents published by Jules Quincherat in 1841–49.

be told. . . . It is an old saying that he who tells too much truth is sure to be hanged. . . . I have sworn as much as I will swear; and I will swear no more."[16]

Or, following the documents much more closely, her answers thus resound when the questioners attempt to force her to submit her case to the Church on earth: "I will obey The Church," says Joan, "provided it does not command anything impossible."

> If you command me to declare that all that I have done and said, and all the visions and revelations I have had, were not from God, then that is impossible: I will not declare it for anything in the world. What God made me do I will never go back on; and what He has commanded or shall command I will not fail to do in spite of any man alive. That is what I mean by impossible. And in case The Church should bid me do anything contrary to the command I have from God, I will not consent to it, no matter what it may be.

In thus maintaining the tone of that—extraordinary—voice, Shaw has, I think, achieved an effect that is in some ways very close to the effect of the "intersection of the timeless with time" which Eliot has achieved in his play, and which he has described in "The Dry Salvages":

> Men's curiosity searches past and future
> And clings to that dimension. But to apprehend
> The point of intersection of the timeless
> With time, is an occupation for the saint—
> No occupation either, but something given
> And taken, in a lifetime's death in love,
> Ardour and selflessness and self-surrender.

An obvious similarity between the two plays may be seen in the tone of satirical wit that runs through both—notably in the ludicrous prose speeches that Eliot's murdering Knights deliver to the audience in self-defense. These have an essentially Shavian purpose: "to shock the audience out of their complacency," as Eliot has recently said, going on to admit, "I may, for aught I know, have been slightly under the influence of *St. Joan.*"[17] The atmosphere of wit is evident also in the first part of Eliot's play, in the cynical attitude of the Herald who announces Becket's return:

16. Cf. Murray, pp. 5-6, 8-9, 14-15, 18, 22, 33.
17. Eliot, *Poetry and Drama*, p. 30.

> The streets of the city will be packed to suffocation,
> And I think that his horse will be deprived of its tail,
> A single hair of which becomes a precious relic.

Or, more important, in the speeches of the Four Tempters, who match
the Four Knights of Part II, and who tend to speak, as the Knights also
do in places, in a carefully calculated doggerel that betrays their
fundamental shallowness:

> I leave you to the pleasures of your higher vices,
> Which will have to be paid for at higher prices.
> Farewell, my Lord, I do not wait upon ceremony,
> I leave as I came, forgetting all acrimony,
> Hoping that your present gravity
> Will find excuse for my humble levity.
> If you will remember me, my Lord, at your prayers,
> I'll remember you at kissing-time below the stairs.

In all these ways Eliot, like Shaw, maintains his action in the "real"
world: and by other means as well. By keeping before us the central
question of our own time: "Is it war or peace?" asks Eliot's priest.
"Peace," replies the Herald, "but not the kiss of peace. A patched up
affair, if you ask my opinion." By the frequently realistic imagery of the
Chorus, made up of "the scrubbers and sweepers of Canterbury." By
the frequent use in Part II of the recorded words that passed between
Becket and the Knights in the year 1170.[18] By throwing our minds back
to the literary forms of the Middle Ages: to *Everyman*, from which
Eliot has taken a good many hints for the tone and manner of Becket's
encounter with the Tempters, and which, as he says, he has kept in
mind as a model for the versification of his dialogue.[19] To this last we
should also add a special device of heavy alliteration (particularly
notable in the Second Temptation), which seems to work in two ways:
it reminds us of the English alliterative verse of the Middle Ages, and
thus gives the play a further historical focus, and it also suggests here a
rhetoric of worldly ambition in keeping with the temptation that
Becket is undergoing:

18. See William Holden Hutton, *S. Thomas of Canterbury. An account of his Life
and Fame from the Contemporary Biographers and other Chroniclers* (London, 1889),
esp. pp. 234-245.
19. Eliot, *Poetry and Drama*, pp. 27-28.

> Think, my Lord,
> Power obtained grows to glory,
> Life lasting, a permanent possession,
> A templed tomb, monument of marble.
> Rule over men reckon no madness.

Both Eliot and Shaw, then, have in their own ways taken pains to place their action simultaneously in the "real" past and the "real" present: an action firmly fixed in time must underlie the shock of intersection.

But of course, in Eliot's play the cause of intersection, the agent of transformation, the saint, is utterly different from Shaw's, and thus the plays become, so obviously, different. Shaw's Joan is the active saint, operating in the world; Eliot's Becket is a contemplative figure, ascetic, "withdrawn to contemplation," holding within his mind, and reconciling there alone, the stresses of the world. His immobility is his strength, he is the still point, the center of the world that moves about him, as his sermon is the center of the play.

One is struck here by the similarity between the total conception of Eliot's play and of *Oedipus at Colonus*. Both heroes, after a long period of wandering, have found, at their entrance, their place of rest and their place of death, in a sacred spot: Becket in his Cathedral, Oedipus in the sacred wood of the Furies or Eumenides. Both heroes maintain the attitude that Oedipus states at the outset: "nevermore will I depart from my rest in this land." Both reveal in their opening speeches the view that, as Oedipus says, "patience is the lesson of suffering."[20] Both are then subjected to various kinds of temptations to leave the spot; both are forced to recapitulate their past while enduring these trials; both remain immobile, unmovable; both win a glorious death and by that death benefit the land in which they die. Both are surrounded by a large cast of varied human sufferers, who do not understand the saint, who try to deflect him from his ways, and who in some cases mourn his loss bitterly: the cry of Eliot's priest at the end is like the cries of Antigone and Ismene:

> O father, father, gone from us, lost to us,
> How shall we find you, from what far place
> Do you look down on us?

20. *The Tragedies of Sophocles,* trans. Sir Richard C. Jebb (Cambridge: Cambridge University Press, 1904), pp. 63, 61.

I suspect that *Oedipus at Colonus* has in fact had a deep and early influence upon Eliot's whole career: "Sweeney among the Nightingales" alludes to this very wood, which Sophocles' Chorus describes as a place where

> The sweet, sojourning nightingale
> Murmurs all day long. . . .
> And here the choiring Muses come,
> And the divinity of love
> With the gold reins in her hand.[21]

The fact that the Muses haunt this wood may throw some light too upon the title of Eliot's first book of essays, *The Sacred Wood,* the book in which he revealed his early interest in the possibility of a poetic drama.

But our main point here is the way in which this deeply religious tragedy of Sophocles, which had already provided a strong formative precedent for Milton's *Samson Agonistes,* now provides us with a precedent for regarding Eliot's saint's play as a tragedy. The precedent may also explain why a strong coloring of Greek-like fatalism runs throughout Eliot's Christian play: a coloring which some of Eliot's critics have found disturbing. But these classical reminiscences of Destiny and Fate and Fortune's wheel remind us only of the base upon which Eliot is building: they do not delimit his total meaning. We can see this amalgamation of Greek and Christian at work in Becket's opening speech—the most important speech of the play, which all the rest of the play explores and illustrates. It is the speech which Becket's Fourth Tempter, his inmost self, repeats in mockery, word for word, twenty pages later, and thus suggests that these Temptations—of pleasure, worldly power, and spiritual pride—are to be regarded as fundamentally a recapitulation of the stages by which Becket has reached the state of mind he displays at his entrance. He believes that he has found a secret cause, and he enters prepared to die in that belief: "Peace," he says to the worried priest, and then, referring to the Chorus of anxious women, continues:

> They speak better than they know, and beyond your understanding.

21. Sophocles, *Oedipus at Colonus,* trans. Robert Fitzgerald (New York: Harcourt, Brace & World, Inc., 1941), pp. 55–56.

> They know and do not know, what it is to act or suffer.
> They know and do not know, that acting is suffering
> And suffering is action. Neither does the actor suffer
> Nor the patient act. But both are fixed
> In an eternal action, an eternal patience
> To which all must consent that it may be willed
> And which all must suffer that they may will it,
> That the pattern may subsist, for the pattern is the action
> And the suffering, that the wheel may turn and still
> Be forever still.

We can worry the ambiguities of those words "suffering" and "patient" as long as we wish: in the end Becket keeps his secret almost as stubbornly as Joan or Oedipus:

> I have had a tremor of bliss, a wink of heaven, a whisper,
> And I would no longer be denied; all things
> Proceed to a joyful consummation.

But halfway between these two passages lies Becket's Christmas sermon, presented as a four-page interlude between the play's two parts. It is one of the most surprisingly successful moments in the modern theater, for who would expect to find a sermon, and an interesting sermon, here? It owes its success to an atmosphere of restrained and controlled mystery, and to the fact that it is not really an interlude at all, but a deep expression of the play's central theme, binding the play's two parts into one. Becket is speaking of this word *Peace*, the word that dominates the play, for all the actors and sufferers in the play are seeking peace, on their own terms. But the meaning of the word for Becket is conveyed only obliquely, by Becket's tone, his poise, his humility, his acceptance, "Thus devoted, concentrated in purpose." He can display only by his own action and suffering what his word Peace means to him, for he is trying to explain the meaning of the unspoken Word that lies locked in the visible and verbal paradoxes of acting and suffering.

And only in this way, too, can Becket display that submission of the will by which he avoids the final temptation of spiritual pride. The Temptations make it clear that Becket has been a proud man—even an arrogant man: the first priest, the Tempters, and the Knights all accuse him, with some reason, of pride. And we hear him speaking at times, throughout the play, and even at the very end, in a harsh, acid tone, which here and there is uncomfortably close to condescension. Eliot's control of the character is not perhaps as firm as we could wish; though there is nothing that a skillful actor cannot handle, for the central conception is clear: like Oedipus, Becket is still a man, and retains the marks of his natural character: but in the sermon we grasp his saintliness.

At the same time Becket conveys to us the essence of the view of Tragedy that we are here considering. Becket's sermon ponders the fact that in the services of Christmas the Church celebrates birth and death simultaneously. Now, "as the World sees," Becket says, "this is to behave in a strange fashion. For who in the world will both mourn and rejoice at once and for the same reason?" And this is true on other occasions, he adds: "so also, in a smaller figure, we both rejoice and mourn in the death of martyrs. We mourn, for the sins of the world that has martyred them; we rejoice, that another soul is numbered among the Saints. . . ."

It is this tension, this double vision, that Eliot presents in his great choral odes. What Eliot has done is to allow everyone in his play except the Chorus and Becket to remain the simplest possible types—simpler even than Shaw's: ciphers who serve their functions: to provide an outline of the action and a setting for the problem. Into the cries of the Chorus he has poured the tragic experience of suffering humanity, caught in the grip of a secret cause: "We are forced to bear witness."

The Chorus opens the play with fear and reluctance and hopelessness, asking who it is who shall

> Stretch out his hand to the fire, and deny his master? who shall be warm
> By the fire, and deny his master?

They know and do not know who it is—themselves—bending to the earth like animals seeking their protective coloring:

> Now I fear disturbance of the quiet seasons:
> Winter shall come bringing death from the sea,
> Ruinous spring shall beat at our doors,
> Root and shoot shall eat our eyes and our ears,
> Disastrous summer burn up the beds of our streams
> And the poor shall wait for another decaying October.

These dead do not desire resurrection; and when their Lord Archbishop reappears to them, they can only cry out, "O Thomas, return, Archbishop; return, return to France. . . . Leave us to perish in quiet." They would like to go on "living and partly living," like Shaw's Dauphin, who irritably shies away from Joan, saying, "I want to sleep in a comfortable bed." Eliot's Chorus starts from this point—by the fireside and the bed—a point which Shaw's chorus of varied actors hardly goes beyond. But Eliot's Chorus moves far beyond this point, undergoing what Kenneth Burke or Francis Fergusson might call a ritual of transformation. They are not at all the "foolish, immodest and babbling women" which Eliot's priest calls them, but the heart of humanity moving under the impulse of a half-realized cause. Under this impulse they have moved, by the end of Part I, into the range of a "stifling scent of despair," which nevertheless is not spreading blindly outwards: for the Chorus

> The forms take shape in the dark air:
> Puss-purr of leopard, footfall of padding bear,
> Palm-pat of nodding ape, square hyaena waiting
> For laughter, laughter, laughter. The Lords of Hell are here.

But after Becket's sermon the Chorus has taken some heart: they no longer seem to fear the spring:

> When the leaf is out on the tree, when the elder and may
> Burst over the stream, and the air is clear and high,
> And voices trill at windows, and children tumble in front of the door,
> What work shall have been done, what wrong
> Shall the bird's song cover, the green tree cover, what wrong
> Shall the fresh earth cover?

From this oscillation between despair and a half-hope arises the play's greatest poetry, as the Chorus moves on far out of the range of ordinary fears and hopes into a nightmare vision that renews and extends the animal imagery, and the dense imagery of taste and smell and the other senses, by which the Chorus had expressed its horror at the close of Part I; but now there is more than horror: the Chorus is moving on here to a vision of humanity's living relation with all being, to a sense that all of creation from the worm to the Prince is involved in this sacrifice:

> I have smelt them, the death-bringers, senses are quickened
> By subtile forebodings . . .

> I have tasted
> The savour of putrid flesh in the spoon. I have felt
> The heaving of earth at nightfall, restless, absurd. I have heard
> Laughter in the noises of beasts that make strange noises . . .
>   I have eaten
> Smooth creatures still living, with the strong salt taste of living things under
> sea . . .
>   In the air
> Flirted with the passage of the kite, I have plunged with the kite and
> cowered with the wren. . . .
>   I have seen
> Rings of light coiling downwards, leading
> To the horror of the ape. . . .
> I have consented, Lord Archbishop, have consented.

Beyond this recognition of responsibility for the action and the suffering, there lies a step into the vision of ultimate horror which they face
just before the murder: a vision of utter spiritual death: the Dark Night
of the Soul:

> Emptiness, absence, separation from God;
> The horror of the effortless journey, to the empty land
> Which is no land, only emptiness, absence, the Void. . . .

This, paradoxically, is their moment of deepest vision, of greatest
courage; the point at which they fully comprehend their need for the
sacrifice about to be permitted, suffered, and which provides the answer to their cries during the very act of the murder:

> Clear the air! clean the sky! wash the wind! take the stone from the stone,
> take the skin from the arm, take the muscle from the bone, and wash
> them. Wash the stone, wash the bone, wash the brain, wash the soul,
> wash them wash them!

Like King Oedipus they are, without quite realizing it, being washed in
this "rain of blood" that is blinding their eyes.

As these cries from the conscience of humanity fade away, the lights
fade out—and then come on again in the foreground with a glaring
brightness—as the four Murderers step forward, make their bows, and
present their ridiculous speeches of defense—in the manner of an after-
dinner speaker: "I knew Becket well, in various official relations; and I
may say that I have never known a man so well qualified for the highest
rank of the Civil Service." Or in the manner of the parliamentary
orator: "I must repeat one point that the last speaker has made. While

the late Archbishop was Chancellor, he wholeheartedly supported the King's designs: this is an important point, which, if necessary, I can substantiate." Or in the manner of the brisk attorney: "I think, with these facts before you, you will unhesitatingly render a verdict of Suicide while of Unsound Mind."

The lights fade out again, the Knights disappear, and then gradually the lights come on once more, to reveal the priests and the Chorus in their old positions. It is as if the Knights had never spoken: the conscience of humanity has been working deep within while the Knights were speaking on the surface, and now the Chorus sums up its discoveries, its transformation, in a psalm of praise, in which once again it affirms a union with the whole creation, but this time in a tone of joy and peace:

> We praise Thee, O God, for Thy glory displayed in all the creatures of the earth,
> In the snow, in the rain, in the wind, in the storm; in all of Thy creatures, both the hunters and the hunted. . . .
> They affirm Thee in living; all things affirm Thee in living; the bird in the air, both the hawk and the finch; the beast on the earth, both the wolf and the lamb; the worm in the soil and the worm in the belly. . . .
> Even in us the voices of seasons, the snuffle of winter, the song of spring, the drone of summer, the voices of beasts and of birds, praise Thee.

Those words from the final chorus may remind us again of the long tentacles of correlated imagery that reach throughout these choral odes: imagery of beasts and birds and worms; of seasons, of violent death, of the daily hardships of the partly living life: with the result that these choral odes grow together into a long poem, interwoven with verse and prose pitched at a lower intensity; and by this interweaving of the odes, even more than by Becket, the play is drawn into unity.

We can see now the effect that these different manifestations of a secret cause have had upon the total construction of our two saint's plays. Eliot's play, focused on a contemplative saint, displays what we might call a semi-circular structure: with Becket as the still center, and the Chorus sweeping out around him in a broad dramatic action, a poetical ballet of transformation. Shaw's play, based on an active saint, develops instead a linear structure, as of a spear driving straight for the mark. It is marred, here and there, by irrelevant or maladjusted witticisms, and the whole character of Stogumber is a misfortune. Yet Joan

and her voices seem to work like key symbols in a poem: appearing in a
carefully designed sequence of different contexts: six scenes, with six
differing moods, moving from farce to high comedy, to a romantic
glimpse of the warrior Joan in shining armor, and from here into an
area of deepening somberness, until, by the fifth scene, the world of
Shaw's play, too, has been transformed—from the foolish to the tragic.
Now we have in his play, too, the dim silence of the Cathedral, with
Joan praying symbolically before the stations of the Cross: her white
raiment revealing the saint whose mission is now nearly complete. The
king is crowned; she has shown France how to win; and now, as her
allies, one by one, and even Dunois, fail to answer the unbearable
demands of the superhuman, Joan goes forth to meet the cheering
crowd who will kiss her garments and line her roadway with palms.
The way is now prepared for the massive trial scene, the tragic agon,
which presents what Eliot calls "a symbol perfected in death."

And then, the Epilogue. Many have found this a disconcerting,
inartistic mixture of farce, satire, and didactic explanation. I agree. But
I do not see why the Epilogue should spoil the play. An epilogue is no
part of the dramatic action: it is the author's chance to step forward,
relaxed and garrulous, and to talk the play over with the audience.
Traditionally, it is true, the epilogue is recited by only one performer—
by Prospero, for instance. There is a slight difference here: Shaw has
had his entire cast recite the Epilogue. But it is still appended commentary on the action, not a part of the action. Moreover, this kind of thing
is not without precedent in performances of tragedy. The ancient
Greeks appear to have liked exactly this kind of release in their festivals
of tragedy, since they demanded that each dramatist, after presenting
his three tragedies, should provide them with their satyr-play, usually of
an uproarious and ribald variety, sometimes burlesquing elements of
the very story that had just been seen in tragic dignity. The Epilogue is
Shaw's satyr-play: a bursting forth of that strong sense of the ridiculous
which Shaw has, during the play proper, subjected to a remarkable
control—remarkable, that is, for Shaw.

It seems possible, then, to find some place, within the spacious area
of tragedy, for our two saint's plays. It seems possible, if we will not
demand an Aristotelian hero, and if we may view the area of tragedy as
a sort of scale or spectrum ranging between the two poles of doubt and

affirmation: or, to put it more precisely, between the pole of fruitless suffering and the pole of universal cause. Not a scale of value, but a spectrum of various qualities, with *A Farewell to Arms* marking one extreme, outside the area of tragedy, and Shakespeare's *Tempest*, perhaps, marking the other extreme. In between, within the area of tragedy, would lie an enormous variety of works that would defy any rigorous attempt at definition, except that all would show in some degree a mingled atmosphere of doubt and affirmation, of human suffering and secret cause. Far over toward the side of fruitless suffering we might find the plays of Ibsen, or *Othello;* somewhere in the middle, *Hamlet,* or *Oedipus Rex;* and far over toward the other side we might find a triad of strongly affirmative tragedies: *Oedipus at Colonus, Samson Agonistes,* and *Murder in the Cathedral;* and still farther over, perhaps hanging on by his hands to the very rim of tragedy—we might even find a place for Bernard Shaw.

XIX/Shaw and Sainthood

Among those of Shaw's plays which deal with figures of human greatness, *Saint Joan* occupies a high rank. In this play and its preface he
describes her as an inspired prophetess and a fighting saint.

It is not enough to state that the canonization of Joan of Arc in 1920,
and the additional fact that his wife further directed his attention to
her,[1] prompted him to dramatize the life of this particular saint in the
years following the First World War. At a period 25 years earlier, when
his opinion of Joan was scarcely favourable,[2] he had dramatized the
historical portrait of Caesar in the light of Mommsen's account. His
choice, at a later date, of the life-story of the Maid of Orleans points to
something more profound, to a change of outlook, since she represents
Shaw's human ideal just as Caesar had done earlier. It was thus an
underlying affinity between these characters and his own ideas at given
times which predisposed Shaw to allow his attention to be drawn to
them and to act further on outside suggestions along these lines.

I shall try to show that Shaw's ideal human figure in the years
between 1910 and 1930 is that of the prophetic and fighting Saint (so
that Joan falls into place as the most significant and unambiguous
expression of this ideal), and its position with regard to his view of the
world more generally. While it is true that his Saint is the product of a

English Studies, XXXVI (April, 1955), 49–63.
    1. Cf. M. Colbourne: *The Real Bernard Shaw,* London 1949, p. 199.
    2. *Three Plays for Puritans* (1900), p. 201.—The Standard Edition of Shaw's Works,
London, Constable 1930 *et seq.,* is always referred to unless otherwise stated.

new and more profound attitude of mind, it is linked nevertheless, and that very clearly, by a natural line of development to both the earlier figures and to the later ones too. It is a useful connexion to bear in mind if we would arrive at a clearer understanding of these later figures. The Shavian conception of Sainthood itself involves a problem—are we justified, for instance, in attaching this label to certain of his characters whom he made to carry his ideals of humanity; and what, in any case, are we to understand by this term in a Shavian context?

No one will, nowadays, find any difficulty in regarding Shaw as an admirer of the Great Man. From his earliest novels he was never content with describing the humanity around him—the picture he drew was always a heightened one. This attitude received support from historical as well as contemporary figures of the kind commonly accepted as great. On them he looked as his models and to them he felt he was linked by spiritual kinship. He agreed with other thinkers of his day in setting them entirely apart from the average mass and in lifting them above the common run of humanity. It would be mistaken, however, to think of him as merely following in a romantic or pseudo-romantic line of hero-worship and cult of the genius: it is precisely because he was in revolt against this attitude that he turned to debunking.. In other words, he revealed and held up for ridicule the all-too-human elements in the fabric of the greatness generally worshipped, while this method helped him at the same time to define more clearly the qualities of geniune greatness and the rights and duties of men of genius.

Even in his early novels we find characters embodying an interpretation of human greatness new in the nineteenth century. These characters view the world objectively, soberly; they are wedded to every-day reality; they are in revolt against all the old aristocratic and middle-class ideals and conventions because of this very individual and original outlook. In their earlier guise they aim at reforming morals and human relationships generally in a self-assertive, individualistic spirit, and later carry on the same attempt as socialists. They are inspired by a sceptical rationalism and they turn against middle-class sentimentality and the

false outward piety of their century.[3] Soon however, Shaw was to create
other characters endowed with more specifically artistic gifts. They
have much in common with the earlier ones, except that in them
prevails an irrational, intuitive vein.[4] His artist-philosophers at the turn
of the century represent a fusion of these two types,[5] and he claimed as
their counterparts in real life such personalities as Bunyan, Blake,
Goethe, Shelley, Wagner, Ibsen, Tolstoy and Nietzsche.[6] For the Shavian artist, art is no end in itself but the expression and the vehicle of a
comprehensive realistic and revolutionary philosophy. Shaw's own attempt at drawing the portrait of this ideal in the John Tanner of his
Man and Superman is unsatisfactory from this point of view—he still
smacks too much of his talkative predecessor, Trefusis, the central
character of *An Unsocial Socialist*. But then, we must be prepared to
see in the artist-philosopher no artist in the narrow sense only but one
whose activity affects the shape of things and influences the course of
events. Thus we arrive at a new and more comprehensive ideal: one
that embraces in its scope the men of action gifted with genius and
which he delineated more particularly in Caesar and Undershaft.[7]
Caesar, for instance, is chiefly a successful statesman, general and
leader of men; but he is also a contemplative, a dreamy genius whose
creative ideas are arrived at by way of intuition and inspiration. But the
harmony and unity achieved in Caesar are impaired already in his
modern successor, Undershaft, and were to be shattered completely in
the following years. The portrait of Undershaft is ambiguous, for while
he too is an active genius and an independent thinker after the pattern
of Caesar, he is at the same time a type of the cynical and ruthless
capitalist. He, in turn, is followed by Mangan of *Heartbreak House*, in
whom the self-seeking capitalist alone remains. And his real successors,
the politicians and statesmen like the Caesar of *Androcles and the Lion*,
the Inca of *The Inca of Perusalem*, and the Napoleon of *Back to
Methuselah*, are but increasingly bitter, satirical portraits of the modern

3. Among them must be reckoned chiefly Harriet Russell in *Immaturity*, Connolly
and Nelly in *The Irrational Knot*, and Trefusis in *An Unsocial Socialist*.
4. Owen Jack of *Love Among the Artists* and, in part, Cashel Byron in *Cashel
Byron's Profession*, and Marchbanks in *Candida*.
5. The very distinction, of course, implies a high degree of oversimplification.
6. *Man and Superman*, p. XXVIII.
7. Undershaft, of *Major Barbara*.

autocrat. Concurrently, a similar decline may be observed in Shaw's artists: they descend to mere romantic boy-poets, and the effect they produce on the stage is as ludicrous in fact as it was intended to be.

Thus after a first peak of creative achievement at the turn of the century, Shaw's male characters in the following years, and until after the First World War, betray a certain lassitude, a resigned and pessimistic attitude to life, which was paralleled in the experience of their author and which paralyzed his power to create ideal human figures.[8] (As the most striking illustration of the attitude, cf. old Shotover in *Heartbreak House*, 1919.) He was steering dangerously close to modern nihilism—but Shaw was also too deeply rooted in the optimistic progressivist philosophy of his day to stand in any real danger from it. No amount of disheartening personal experiences could shake a metaphysical conviction which at this very date takes a decisive turn and gains in strength, thereby giving his life an increasingly religious colouring. It appears at first in a somewhat rationalistic guise as his belief in a Life Force immanent in living nature which is responsible for all progress, both organic and spiritual, and reaches its highest point of development in man, where it informs his instinct, his will and his imagination no less than his reason. These views were partly derived from his own experience and more particularly from the thought of forerunners and contemporaries such as Schopenhauer, Darwin, Butler, Nietzsche. They became more and more of a conviction and a faith with him—he grew no longer even to oppose them to religious faith but accorded them an equal status.[9]

This inner development is reflected in some of Shaw's characters who can be regarded as the forerunners of his Saints. As his own faith grew, he became convinced that it was only in men who had faith—in his sense of the word—that the Life Force was given a chance to shine forth in all its strength. He stresses this new element and sets it up against the *savoir-faire* and practical success of the man of action.

8. cf. Julius Bab: *Bernard Shaw*, Berlin 1926, pp. 256.

9. For Shaw's philosophy, see C. E. M. Joad: *Shaw*, London 1949. The development taking place in Shaw's mind can be further observed in the use he makes of religious expressions in preference to philosophical ones. This becomes apparent after 1905. Thus, 'God', 'religion', are frequently used for 'Life Force', 'philosophy', etc., His mistrust of religion (or what he understands by it) can be seen as late as 1903: ' . . . religion . . . is for me a mere excuse for laziness.' Cf. also other statements in the Preface to *Androcles and the Lion* and *Back to Methuselah*.

This discord in his mind was not, however, healed straightaway, and in *John Bull's Other Island* he confronts the rational, practical Larry Doyle with the other-worldly mystic, Peter Keegan, without taking sides for either.[10] A similar tension can be observed between Undershaft and Barbara—here the gulf is only just bridged by Cusins.[11] But in both cases the last word remains with the new Saints, and Shaw's course is set. The new ideal at last conquers triumphantly in Lavinia, Blanco Posnet[12] and, most gloriously, in Saint Joan. They are the dominant characters in their respective plays. Their destiny is shaped by a religious conviction, for whose sake they are prepared to risk their lives.

It is no accident, moreover, that Shaw's new attitude to life is reflected chiefly in his female characters. At the time of *Man and Superman* he had assigned woman no higher task than that of propagating the species and providing for the continuance of life, while it fell to the male to ensure spiritual progress. In actual fact, even his early heroines showed a tendency to undermine and refute this theory by their obvious intellectual superiority over the men and by their definitely unfeminine disposition. He now further invalidated it by creating women of great intellectual power, with something, indeed, very close to genius, to whom he accords the same functions as to the men of genius. (It should be noted, incidentally, that the 'genius' stands on a sexually neutral plane, high above the philistine and limited average of either and both sexes.) The First World War brought home to Shaw the political inability of man and the dangers inherent in the dynamic masculine genius and so, by contrast, increased his belief in the mission of woman. It was in this atmosphere that *Saint Joan* took shape and that his ideal of sainthood was fully worked out in her.

The evolution of Shaw's human ideal has been pursued sufficiently far in its broad outlines, for us to be able now to examine a little more closely the meaning and nature of his Saint. And here we must turn not to the figure of Joan, but that of Christ, and to Shaw's attitude to a

10. cf. Eric Bentley: *Shaw als Neunziger.* Amerikanische Rundschau, Vol. II, No. 10, 1946.

11. The break is not so complete, for Undershaft regards himself as a mystic and Barbara is active as a member of the Salvation Army.

12. Lavinia in *Androcles and the Lion,* Blanco Posnet in *The Shewing-Up of B. P.:* a sudden experience brings about the conversion of the latter from a life of profligacy.

personality which had been occupying his thoughts for some years before the outbreak of the War.

If one man in all the world can be found, now or forever, to know that you did wrong, that man will have either to conquer the world as I have, or be crucified by it.[13]—Thus Shaw's Caesar to Queen Cleopatra, who has just had one of her ministers executed in cold blood. This sentence can be taken as an intentional reference to the destiny of Christ, by which he recognizes it as a career worthy of a man of genius. At the time, however, he selected and dramatized the activities of the Caesar, the advocate of power who conquers the world about him by action and for the sake of action. But ten years later, when we read the following, we realize that Shaw's ideal was due for a change: 'Great religious leaders are more interesting and more important subjects for the dramatist than great conquerors.'[14] He now toyed with the idea of converting the life of Mohammed into a play[15] (this project was never realized) and during the next few years the figure of Christ continually occupied his mind.[16]

This shift of emphasis does not, however, represent as dramatic and sharp a break with his former attitude as might be inferred from this scheme. The new outlook was already foreshadowed in the character of Caesar whom Shaw had conceived as a kind of modern Puritan full of a lofty moral code, opposed to the principles of vengeance and retribution, and devoted to the welfare of his subjects. It was his own interpretation of Nietzsche's 'Caesar mit der Seele Christi'.[17] We shall see, moreover, that his view of Christ is extremely unorthodox, that he cannot accept without a good deal of criticism even this figure remodelled wherever the facts allow to suit his ideal.[18]

At the very outset, he differs in this, that Christ, for him, is not the

13. *Three Plays for Puritans*, p. 180.
14. *The Doctor's Dilemma and Other Plays*, (1910), p. 387.
15. *Op. cit.*, p. 387.
16. See his essay *On the Prospects of Christianity*, prefaced to *Androcles and the Lion*.
17. Fr. Nietzsche: *Also Sprach Zarathustra*. Leipzig 1932, p. 500.
18. We are not concerned here with establishing in how far Shaw departed from the accepted truth in his portrayal of Christ. I refer to it simply because it is illuminating for his idea of the Saint.

only-begotten Son of God sent by Him to earth to deliver mankind, but simply a great prophet and the founder of a new religion, no more and no less than others with a similar mission.[19] Shaw proposes to examine critically whether his message has any relevance for the modern world, to pass judgment on him as an historical figure seen from a sober and objective point of view—as he regards it. In this voyage of discovery, he steers by the light of the Gospels of St. Matthew and St. John, rejecting that of St. Luke on the grounds that he was too much of a literary man and turned Christ into a sentimental pacifist, into the 'gentle Jesus meek and mild'. It was this very aspect, dear to the Victorians, that had first repelled Shaw.[20]

What he respected in Christ was, above all, the preacher of social reform and of a new way of life—i.e. Communism and altruism, not the Saviour of orthodox Christianity, with his message of a transcendent Power. According to Shaw, Christ discovered his revolutionary message within himself by virtue of the 'inner light'[21] or 'divinatory instinct,'[22] as he calls this faculty. In the new Shavian creed, its presence is the first condition of human greatness for it enables the Life Force to manifest itself most powerfully. He believes in a steady upward evolution, an ever higher degree of organization, a 'wider, deeper, intenser, self-consciousness, and clearer self-understanding.'[23] Men of genius represent a higher mode of life, they stand on a higher level of consciousness than the rest of mankind. For this reason their ideas, which they receive by intuition and develop by reason, are truths pointing the future for all men.[24] Shaw singles out for praise and approval those whose activities made themselves felt in his own particular spheres of interest: in ethics and religion, in social and political relations.[25] Fur-

19. *Androcles and the Lion,* p. 31.
20. *Op. cit.,* pp. 34, 83.
21. *Op. cit.,* pp. 68, 145.
22. *Op. cit.,* p. 41. It is more usual for Shaw to speak of the 'imagination'. Also see p. 182 in this essay.
23. *Man and Superman,* p. 123.
24. Cf. C. E. M. Joad in S. Winsten: *G.B.S. 90—Aspects of Bernard Shaw's Life and Work.* London, 1946, p. 67.
25. Cf. a statement he made earlier when the artist was still the embodiment of his ideal type: '. . . the distant light of a new age . . . Discernible at first only by the eyes of the man of genius, it must be focussed by him on the speculum of a work of art, and flashed back from that into the eyes of the common man.' *Plays Pleasant,* p. viii.

ther, he respects those only who give themselves whole-heartedly to their vision with all their faith and all their strength, by trying to make it a living reality in the world around them. He demands action on the part of intellectual creators: this much is residual from his earlier conception of the genius, but now a heavier stress is laid on the creative impetus, and its whole definition and content have undergone a transformation. And Christ would have won Shaw's more unqualified approval had he been politically active in the fashion of a Moses or a Mohammed.[26] It appears that he considers it is not enough that the teaching and the comfort should reach single, isolated individuals. The Statesman whose ideas take practical effect on a larger scale, who can, where necessary, compel the slack and the retrograde by force and similar doubtful expedients to work for their own salvation, has his full support.[27]

Nevertheless, the ruthless fanatic whose sympathies are limited to his own ideas and who cares nothing for those they concern, does not represent Shaw's ideal. The whole question is one of policy. Thus he approves of Christ for his inability to prevent himself from carrying help to the mass of humanity, even though this proved harmful to him and detrimental to his teaching. (It appears, according to Shaw, that Christ was ashamed of his power to work miracles and saw in them a danger for the superstitious crowds.)[28] Shavian Saints are required to live entirely in the here and now: they must strive to lead men to a 'nobler and richer existence.'[29] They are leaders and patterns of humanity whose whole life is devoted to their task—but there is no need in all this for either ascetic practices or the martyr's death.

He is therefore delighted to find that Christ preached neither renunciation of this world nor humility, that he was no uncultivated ascetic hermit like the Baptist, but rather a genial, generous man who commanded his fellow-men to love one another and be joyful. His Christ preaches no 'slave morality,' he does not belong to the lower classes,

26. *Androcles and the Lion*, p. 3: 'Jesus ... if a modern practical statesman ...' Moses and Mohammed are mentioned several times.
27. Cf. later statements as in *The Intelligent Woman's Guide to Socialism, or Everybody's Political What's What.*
28. *Androcles and the Lion* p. 24.
29. *Op. cit.*, p. 145.

but is well-bred, well-mannered and self-assured; and even though he is ill at ease in 'Society,' he enjoys a happy, easy conviviality.[30] In common with all Shavian geniuses, he has outgrown the standards of his own times and is therefore engaged in an unrelenting struggle against their defenders—hence his hatred of the Pharisees and scribes, who found their hierarchy further threatened by his disregard of accepted forms and social doctrines. Timely action on their part to remove him results at last in his death on the Cross.

Shaw sees a perfect correspondence between Christ's natural inclinations and his whole combative existence which leaves no room for an evidently superfluous exercise of self-discipline or self-conquest. For the same reason and because family ties are considered as an obstacle for the man of genius, Christ remains celibate. The fact that he was also the Son of God remains totally outside these arguments. Shaw then attacks consented martyrdom, for the man with a mission to fulfill must preserve his life as long as he can, to this end. He is roused to sharp criticism by this feature in the life of Christ which, unlike many other inconvenient facts, he found impossible to omit or tone down. He cannot share the Christian view of Christ's death as atonement. To him, Christ, who at first seems perfectly healthy and normal, is dazzled by the words of Peter: 'Thou art the Christ, the Son of the living God,' and is doomed thereafter to mental aberration, to a delusion with regard to his own divine origin. As a result, he becomes arrogant, dictatorial towards his disciples and friends, and is finally swept into an erroneous belief in the necessity for martyrdom.[31] According to Shaw again, it should have been Christ's first concern to ensure the success of his teaching and, without rating his life too high, he should not have exposed it to unnecessary dangers. The passive role assumed by Christ at his trial by the Romans he finds particularly difficult to forgive,[32] and this deliberate acceptance of suffering and death he can never understand as anything but a perversion of healthy human instincts.[33] In

---

30. *Op. cit.,* p. 31: 'Jesus's manner throughout is that of an aristocrat, or at the very least the son of a rich bourgeois, and by no means a lowly-minded one at that.' Also p. 22.

31. *Op. cit.,* pp. 27, 79, 83.

32. This trial would have furnished an excellent play. For a brief attempt in which the 'healthy' Christ is made to speak see Shaw's preface to *On the Rocks.*

33. *Op. cit.,* p. 22: ". . . the inveterate superstition that suffering is gratifying to God."

consequence he rejects the whole Christian doctrine of redemption in which he sees an attempt of the individual to escape responsibility for his own actions and their results. He would like to see it replaced by a realization that the arduous road to perfection leads through many pitfalls, that errors are the necessary condition of improvement, that their remedy lies in good works—not in penance and remorse which paralyse the will to fresh activity. In other words, Shaw would have humanity look onward, forward, towards a world waiting for betterment, not inward and away from it, wasting energy on introspection. No sin can attach to the sort of man who 'tirelessly strives onward' in the manner of Faust, who tries by constantly renewed attempts to bring ever nearer to perfection efforts which meet at first with only partial success or even failure. Conscience and a sense of honour should provide the necessary safeguards and the stimulus for such action.[34]

Thus, granted the fact that Shaw totally fails to understand the meaning of Faith according to the Church if only because he inhabits a fundamentally different mental climate, it becomes clear that to him (as to many English thinkers) it is not the abstract guiding principles but the actual content of a life that matters. He would have subscribed in full to the motto: 'Conduct matters more than creed.' But it must be stressed once again that Shaw did not belong to that modern school of thought which renounces all metaphysical foundations. His practical ideas and his efforts to educate men in the conduct of their lives derive their whole strength from his philosophy of the Life Force in which he steadfastly went on believing.

He even tried to discover a similar belief in Christ and interpreted certain passages in the Gospel of St. John to fit in with his theory. He alleges, for instance, that St. John, in contrast to St. Matthew and St. Mark, made Christ a cultivated man, a 'sophisticated mystic,'[35] one, in other words, who shared his own conception of God. Such sayings as 'I and the Father are one', 'God is spirit', etc., are seen as the far-off dawn of the Life Force doctrine. In the kind of *unio mystica* which he envisaged, God is man and man a God. He refers for support to the 82nd Psalm: 'I have said, Ye are gods; and all of you are children of the

34. *Op. cit.,* p. 91.
35. *Op. cit.,* p. 39.

most High', and in its spirit exhorts men to become fully aware of their place and their responsibilities in this world. Thus the duty of carrying out God's work upon earth is laid on man: he is the instrument and an incarnation of God,[36] and it therefore also falls to his lot to mete out mercy and justice in the name of the Godhead.[37]

This outline of Shaw's critical interpretation—with all its wrong-headedness and lack of historical sense—at least helps to focus the pattern of his mind and the standards of value by which he measured human behaviour. In *Saint Joan,* the play he was to write some years later, these values are given a definite and perfected shape.

We have seen how, in the space of some 20 years, Shaw's ideal of the human character underwent a profound change. After the earlier one had been found wanting, he turned for a new one to the great religious teachers and innovators. By their exemplary conduct and by the dynamic quality of their minds, they too had been leaders. Among them was Joan of Arc, who had recently been canonized. As a woman, moreover, she commended herself to Shaw, whose bias in favour of female characters, particularly after the War, we have already discussed. He now proceeds to turn her into a 'genius'. Like her predecessors, Candida, Cicely, and Barbara, she is driven by a maternal instinct to help others and she is a rational creature with common-sense, political understanding and the indispensable practical ability of his earlier heroes. She fulfils the Shavian conditions of genius by being able to see things as they are, with a clear, spontaneous vision cutting through all the obstructions of conventional delusions. All this is well within the limits of empirical, rational thought. But she is also equipped with a creative imagination which enables her to apprehend new and divinely-inspired truths and which alone can raise the rational faculties on to that higher plane we recognize as genius. Shaw succeeded in presenting

36. *The Black Girl in Search of God,* (1930), p. 15: 'Jesus . . . suggests that godhead is something which incorporates itself in man . . .' etc.
37. *Androcles and the Lion,* p. 41.

in St. Joan an artistically satisfactory synthesis of all his ideal requirements.[38]

Her visions, which Anatole France, for one, rejected as mere hallucinations, Shaw takes seriously; they are products of her creative imagination, prophecies 'divinely inspired'[39] springing from the activity of the
Life Force within her.

But since the visions of the inspired imagination are human as well as
divine in origin, there is a danger they may be not only creative and
prophetic but false and illusory. Shaw immediately attempts to dispose
of this paradox in his philosophy by rational arguments. To quote one
example: Joan's voices announce to her in the prison at Rouen that
deliverance is at hand. She trusts them until reason tells her that such a
deliverance is a practical impossibility. He therefore regards it as the
duty of empirical reason to test the practical validity of. intuitions, and
this leads him to distinguish between realistic vision and romantic
illusion (or fancy). For while the former is constructive and creative,
the latter, which refuses to submit to rational tests, is no more than a
delusion.[40]

But Joan is a realistic genius and her visions have a meaning for the
future. These visions, 'divinely inspired' though they may be, still arise
out of her and require no outside interpreter to make them plain to her:
she is 'self-elected'[41] and has no need of dogmatic truths or traditional
institutions through which to receive them. She is thus, of necessity, a
revolutionary, whose very aim is to clear away traditional modes of life
to establish her new standards. Shaw quite consequently makes her the
opponent of feudalism and a pioneer of the modern age where social,
political, and religious ideas are concerned and puts into her mouth
words which herald the French Revolution, modern nationalism, and
Protestantism.

It is the untiring energy of mind and heart and body with which she
fights for her ideas that makes her worthy in Shaw's eyes to embody his

---

38. Again, we are not concerned with the historical accuracy of Shaw's presentation
of the Maid of Orleans. The point at issue is the subjective interpretation underlying the
presentation of any historical and biographical material.

39. *The Black Girl in Search of God,* p. 3. *Saint Joan,* p. 14.

40. *Misalliance,* p. 103.

41. *Saint Joan,* p. 37.

ideal. She rides and fights, a woman in warrior's armour, with the French army, brings about the coronation of the Dauphin, mediates statesman-like between him and his lieges and vassals, and finally on her own responsibility undertakes a bold attack on Paris in which she is captured by the allies of the English.

In spite of her preoccupations with great political aims, the problems of ordinary humanity remain present to her. Her own belief in the divine origin of her ideas inspires courage in her companions, just as the purity of her life and her spiritual greatness cleanse all around her: she is, in every respect, a leader and a model. She rejects marriage the better to devote herself to her task. Shaw is anxious here to make quite plain that Joan was sexually normal and by no means unattractive. She arrives at her decision (like Christ!) not from ascetic self-denial but because the 'heroic' life seems to her the one most suitable for her, the most natural and the richest. It also means the total rejection of what appear the things most desirable in life to the average person such as love, family-life, mass-amusements.

He again stresses the class-motif: she does not belong to the lower strata but nevertheless easily enters into the minds of simple, humble people who acknowledge her greatness and trustingly submit to her leadership. The aristocracy and the clergy, on the other hand, regard her as a dangerous rebel and condemn her to death for this reason,[42] not because of any imputed heresy or witchcraft. In total contrast to Shaw's Christ, she never deludes herself as to the necessity for her death as a martyr. When, after capture, she stands before her judges, she fights for life and freedom and is prepared to 'recant' her heresies to this end until she realizes that life-long imprisonment is the best she can hope for, and is brave enough to prefer death to this—'a decision which shewed not only the extraordinary decision of her character, but also a Rationalism carried to its ultimate human test of suicide.'[43]

Joan's destiny is not wrecked by a tragic flaw, by 'hubris', but because she and those around her are only human beings, and in these Shaw had lost his absolute faith. The great are always alone: they are so far ahead of their times that there is no other being to understand

42. *Op. cit.*, pp. 23, 106, 108.
43. *Op. cit.*, p. 18.

them. Only a superman, like Shaw's Caesar, could carry such a burden. The few minor faults attributed to him could not obscure his unquestionable superiority over the world about him; he made history and was not ready to die until he was satisfied that he had accomplished his task. Joan is not of such stature: she is too young, too unprepared and in the last resort, too lacking in the skill and far-sightedness required in dealing with a recalcitrant world. She is not less great than Caesar, but her greatness is of a different order: she is always deeply involved in human problems and never stands above or away from them.[44] Shaw's gaze has shifted to the inner man; he no longer measures greatness by success and apparent outward perfection. Indeed, Joan is imperfect in many respects: she makes mistakes and dies with her work still unfinished. But the decisive factor must be sought elsewhere: for 'having practiced heroic virtues,'[45] her life was that of a Saint who through prophetic vision opened up new paths of humanity and followed these herself as a pioneer. In the epilogue Shaw proceeds to tone down the effect of her death and indicates that her fight was not in vain: France is liberated, the ideas of our own contemporary world clear her from guilt and she is canonized a Saint of the Church; her ideas, at one time considered revolutionary, have become common property, the commonplaces of our age.

In his characterization of St. Joan, Shaw made use of the Catholic definition of the Saint as a starting-point, apparently unaware of any differences between the tenets of the Church and his own views. A saint, he states, is a person 'who having practiced heroic virtues, and enjoyed revelations or powers of the order which the Church classes technically as supernatural, is eligible for canonization.'[46] Now it is true that the Roman Church requires of its saints the performance of two accredited miracles, and an heroic life. But is this, in fact, sufficient to make Shaw's Joan, the embodiment of his human ideal at that epoch, a saint, in the Christian or any religious sense at all?

For Shaw, the revelations are products of the prophetic imagination.

---

44. Cf. Joan's monologue in Rheims Cathedral with that of Caesar in front of the Sphinx.
45. *Op. cit.*, p. 7.
46. *Op. cit.*, p. 7.

His geniuses call it 'divine' because they sense in it the workings of that Life Force immanent in all living things. The specific miracles of healing and leadership he explains rationalistically as hypnotic forces or as 'magnetic field.'[47] For the Christian, conversely, the miracles of Saints stem from the ineffable, inexplicable power of God. They neither require nor indeed allow of any explanation: the very fact of their inconceivability is the warranty of their miraculous nature.[48] By the same token, God is absolute transcendence, perfect in Himself, independent of man and independent of development and growth in time.

The divergence of the Shavian from the Christian interpretation of 'heroic virtue' is equally glaring. For the Christian, life on this earth is but a part of a higher, eternal life in God and for this reason, all culture, knowledge and progress have no ultimate meaning seen in themselves and in isolation from the greater truth. The only factor deserving of attention in this life is to prove oneself worthy of God's love, to 'remain or progress in Christliness, in a state of Grace.'[49] This may be achieved by fulfilling the twofold commandment of love: the love of God and an active life spent in the service of one's neighbour. But this achievement is a difficult one, for man is essentially sinful, and to remain on the right path he must exert himself over and over again and triumph over himself in a series of heroic actions. Asceticism is regarded as one of the means to this end. The Church does not recommend ascetic practice for its own sake but the Christian 'in his fight against sin and all that induces sin, in his progress to saintliness and his striving after blessedness viz. recognition in the eyes of God, is greatly assisted by particular practices such as askesis.'[50] Thus, for the Christian saint who performs these heroic actions, asceticism is a virtual necessity.

The heroic performances Shaw requires of his heroes are of quite a different order. We have seen that they are, in the first line, leaders and

47. *Op. cit.*, p. 83.

48. Shaw appears to acknowledge such a miraculous power when, with Joan's appearance at Orleans, the wind suddenly changes favourably. But even here it remains an open question whether it was not an accidental effect interpreted by men as a miracle subsequently. (*Saint Joan*, sc. III.)

49. *Die Religion in Geschichte und Gegenwart (RGG)*, column 579. (My Translation.) (Rust-Scheel.)

50. *Op. cit.*, col. 579. Translated.

prophets. Their highest aim is to establish progress in this world—the beyond, except as a concept of futurity, does not exist for them. Their heroism consists in their courage, a total acceptance of their mission and an unshakeable faith in it, and also in the particular scale of moral values which orders the conduct of their exemplary lives. These are determined by natural disposition, not evolved by continual self-conquest and self-denial. Shaw's Saints do not remain in a state of sin, because they expiate any earlier failings by unceasing social, political and moral activity. Heroic living here does not necessarily imply suffering, but predestination, a distinction conferred from all time on chosen individuals and one which sets the genius or the Saint apart from the rest of humanity. The failure of the great mass of the people indeed is not due to temptation and sin, but rather to the mental or physical shortcomings which fatally incapacitate them in the struggle for new truths.

In the case of Shaw's Saints, then, there can be no question of any orthodox form of holiness, in spite of some apparent similarities. Thus, for instance, in both cases personal life has been renounced and merged entirely in the service of the fellow-man; both types are patterns of purity, goodness, love and charity. But in these respects, the saints of all religions are alike.[51] But doing good is not the whole meaning and purpose of holiness, which looks to religion, to a spiritual reality for its final definition and essence.[52] It is here that the gap widens. Shaw goes further even than Calvinism with its insistence on practical morality as against faith: for while the asceticism of the Puritan, directly concerned with this world though it is, with his indefatigable labouring after success is only to prove he is one of God's elect, the same tendency in Shaw's Saint derives its significance solely from a vitalistic conception of human progress and development. His view of human greatness consequently lacks any religious background or foundation, except in a

51. Cf. Schopenhauer on the Saints of the Hindoos and Jaspers in *Psychologie der Weltanschauungen*, Berlin 1919, p. 87.—I need not institute a comparison between Schopenhauer's ideal of the Saint and that of Shaw; it is even further removed from this than the Catholic one, because it is to renounce all worldly activity for the sake of a purely contemplative life.

52. *Die Religion in G. & G. (RGG)*, col. 1722, col. 1738: 'Der Heilige ist . . . diejenige menschliche Erscheinung, in der sich die numinale Lebensessenz am dichtesten aufsammelt.' (Das Numinose: das religiöse Grund- and Urgefühl.)

very broad sense. Hence, though Lavinia, Barbara and Joan believe in
the existence of a divine power they experience in dreams and visions
and for which they live and work and even die, they do not submit to it
humbly as to an Absolute in the face of which all human strength is as
nought.[53] In fact, their attitude to their God is self-assured; they trust in
his dependence on them. As Barbara proudly asserts: 'Let God's work
be done for its own sake: the work he had to create us to do because it
cannot be done except by living men and women. When I die, let him
be in my debt, not I in his; and let me forgive him as becomes a woman
of my rank.'[54] In the final analysis, it is the rationalism that proclaims
man the measure of all things, which remains supreme in Shaw and his
heroes. This rationalism, however, is tempered by certain considerations: thus he several times describes his Saints and others inspired by
similar motives as 'mystics', or again, mystics (such as Blake) as thinkers
closely related to them.[55] This concept may help us in clarifying the
precise nature of Shaw's religious feeling. In mystical experience (in the
normal use of the term) the cleavage between subject and object is
temporarily healed and the receiver of the experience is made one with
God. The significance of the phenomenal world dwindles in proportion
and is seen as no more than the secondary consequence, the extension
of and decline from the Absolute. The aim of the mystic is to achieve
an increasingly intense and forever renewed unity with God.[56] This kind
of mysticism cannot be traced anywhere in Shaw, except perhaps in the
figure of Keegan who is not, however, an ideal figure so much as a
deliberate portrait of a typical Irish mystic.

But Prof. Karl Jaspers, in his book *Psychologie der Weltanschauungen,* distinguishes yet another kind of mysticism from this traditional,
commonly accepted one: its representative he sees in Kant. While the
'genuine' mystic may, by his continual striving for ever closer communion with God, easily be seduced into concentrating upon and cultiva-
ting exclusively a technique of experience, the mystic in Jaspers' sense

---

53. Cf. in contrast to their attitude the definition of the Holy in *op. cit.,* col. 1722;
and R. Otto: *Das Heilige,* Berlin 1917.

54. *Major Barbara,* Odham Edition, London 1951, p. 503.

55. Undershaft regards himself as a mystic. In *Saint Joan* (p. 11) the revelations
vouchsafed to Joan are compared with those of Blake and Swedenborg. Cf. *Pen Portraits,*
p. 152.

56. Jaspers, *op. cit.,* p. 393.

is returned to the world at the very moment of communion. In him 'a longing for the objective world arises from the mystical experience itself and at the same time tends to return to new mystical experience'. Thus a perpetual motion as of a pendulum swinging from interiority to exteriority and vice-versa is set up. 'The infinite range of objective action, thought and creativeness forever expand the circle (of experience) spiral-like, and the mystical experience in turn appears more intense and more significant at each repetition, since it results from an increased receptivity and openness to the external world.'[57] This process enables the soul to undergo an unending series of metamorphoses, concluding in the Idea which embraces communion of every kind, with the self and with the external world and comprises both subject and object. Jaspers calls this mystique (that of Kant) 'one belonging to this world, at once the highest aim (Überbau) and the source and cause of all activity in this world,'[58] and opposes it by the mystique of Plotinus, the mystique of the Absolute.

A mystical experience of this type might well be that of Shaw and of his Saints. Joan's visions and voices might be explained as this species of experience of the divine which she goes on to project creatively into this world, translating it into objective terms in order to derive from here renewed stimulation for further experience. Shaw's very idea of the Life Force would then appear as a development of this mysticism. It is the ultimate irrational basis of all modern philosophies and possibly the typical and the only acceptable form of mysticism for modern Western man, who is so deeply involved in the technical civilization made by him that he no longer can dissociate himself from it completely. Indeed, such a dissociation is not even desirable in his eyes: it appears as an attempt to escape his responsibilities and the task set to him. On the other hand, this modified form of mysticism would enable him to put this world at a sufficient distance to realize that it is but the symbol of a higher reality which has to be sought elsewhere even though it is bound to be for ever hidden from him.

The question remains, whether it is permissible at all to speak of 'mystical experience' in the case of Shaw and his Saints. The answer to

57. *Op. cit.*, p. 394. (My Translation.)
58. *Op. cit.*, p. 398. (Tr.)

it rests, in the last resort, upon personal judgment. One may feel that
the words spoken by Lavinia or Joan to their God are real and sincere,
and thus discern in them the key to Shaw's theory of the Life Force
and a true experience of transcendental values (even though it must be
remembered that he regards the Life Force as immanent).[59] Or again,
one may remain unconvinced by these utterances which are heard,
indeed, but rarely, in a rhapsody of dominantly rationalistic character,
and then one is bound to see in Shaw a scoffer and a jester, a shallow
progressivist or, at best, a social critic with an eye to outward things
only. It is my belief that the statements of Shaw which point to a
deeper experience should be taken as sincere and deserve serious
consideration. The fact that they occur but rarely in his work may be
due to the fact that he was one of those excessively shy and sensitive
natures which do not willingly or easily disclose their innermost
thoughts and, for the same reason, prefer to appear in the role of a
Mephisto or a comedian. The shell of rationalism upon him is thick
indeed—but it discloses at last a kernel of great delicacy and a surprising openness to spiritual experience.[60] There can be no other explanation of the stress he lays at all times and throughout his career on the
irrational element in all creativeness, whether it be that of the artist,
the statesman, or the Saint.

To sum up: the mixture of Saint and Realist[61] in Shaw's representatives of ideal humanity is not accidental. It is rather an expression of
the mental activity of the modern mystic as Jaspers describes him—in
other words, of Modern Man *par excellence*, with his particular form of
metaphysical experience. We are no longer in sympathy with Shaw's
intense optimism and his faith in progress, and therefore unable to
accept the importance of his prophetic and fighting men of genius as
heralds of a better future, as leaders of men on the road towards moral
and spiritual perfection. But his real achievement cannot be denied, for
he rediscovered and pointed out the necessity for spiritual, metaphysical ties on the part of these leaders, quite apart from mere ability,
practical sense and dynamism. It is thus that he broke through the
limitations of the Superman and evolved a newer ideal which occupies
an important place and stands as a landmark in the contemporary
development of the idea of leadership.

59. So does M. Colbourne in *op. cit.*, p. 242.
60. Cf. A. Henderson: *Bernard Shaw, Playboy & Prophet*. New York 1932, p. 574.
61. Cf. Jaspers's definitions of these types in *op. cit.*, p. 387.

✍ JOHN FIELDEN

XX/Shaw's *Saint Joan* as Tragedy

"What more do you want from a tragedy as great as that of Prometheus?" Bernard Shaw said one day to his Boswellian biographer, Archibald Henderson, as they sat discussing *Saint Joan.* "All the forces that bring about the catastrophe are on the grandest scale: and the individual soul they press upon is of the most indomitable force and temper."[1] Certainly this remark suggests that Shaw himself considered *Saint Joan* a tragedy. Critics, however, while willing to admit the play's standing in the forefront of twentieth century drama, have been inclined to consider it as a play of religious ideas, rather than as a tragedy.[2] Eric Bentley, in his *Bernard Shaw,* writes that in *Saint Joan,* Shaw essays "what in his discussion of *Man and Superman* he called a tragic conflict—that is, an irreconcilable conflict," the clash of the irrestible force of Joan's genius meeting the immovable object of social order.[3] But this is as far as Bentley will go. Two more recent essays, "The Saint as Tragic Hero," by Louis L. Martz, and "Shaw and Sainthood," by Hans Stoppel, concern themselves with the problem of Joan's "sainthood," both concluding that while Shaw was not naive enough to base his conception of The Maid on traditional Christian notions of sainthood, he nevertheless failed to create a tragic protagonist along

Twentieth Century Literature, III (July, 1957), 59–67.
1. Archibald Henderson, *Bernard Shaw: Playboy and Prophet* (New York, 1932), 543.
2. In his brilliant reviews of the first London production of *Saint Joan,* Desmond MacCarthy labeled the play thusly: "*St. Joan* is not a chronicle play. It is not primarily an historic drama. It is a religious play." Desmond MacCarthy, *Shaw* (London, 1951), 162.
3. *Bernard Shaw* (Norfolk, 1947), 172.

Aristotelian ideas of the tragic hero because he never established the responsibility for Joan's fall as primarily her own. "Joan's destiny is not wrecked by a tragic flaw, by 'hubris'," Stoppel asserts, "but because she and those around her are only human beings, and in these Shaw had lost his absolute faith."[4] Martz similarly considers Joan free of the taint of hubris. "Thus Joan's apparent resemblance to the Aristotelian hero: her extreme self-confidence, her brashness, her appearance of rash impetuosity—all this becomes in the end a piece of Shavian irony, for her only real error in the play is the one point where her superb self-confidence breaks down in the panic of recantation. And so the hubris is not Joan's but Everyman's."[5]

Neither of these articles, however, takes quite the extreme position advanced by Sylvan Barnet in his "Bernard Shaw on Tragedy," recently published in *PMLA*, for both Stoppel and Martz admit that *Saint Joan* at least hangs by its hands, as Martz puts it, to "the very rim of tragedy."[6] Barnet not only accepts the traditional view of Joan's failure as a tragic protagonist ("But Joan is not hubristic, either in an Aristotelian or Shavian sense."), but goes beyond this to assert that Shaw was incapable of writing tragedy. Barnet's argument is based upon the curious belief that since Shaw subscribed to "a teleological principle, believing that the universe is not a chaos of discrete phenomena but an evolving purposeful organism," this made Shaw a romantic, an optimist, and hence incapable of creating in *Joan* a tragic drama. "Most teleological views are hostile to the idea of tragedy," writes Barnet, "for they see some great purpose in the bafflements and defeats which are the stuff of tragic drama."[7]

There are, of course, arguments for another view of *Saint Joan*, and it will be the purpose of this article to make a case for *Saint Joan* as a play cast deliberately in the framework of classical tragedy and to reestablish Joan as a heroine fit for this genre.

I

Shaw's title to his play, *Saint Joan: a Chronicle Play in Six Scenes*

4. *English Studies*, XXXVI (1955), 59.
5. Included in *Tragic Themes in Western Literature* (New Haven, 1955), ed. by Cleanth Brooks, p. 160.
6. Ibid., 177.
7. PMLA, LXXI (December, 1956), 889.

and an Epilogue,[8] offers little consolation to one who is engaged in a
defense of this drama as tragedy. Little help, also, is afforded by the
preface, for only by inference here can one establish that Shaw had in
view an analogy between *Saint Joan* and the type of classical tragedy
most of us consider when we use the term *tragedy.* In one part of the
preface, Shaw refers to the length of *Joan* as the "well-established
classical limit of three and a half hours practically continuous playing"
(p. lxi), and at the end of the preface, refers to the theatre in general as
"purgatorial in its Aristotelian movements" (p. lxii). But when one
analyzes carefully what Shaw has to say about *Saint Joan* in the section
of his preface called "Tragedy, not Melodrama," he finds that although
Shaw at one point refers to his drama as "high tragedy" (p. lvi), he
defends his statement only by claiming that the play is not melodrama
because Warwick and de Stogumber, the representatives of English
feudal aristocracy and nationalism respectively, and Cauchon and the
Inquisitor, Lamaitre, symbols of Church authority, are not presented as
villains but rather as judicial and pious murderers. He concludes that
this oxymoron infuses his tragedy with an element of comedy. Yet, one
might say that Shaw, who said in life almost too much about everything, here said too little, for it is just this point that does raise *Saint
Joan* above the melodrama—and above the expository chronicle play. It
is this ambivalence of Shaw's attitude toward the tragic conflict revealed in his play, his ability to recognize both the justice and the
cruelty of the actions of church and state that brings the play to the
level of high-tragedy. "The two sides of everything," wrote Henry
Alonzo Myers, "are the well-known materials of modern tragedies,
which must end, if the artist fails to see the pattern of justice in 'the
two sides of everything' . . . on a note of futility and hopelessness."[9] The
Hegelian attitude toward tragedy, that which holds that out of the
division of the ethical substance comes a synthesis that transcends both
lesser, sundered goods, is clearly Shaw's in *Saint Joan.* This transcendent view of tragedy does not in itself preclude *Saint Joan's* being

8. (London, 1924); parenthetical page references will refer to this first edition.
9. *Tragedy: A View of Life* (Ithaca, 1956), 101.

classified as high tragedy, although it does supply grist for the mills of those who would view the play as "Christian tragedy" (hence not tragedy at all) and Joan as "saint."[10]

If Shaw were to have presented The Maid to us as a saint, she would have failed as a classical tragic protagonist only if she were at the same time presented as merely an agent in the hands of supernatural forces. The mere fact that she was in communion with some actual or imaginary powers seems to have little to do with her standing as tragic heroine, since the noting of omens and signs, the consulting of oracles, the heeding of the admonitions of friendly gods, are indeed standard in Greek tragedy. Arguments, also, that since Joan has been canonized she therefore must have led a life flawless in every respect seem based upon an unfamiliarity with the lives of some of the more outstanding saints of christendom. Shaw makes it clear to readers of his preface that the word "saint" in his play's title refers to the official honor bestowed by the Roman Catholic Church upon Joan at her canonization in 1920. Nowhere, either in his preface or in the text of the play, does he imply that he is dealing with the perfectly virtuous person whom Aristotle thought unsatisfactory as a tragic protagonist. "A saint," Shaw writes in the preface, "is one who having practiced heroic virtues, and enjoyed revelations or powers of the order which The Church classes technically as supernatural is eligible for canonization" (p. x).[11]

Shaw's preface indicates similarly that Joan's "voices" are to be considered "technically" supernatural. Shaw regards them merely as a production of Joan's imagination (p. xiv), and indeed an iconography of her common sense, since "they never gave her any advice that might not have come to her from her mother wit exactly as gravitation came to Newton" (p. xv). Episodes in the first three scenes of the play seem intended to convey this realistic interpretation of Joan's powers to audiences who have not had the advantage of reading Shaw's preface. In the first scene, this exchange occurs between Captain Robert de Baudricourt and The Maid:

10. Cf. Laurence Michel, "The Possibility of a Christian Tragedy." *Thought*, XXXI (Autumn, 1956), 127.

11. It is to be noticed that Shaw does not define the saint as "virtuous," but as one having practiced "heroic virtues," virtues heroic in their ascendancy over the vices and vanities inherent in human frailty.

ROBERT: How do you mean, voices?
JOAN: I hear voices telling me what to do. They come from God.
ROBERT: They come from your imagination.
JOAN: Of course. That is how the messages of God come to us (p. 11).

In the next scene, Shaw arranges dramatically another illustration to indicate that Joan's "supernatural" powers emanate from her common sense. After Gilles de Rais (Bluebeard) has assumed the throne in Charles' place to test Joan's ability to divine the true king, the possibility that Joan will accomplish something miraculous in so discovering the Dauphin is dispelled by the duologue between La Trémouille and the Archbishop of Rheims. "She will know what everybody in Chinon knows," says the Archbishop, "that the Dauphin is the meanest-looking and worst dressed figure in the Court, and that the man with the blue beard is Gilles de Rais." And to La Trémouille's scandalized observation that this would not be a miracle at all, the Archbishop replies: "A miracle, my friend, is an event which creates faith. That is the purpose and nature of miracles. They may seem very wonderful to the people who witness them, and very simple to those who perform them. That does not matter: if they confirm or create faith they are true miracles" (p. 23).

In the third scene of the play, Joan meets Dunois on the banks of the Loire, as he and his forces wait hopelessly for the west wind which will enable his boats to cross the river and relieve Orleans. Shortly after her arrival, the wind does shift, and Dunois' boats push out across the water. Yet this occurrence does not seem to have convinced Dunois of Joan's powers of anything but good fortune, for even during the exciting moment following the wind's change, it is Dunois' page who shouts, "The Maid! The Maid! God and The Maid!" Dunois' cry is the more conservative "For God and Saint Dennis!" (p. 38).

These—the "voices," the identification of the Dauphin, and the changing of the wind at the Loire—constitute the "miracles" of Joan that Shaw wishes to dramatize. In each of these scenes, Shaw has introduced speeches which cast doubts upon the miraculousness of the events which have transpired. But while it is true that in the text of the play Shaw has dealt with Joan's "voices" and "miracles" in a rational fashion, it must be admitted that he has obfuscated his attitude toward

Joan in the section of the preface entitled "The Evolutionary Appetite." Here he observes:

> But that there are forces at work which use individuals for purposes far transcending the purpose of keeping these individuals alive and prosperous and respectable and safe and happy in the middle station in life, which is all any good bourgeois can reasonably require, is established by the fact that men will, in the pursuit of knowledge and of social readjustments for which they will not be a penny the better, and are indeed often many pence the worse, face poverty, infamy, exile, imprisonment, dreadful hardship, and death (xvi-xvii).

Continuing in this Bergsonian vein, Shaw asserts that "The diverse manners in which our imaginations dramatize the approach of the supernatural forces is a problem for the psychologist, not for the historian." He cautions the historian not to classify Joan's visions with those of the lunatic or drunk, and observes that "the simplest French peasant who believes in apparitions of celestial personages to favored mortals is nearer to the scientific truth about Joan than the Rationalist and Materialist historians and essayists who feel obligated to set down a girl who saw saints and heard them talking to her as either crazy or mendacious" (p. xvii). Shaw's claim that Joan's voices are merely the dramatic symbol of her common sense, but that paradoxically her common sense is the result of pressure upon her of the super-personal "evolutionary appetite," has supplied the basis for Barnet's denial of Joan as a tragic heroine. This denial is predicated upon the belief that Shaw's subscription to a "teleological principle," which holds that "the universe is . . . an evolving purposeful organism," led him to presenting his public with a Joan who is merely a tool in the hands of the mysterious forces of the cosmos. Barnet refers us to the preface to *Man and Superman*, asserting that "Shaw correctly foresaw that such a figure as Joan could not be a tragic hero for him," where Shaw wrote:

> This is the true joy in life, the being used for a purpose recognized by yourself as a mighty one; . . . the being a force of Nature instead of a feverish selfish little clod of ailments and grievances complaining that the world will not devote itself to making you happy. And also the only real tragedy in life is the being used by personally minded men for purposes which you recognize to be base.[12]

12. Barnet, "Bernard Shaw on Tragedy," 899, quoting Shaw from pp. 163–164 of Shaw's *Prefaces* (London, 1934).

St. John Ervine, in his recent biography of Shaw, refers to this passage as the "focal point of his [Shaw's] religion." Ervine's discussion concerning this quotation is too long to relate fully, but the points Ervine makes here are that it is "not easy to know what he [Shaw] meant by the Life Force," nor whether Shaw came to "a decision about the function and purpose of man that is clear and explicit." There is no assurance, moreover, claims Ervine, "in G. B. S.'s doctrine that the Life Force has a clear understanding of its intention or that it can perform what it wishes to do." It acts upon "the principle of trial and error," seeking "a perfection it does not yet possess." Certain conclusions adverse to Shaw's creed, warns Ervine, may be drawn from too summary an account of Shaw's philosophy of creative evolution. "One is that there is no freedom of choice for man," and this is the adverse conclusion that concerns us here.[13]

We must see that Shaw intends us to feel that Joan, so far as her actions and choices are concerned, was a free agent. There was something extra-personal urging her on, out of the "middle station in life" to do that which she felt must be done. This force, surging through her dramatic imagination, influenced her choices, yes, but did not preclude them. Nothing would be more antagonistic to Shaw's social philosophy than the proposition that the individual cannot will his destiny, at least to a considerable part.

One might say, in answer to Barnet, that the presence of an outside force, some "divinity that shapes our ends," is one of the prime requisites of classical tragedy. It has traditionally been one of the aims of tragedy to depict man in relation to some ordering force or fate, and not in relation to a meaningless, chaotic, or mechanistic void. On this point, Herbert J. Muller, in *The Spirit of Tragedy,* writes: "Above all, tragedy is centered on the problem of . . . [man's] fate, not merely his failures in love, business, or war, nor his sufferings from political or social injustice, but his relations to his total environment, his position in the universe, the ultimate meaning of his life."[14] Shaw, in *Saint Joan* attempts to draw an "ultimate meaning" from The Maid's life. He does not present his tragic protagonist as meeting her fate in a universe devoid of meaning or of "teleological principle" as does Sartre in his

13. *Bernard Shaw: His Life, Work and Friends* (New York, 1956), 390–391.
14. (New York, 1956), 14.

existentialist tragedies or Hauptmann in his naturalistic dramas. Joan is driven by fate to accomplish her mission just as Orestes, Oedipus, and Hamlet are driven to find, tragically, the unknown murderers, Lear to hear Cordelia's love, Solness to climb the heights once more. "Swerve me!" cried Ahab. "The path of my fixed purpose is laid with iron rails, whereon my soul is grooved to run." Yet no one seriously claims that the driving force of fate precludes these titans of literature from being considered as tragic heroes. It is the choices of action determined by the not quite perfect character of the hero, choices made in the shadow of urging, hovering fate, that determine the tragic hero's doom. And it can be shown that it is The Maid's freely-made choices, made in the exultation of pride, that bring her to the stake. For the Greek sin of hubris occurs when man acts as if he were akin to the gods, forgetting his lowly human station. So, in Shaw's play, Joan acts.

II

Joan's tragic error takes place in scene five of the play. Prior to this scene, she is self-assertive, but hardly self-important. Her demands are great for France and minor for herself. She requires armies to further the commands of her voices that she lift the siege of Orleans and crown the Dauphin at Rheims, but only common armor and horse for herself. When she discovers Charles hiding among his courtiers she falls to her knees, hardly daring to look upon his regal countenance. After she receives the Archbishop's blessing, she falls to her knees once more fervently to kiss the hem of his robe. When the wind changes so that Dunois' forces can cross the Loire she is blinded by tears of gratitude to God. It is necessary to recognize the change in Joan that occurs in scene five to appreciate Joan as a tragic heroine.

In this scene, we are introduced to an altered Joan, who complains about the dullness of the peaceful life and who is reluctant to resume the hum-drum life of a fifteenth-century village maiden. "I am such a coward: I am frightened beyond words before a battle; but it is so dull afterwards when there is no danger," she cries, "oh, so dull! dull! dull!" Dunois cautions her about her immoderacy. "You must learn to be abstemious in war, just as you are in your food and drink, my little saint" (pp. 55–56). Next, Joan complains about the resentment she has met at court and defends the correctness of her every move. She denies that she seeks honors, but she wants the love and praise of Charles and his court. Her self-concern suggests that of the bored, dissatisfied "new woman" of Ibsen.

The Dauphin has been crowned Charles the Seventh by her in the Cathedral of Rheims; the seige of Orleans has been lifted and other battles fought and won. The mission given her by St. Catherine and St. Margaret (of, if one chooses, by the life force acting through her genius) has been completed. But English forces are still camping on French soil. Despite the fact that her mission has ended, Joan impulsively decides to attempt the final expulsion of the English, beginning with an attack on Paris. Before the decision is announced, however, Shaw presents Joan, for the first time in the play, in onstage communion with her voices. They speak to her through the bells, she informs Dunois. At the quarter-hour, they say "Dear-child-of-God"; at the half-hour, "Be-brave-go-on"; at three-quarters, "I-am-thy-help"; and at the hour, the great bell tolls, "God-will-save-France." It is then, Joan says, "That St Margaret and St Catherine and sometimes even the blessed Michael will say things that I cannot tell beforehand" (p. 57). But Joan pro-nounces her decision to attack Paris after the bells have chimed the quarter-hour (saying "Dear-child-of-God") and not after the clanging of the great bell of the hour, when Joan claims the voices tell her things she does not know beforehand. Just what Shaw intends us to make of this is difficult to determine. But it does seem possible that he is indicating that Joan's claim that her voices told her to attack Paris represents a self-deception, that she is from this moment on listening neither to her voices nor her commonsense, but is doing merely what she emotionally wants to do. Certainly it is clear from the evidence Shaw gives us in this scene that Joan is thinking more of relieving her feelings of *ennui* than she is of the needs of France.

The change in Joan becomes increasingly apparent. She stamps her foot with impatience at the King when he suggests making a treaty with the Burgundians, where she formerly had thrown herself to her knees at his feet. She puffs with delight upon learning that the Burgundians have received an offer of 16,000 pounds for her capture, and over-rides Dunois' admonition that since "God is on the side of the big battal-ions," her proposed attack on Paris will bring certain defeat. As Shaw's stage directions order, she speaks "roughly" to the Archbishop and demands that he inform Charles that what *she* says is God's will *is* God's will, and elicits from the prelate a comment which in its last two sentences seems to underscore the point that Shaw is making in this scene.

> If I am not so glib with the name of God as you are, it is because I interpret his will with the authority of the Church and of my sacred office. When you first came you respected it, and would not have dared to speak as you are now speaking. You came clothed with the virtue of humility; and because God blessed your enterprises accordingly, you have stained yourself with the sin of pride. The old Greek tragedy is rising among us. It is the chastisement of hubris (p. 60).

While it is frequently useless to speculate upon what an author has in mind when he writes a certain speech, or uses a particular word, it seems important to our discussion to call special attention to the Archbishop's use of the word "hubris" and his reference to "the old Greek tragedy." How a playwright could make this reference to classical tragedy and not mean to communicate anything to his audience is difficult to imagine. And when a speech such as this fits in perfectly with other indications in the play and in the preface that Shaw was at least considering his play from the standpoint of classical tragedy, it is of a significance difficult to cast aside.

Critics of the play, however, have been inclined to lift the charge of hubris from the shoulders of The Maid and place it elsewhere. Martz opines, "... the hubris is not Joan's but Everyman's." And Barnet believes "... the judges or the archbishop ... see hubris where there is none.. .."[15] But in terms of the action of the play and of the medieval thought it reflects, Joan was hubristic. To Shaw, who did not believe in a personal diety but in an *élan vital* which surges through all living creatures in its search for perfection, the gods of this play, gods whose powers Joan usurped and to whom Joan was hubristic, are the great forces of the age—Feudalism and the Universal Church. Critics who argue that Shaw did not believe Joan hubristic toward the living, personal God of the medieval church fail to appreciate the point Shaw makes in *Saint Joan*. She does not act akin, if not superior to the God-

15. Barnet, "Bernard Shaw on Tragedy," 898.

like forces of her age. She declared the supremacy of the individual conscience over church dictate; her appeal to French nationalism rang the deathknell of international feudalism. For these sins, social more than spiritual, Joan is brought to the stake. She rides off against the Burgundians, no longer in her simple soldier's armor, but clothed in a majestic surcoat of gold. It is by this cloak of gold, the symbol of her vanity,[16] that she is pulled from her horse and captured.

III

This, then, is the basis for my contention that *Saint Joan* is a play conceived within the framework of classical tragedy. Criticisms based on the assumption that it is a Christian tragedy and hence not a tragedy at all seem founded upon a misreading of the play and on an incomplete understanding of Shaw's attitude toward Joan's sainthood. The play seems clearly to contain the elements of classical tragedy. It tells the story of the rise in fortune of a good person who falls to death because of pride and a tragic error; it is serious and of great magnitude; embodied in it, moreover, is timeless myth. Who could be more a scapegoat than the Joan Shaw presents to us ultimately sacrificed on the altar of religious and social conformity?

It contains, furthermore, dramatic elements which elicit the catharsis of pity and terror customarily demanded from high tragedy. Such a magnificent scene as the fourth, where Warwick and Cauchon discuss the reasons why Joan must be crushed, impart to the spectator a certain cold horror as he realizes that the great forces of international feudalism and church await with eager expectation the mistake on Joan's part which will bring her into their grasp. And in scene six, when the stage darkens, and the glow of the fire burning high in the courtyard is seen flickering across the emptied stage, the audience realizes that this is the dramatization of the burning of a real girl—that this really happened. Vague considerations that she was, after all, technically classified as a saint, and that this is just a play of ideas, not a tragedy, fade then into nothingness.

---

16. The Inquisitor: This is not a time for vanity, Joan. You stand in great peril.

Joan: I know it: have I not been punished for my vanity? If I had not worn my cloth of gold surcoat in battle like a fool, that Burgundian soldier would never have pulled me backwards off my horse; and I should not have been here (p. 83).

This is the end of the play proper. Critics have argued quite validly that the epilogue, loquacious and tinged with humor as it is, destroys the mood achieved by scene six. But does the epilogue injure the play's organic unity? It would, I think, if the epilogue were in form and tone equal to that of the body of the play. But its very differentness sets it apart from the rest of the drama, as an epilogue should be separated. In form it is expressionistic. Its characters are presented as components of a dream of Charles'; no attempt is made to make the epilogue realistic: the entrance of the "clerical-looking gentleman in black frock-coat and trousers, and tall hat in the fashion of the year 1920" should be enough to dispel any notions that this is really Joan we are seeing, that she is hale and hearty and sitting on the right hand of God. It is a gloss upon the point of the play, an attempt to universalize Shaw's proposition that each age (not only Joan's) brings to the cross or stake those who assault the moral or social conventions. We may well object to Shaw's persistence and claim that we need no such reminder as the epilogue. But the epilogue will seem more acceptable if we think of *Saint Joan* as a play adhering in a loose sense to the form of Greek tragedy, for in the chant-like passages of the epilogue we are harked back to the ancient choruses commenting on and drawing from the moment of plays the universal truth. Its ending, "How long, O Lord, how long?" is neither pessimistic, nor optimistic, and certainly not cynical. In Joan's fall is implied a new resurrection, and in this resurrection another fall. This is the world; this recognition is the tragic spirit. "How long, O Lord, O Life Spirit, O Man, how long?"

✒ J. I. M. STEWART

XXI/That Sure Mark of Greatness: *Saint Joan* and Its Imperfections

Saint Joan (1923) achieves a unique and almost perfect integration of high comic powers with strong convictions. The result is certainly Shaw's outstanding play, conceivably the finest and most moving English drama since *The Winter's Tale* or *The Tempest*. It owns that sure mark of greatness: a stature that remains intact after every consideration has been given to evident and undeniable imperfections. A preserved admiration for it amid the changed literary fashions of the mid-twentieth century may fairly be set, along with a similarly preserved admiration for the poetry and prose of Hardy and the short stories of Kipling, among the touchstones of a good and catholic literary taste.

There is, at the simplest, a new tact in the use of laughter. Two instances of this occur at the end of the first scene. Robert de Baudricourt, the military squire who eventually agrees to send Joan to the Dauphin, is a man of the commonest clay, disguising behind aggressive bluster a decided weakness of will. When Joan, receiving his grudging permission to go forward, cried out 'Oh, squire! Your head is all circled with light, like a saint's', the dramatic effect—which is of the sudden and overwhelming order of Miranda's 'Oh brave new world'—is enhanced alike by the antecedent comedy of his character and by the immediate touch of genius in the stage-direction telling us that he has 'looked up for his halo rather apprehensively'. There is the same fusion of our laughter with deep emotion in the moment upon which the

Extracted from "Shaw" in J. I. M. Stewart, *Eight Modern Writers*, Vol. XII of *Oxford History of English Literature* (Oxford, 1963), 179–82. Retitled by the editor.

scene closes—a moment which looks forward to the Archbishop's definition of a miracle as an event which creates faith, while at the same
time knitting perfectly with the comedy of the 'three Barbary hens and
the black' upon which the action has opened:

> *Robert, still very doubtful whether he has not been made a fool of by a crazy
> female, and a social inferior to boot, scratches his head and slowly comes back
> from the door.*
> *The steward runs in with a basket.*
> STEWARD. Sir, sir—   `
> ROBERT. What now?
> STEWARD. The hens are laying like mad, sir. Five dozen eggs!
> ROBERT (*stiffens convulsively; crosses himself; and forms with his pale lips the
> words*) Christ in heaven! (*Aloud but breathless*) She did come from God.

Or, again, there is the handling of John de Stogumber, the Earl of
Warwick's chaplain, whose charge against Joan is that she 'denies to
England her legitimate conquests, given her by God because of her
peculiar fitness to rule over less civilized races for their own good' and
who takes it as self-evident that the Archangel Michael talks in English
if he talks at all. We have had this character before in the Britannus of
Caesar and Cleopatra, and are constrained to admit that farcical anachronism could no farther go. But when, in the end, it is de Stogumber
who is chosen by the dramatist to bring before us the physical horror of
Joan's end, the joke is not dropped but transmuted in the one point of
comfort the wretched man can see: 'She asked for a cross. A soldier
gave her two sticks tied together. Thank God he was an Englishman! I
might have done it; but I did not: I am a coward, a mad dog, a fool. But
he was an Englishman too.'

Neither in minor matters of this sort nor in the play as a whole is it
an essentially historical imagination that is at work. 'There is a new
spirit rising in men', the Archbishop says in the second scene; 'we are at
the dawning of a wider epoch.' And in the fourth scene Warwick and
the Bishop of Beauvais look forward apprehensively to dangers for
which they coin the names Protestantism and Nationalism. These characters carry, of course, the burden of making intelligible to us what
could scarcely in actual fact be intelligible to themselves, and Shaw has
both achieved this with a brilliant lucidity in the play and cogently
defended in his preface its dramatic propriety. Even so, we are rather
sharply aware that his interest is not in the pressure and density of an

actual historical situation. Rather it is in Joan in her most representative quality as one of those who have been—in the words used at her canonization—endowed with heroic virtues and favoured with private revelations. To some extent at least Shaw the disciple of Butler has given place to Shaw the disciple of Bunyan. He shows no inclination, indeed, to the truths of revealed religion. Joan's voices do not come, as she supposes them to do, from a God in any sense acceptable to believing Christians. They simply represent, the preface tells us, the 'pressure upon her of the driving force that is behind evolution'. The evolution is very much that of Samuel Butler and the brothers Barnabas still. The preface speaks of 'the fountain of inspiration which is continually flowing in the universe' and of 'the eternal soul in Nature'. It condemns the 'rationalist' view that 'new ideas cannot come otherwise than by conscious ratiocination'. And it asserts that 'no official organisation of mortal men. . . . can keep pace with the private judgment of persons of genius'. This is the crux. The spirit bloweth where it listeth. It is the parlourmaid and not the statesman or philosopher who first lives for three hundred years;[1] it is the ignorant country girl and not the learned and humane Inquisitor whom the Life Force categorically commands. 'The voices come first' Joan says, 'and I find the reasons after.' Joan's faith in her voices is the obverse of Shaw's deepening scepticism before human institutions. Of these institutions he takes the medieval Catholic Church as supremely representative. For that Church as he sees it he contrives the effect of a wonderfully fair hearing. There is a transcendent instance of this immediately before Joan is brought in for trial. Ladvenu, a young Dominican, asks: 'But is there any great harm in the girl's heresy? Is it not merely her simplicity? Many saints have said as much as Joan.' The Inquisitor replies that heresy begins with people who are to all appearance better than their neighbours. And his speech is perhaps the finest—as it is certainly one of the longest—in all the plays.

Yet Shaw's final antagonism to the Church's point of view is absolute. There can be no blessing on councils, synods, and assemblies—unless indeed they have the grace to receive that wisdom which comes into the world only through the channel of the inspired individual. In

1. In *The Thing Happens,* the third play of Shaw's *Back to Methuselah* cycle. [Editor's note]

Shaw's decline this persuasion led him into a strangely uncritical approbation of the new absolutisms rising in Europe. If it leads him first to his finest play, he has his heroine to thank for it. He has been a playwright for thirty years—and now, at the end of a long line of brilliant inventions, there stands at last a real human being. A young woman whose intervention in the dynastic struggles of the fifteenth century is to be received as a manifestation of the Life Force, urging ever higher the human race at large, seems a conception of dubious dramatic promise, and one could have had, before the event, very little assurance that Shaw's Maid would not be of the same order as Schiller's or Mark Twain's. In fact, she is a major dramatic achievement. Nor does she simply rise clear of the persons, events, and profuse speechifyings surrounding her. Rather she raises them to her own plane, and is thus literally the making of the play. She is a Shavian heroine—distinguishably, one may say, the creation of the writer who discerned in the Helena of *All's Well* one of the finest of Shakespeare's women. At the same time she is the true sister of Catherine of Siena and Theresa of Avila. And this is perhaps Shaw's work rather than history's.

🖎 DANIEL C. GEROULD

XXII/*Saint Joan* in Paris

Of the seventeen comedies by Shaw produced in Paris during the author's lifetime, only one, *Saint Joan,* was an unqualified success. Prior to the performance of *Saint Joan* in 1925, seven of Shaw's plays had already been produced in Paris, but none of them had enjoyed much popular or critical success.[1] By the 1920's all efforts to establish Shaw as a major modern dramatist appeared to have failed in France.

The critics saw Shaw primarily as a satirist of British society and felt that his theatre would remain forever incomprehensible to the French because of its special national flavor.[2] The difficulty had been compounded by Shaw's deliberate choice as his authorized translator of Augustin Hamon, a French socialist, who by his own admission knew little English when he began his task and absolutely nothing about literature or the drama, either in French or English. His inept translations and extravagant claims about Shaw's revolutionary philosophy alienated even those among the French public who might have developed an interest in Shaw's theatre.

After the total failure of *Pygmalion* in 1923, there was no new production of a Shaw play for a year and a half, and it appeared that Shaw was forever destined to be misunderstood in France and that he would never know either the popular success or critical acclaim which

The Shaw Review, VII (January, 1964), 11–23.
    1. Francis Ambrière, "Les Grandes premières: *Sainte Jeanne* de Bernard Shaw," *Les Annales (Conferencial),* October, 1951, p. 46.
    2. Louis Gillet, *"Sainte Jeanne," Revue des deux mondes,* XXII (August 1, 1924), 688.

he by then enjoyed in England, America, and Germany.[3] To critics like Henry Bidou and Gabriel Marcel, who knew and esteemed Shaw's plays in English and had seen them performed in England, there seemed to be fundamental and perhaps insuperable barriers of language, thought, and feeling between Shaw and the French. On the other side of the channel, Shaw's patience had come to an end: if the French found his humor parochially British, Shaw found the whole Parisian stage provincial and reactionary. He defended his choice of a socialist translator who knew nothing of the Parisian stage, arguing that only a fellow socialist would protect his plays from falling into the hands of unscrupulous men of the theatre who would distort their social message for commercial gain. The year before the French production of *Saint Joan* Shaw contributed an article to a French drama magazine in which he made the following unflattering remarks about the French theatre and its public:

> It seems to me that the theatre in France addresses itself less and less to an intelligent public; the public is in fact so stupid that an explanation of the play must be printed on the program to help the spectators to understand what they see. The other day I saw a program of *Arms and the Man* which carefully explains that the tragic figure of my play is a buffoon who must not be taken seriously. It is pitiful, because an appreciation of my plays has become a proof of civilization, and up to the present France is almost at the bottom of the form. Nothing however can be done. I have educated London, I have educated New York, Berlin and Vienna; Moscow and Stockholm are at my feet, but I am too old to educate Paris; it is too far behind and I am too far ahead.[4]

Then, on April 28, 1925, the situation changed overnight with the production of *Saint Joan* at the Théâtre des Arts by Georges and Ludmilla Pitoëff. Shaw achieved a tremendous and lasting success on the Parisian stage with this production, which is still considered one of the great French theatrical events of the century.[5] For the Pitoëffs, it was the greatest success of their career;[6] *Sainte Jeanne* ran for over one hundred performances in 1925 and was revived year after year for the

3. Ambrière, *Les Annales,* October, 1951, pp. 45-46.
4. Quoted by James Graham in "Shaw on *Saint Joan,*" *The Sunday New York Times,* April 13, 1924.
5. Ambrière, *Les Annales,* October, 1941, pp. 44-45.
6. Henri-René Lenormand, *Les Pitoëff: souvenirs* (Paris: Odette Lieutier, 1943), p. 112.

next ten years. With only a few exceptions the critics praised both the play and the performance with a warmth accorded to none of Shaw's other works. Had Shaw at last succeeded in educating the French and in forcing them to accept him on his own terms? Or had the French, aided by Saint Joan and the Pitoëffs, really won the battle by transforming Shaw to suit their own taste, after first eluding the vigilance of Shaw's appointed guardian, Hamon? In order to answer this question it is necessary to discover what the French critics thought of the play itself as distinguished from the French performance.

In the year preceding the French production much had been written in Parisian newspapers and magazines about Shaw's play, including long reviews of the play based on the English text or on the New York and London performances. The chief cause of this pre-performance interest was the curiosity and apprehension aroused by the announcement that Shaw had written a play on a subject particularly sacred to the French. Many thought that Shaw was peculiarly ill-suited to write about Joan of Arc and could imagine his attitude towards the saint only as a desecration or grotesque caricature.[7] However, the critics who knew the play in English all agreed that the fears about Shaw's treatment of Joan were totally groundless, and they hastened to assure their readers that Shaw had been respectful of the Saint.

However, despite Shaw's unwonted reverence, the French critics who knew the play in English agreed that Shaw was by nature unable to understand the mystic force animating Joan and that his rational explanation of her voices and miracles was by no means satisfactory. Shaw was devoid of the poetic gifts necessary to enter even only imaginatively into the miraculous spirit of the middle ages.[8] This failure to grasp the religious quality of Joan as a saint was felt to be the capital defect in Shaw's play. At this point Saint Joan was by no means acclaimed as an unqualified masterpiece since the French critics had many important reservations about Shaw's conception of Joan.

Several months before the French performance of Saint Joan, the French dramatic critics had again engaged in a discussion about the saint on the stage when François Porché's La Vierge au grand coeur

7. Gillet, Revue des deux mondes, XXII (August 1, 1924), 687.
8. Ibid., 695.

was presented at the Théâtre de la Renaissance in January, 1925. In attempting to explain Porché's failure, the critics set out to define the requirements of an historical play dealing with Joan of Arc and to point out the dangers of the subject. They agreed that it was a very difficult subject,[9] if not absolutely impossible.[10] The story was too well known to interest a twentieth-century audience who constantly demanded the unexpected and surprising; such an historical character was incompatible with the mentality of the public.[11] The French national heroine had never and could never succeed on the stage, the critics concluded.

The religious inspiration for a play about Joan of Arc posed a serious problem. In this respect, Porché's honorable intentions were of questionable value, since the inspiration of his play seemed less spontaneous than the result of a conscious effort to write an edifying and pious work.[12]

In Porché's play, Saint Michel constantly appears directly to Jeanne, and at the end of the play Sainte Marguerite, Saint Gabriel, and a whole host of angels participate in Jeanne's apotheosis. Such a use of the supernatural, with the stage techniques of a fairy play, seems factitious and compromising.[13] As a result of Porché's attempt to infuse religious spirit into his play, he makes the fatal error of creating a Jeanne d'Arc who talks too much and too poetically. Porché's heroine declaims endlessly with a false poetic lyricism, whereas the prime requirement for an acceptable modern Jeanne d'Arc would be that she avoid all rhetoric.[14]

In fact, Porché's treatment of Jeanne d'Arc, with its emphasis on her inner drama and her religious inspiration, was in accord with the French tradition of plays on this subject since 1890. The great majority were lyric in tone and written in verse, and they all stressed her divine inspiration and mission rather than her plight as a victim of the machi-

9. André Billy, *"La Vierge au grand coeur,"* Mercure de France, CLXXVIII (February 15, 1925), 186.

10. Gaston Rageot, "Le Personnage historique et le théâtre d'aujourd'hui," *Revue politique et littéraire,* February 7, 1925, pp. 137–38.

11. *Ibid.*

12. Gabriel Marcel, *"La Vierge au grand coeur,"* L'Europe nouvelle, February 7, 1925, p. 190.

13. *Ibid.*

14. Pierre Brisson, *"La Vierge au grand coeur,"* Annales politiques et litteraires, LXXXIV (February 8, 1925), 140.

nations of church or state.[15] In keeping with this tradition, Porché totally omits any account of Jeanne's struggles with worldly powers, including the trial.

This lyric tradition seemed outmoded for the 1920's; a new conception of the Joan of Arc play was needed. Pierre Brisson suggests that only by abandoning the usual treatment accorded to Jeanne can the pitfalls of this too familiar subject be avoided. In order to have freedom and originality, a play about Jeanne d'Arc would have to center not on the story of the saint herself but rather on the worldly struggles of those about her.[16]

If we relate what the French critics said of Shaw's *Saint Joan* in English to their discussion of Porché's *La Vierge au grand coeur* and of the problems of the Jeanne d'Arc play, it is possible to draw the following conclusions about the chances of success for Shaw's play in performance on the Parisian stage. In the first place, Shaw's abandonment of the customary lyric manner and rhetorical piety could not but be welcome to the French for whom the subject had seemed thoroughly exhausted. The theatre and poetry in France had for some time been going in opposite directions, and since the war *le théâtre en vers* was virtually dead.[17] By choosing the non-poetic theatre for his treatment of Joan, Shaw would bring to the French a new conception of a history play on the life of the saint. Further, his emphasis on the conflicts between Joan and the powers of church and state would represent a desirable departure from the lifeless French tradition. However, Shaw's treatment of Joan's religious inspiration and mission seemed unlikely to satisfy the French demand for the kind of mystic interpretation found in Péguy.

On the basis of the evidence available before the performance, there would be no way to predict the great success which Shaw's play was to enjoy in France or the French critics' praise of it as a masterpiece of

15. Arabella Lorraine Pierson, "Jeanne d'Arc in French Drama 1890–1928," (abstract of a Ph.D. dissertation, Dept. of Romance Languages, University of Illinois, Urbana, Illinois, 1930), 4, 22.

16. Régis Gignoux, *Comoedia*, quoted in the supplement to *La Petite illustration* of February 28, 1925, which contains the text of Porché's play and short extracts from critical reviews. The pages are not numbered for these extracts.

17. Albert Thibaudet, *Histoire de la littérature française de 1789 à nos jours* (Paris: Librairie Stock, 1936), 559.

Shakespearian stature. In fact, we should expect to find numerous reservations about Joan herself, even if there were much interest in the originality of Shaw's approach to a well-known historical subject.

At this point the Pitoëffs and their contribution must be considered, since unlike Shaw's other plays which were presented in France, *Saint Joan* remains inseparably linked to a particular production and above all to a particular actress. It is impossible to explain the play's great success without taking into account all the aspects of the Pitoëffs' production: the handling of the text, the staging, and Ludmilla Pitoëff's performance as Joan.[18]

Emigrés from Russia, the Pitoëffs played an important role in the French theatre of the 1920's, introducing such foreign dramatists as Pirandello and Chekhov to the French public. Although their only previous staging of Shaw had been a minor production of *Androcles and the Lion* that attracted little attention, they were anxious to attempt another Shavian comedy.

The Pitoëffs were enthusiastic when they first read the English text of *Saint Joan* which Shaw himself had sent them, but they were appalled as soon as they saw what Augustin Hamon, aided by his wife Henriette, had made of it in translation. It was a hopeless task, however, to suggest changes or improvements to the Hamons since they clung stubbornly to their rights as authorized translators and had in the past refused to change even a word. The only alternative for the Pitoëffs was to undertake a revision secretly on their own authority. For the first time the performers revolted against Hamon's translation, and contrary to Shaw's expressed•wishes and legal rights, they had the French text completely revised by a professional man of the theatre. Exactly what Shaw had feared and tried to prevent by authorizing a fellow socialist as translator had finally come to pass.

The Pitoëffs turned for help to their friend Henri-René Lenormand, a young playwright already well-known on the Parisian stage for *Le Temps est un songe* and other plays. Lenormand, in his book on the Pitoëffs, tells how he and Ludmilla spent several weeks working together on a revision of the text.[19]

18. Gabriel Marcel, *"Sainte Jeanne," L'Europe nouvelle*, May 9, 1925, p. 620.
19. Lenormand, 121-22.

In this way, the text used in the French production of *Saint Joan* was not the same one published by the Hamons. The Parisian critics, unaware of the secret revision, made no adverse comments on the translation and for the first time appeared satisfied with what they thought was the work of the Hamons.[20] The critic of *Le Temps*, who had found the French version of *Pygmalion* execrable, was happy to be able to congratulate the Hamons on their brilliant translation of *Saint Joan*.[21]

However, the secret of the Lenormand revision soon leaked out and brought down the wrath of Hamon and Shaw on the heads of the conspirators. When André Antoine disclosed in a review of the play that the translation had been retouched, Hamon replied in an open letter that this accusation was a slander which in England would be punishable under British law.[22] Shaw, when he learned what had happened, contented himself with writing angry and ironic letters in which he thanked Lenormand for his help and wished him as much success with his own plays.[23] Thus, the Pitoëffs' handling of Shaw's text went directly counter to the author's intentions in such a way as to produce discord between Shaw and the French artists who thought they were serving him best.

The same lack of harmony between the dramatist and his French interpreters manifested itself in other aspects of the Pitoëffs' production. Georges Pitoëff's conception of *Saint Joan* was highly personal and led him to stage and direct the play in a strikingly original fashion. Pitoëff conceived Shaw's play as a mystic drama centering completely around Joan's saintliness. "I want the audience to feel only one thing: that Joan is a saint," he wrote of his production and its atmosphere of religious mysticism.[24] He used as his basic frame for the stage a triptych which was present in all the scenes of the play and which from the beginning prepared the audience for the miraculous.[25]

20. *Ibid.*, 125.
21. André Rivoire, *"Sainte Jeanne,"* Le Temps, May 4, 1925, p. 3.
22. Aniouta Pitoëff, *Ludmilla, ma mère: vie de Ludmilla et Georges Pitoëff* (Paris: René Julliard, 1955), 141.
23. Lenormand, 125.
24. Georges Pitoëff, *Notre théâtre*, ed. Jean de Rigault (Paris: Messages, 1949), 21.
25. John Palmer, "The Productions of George Pitoëff, "*The Fortnightly Review*, CXVIII (August 1, 1925), 212-13.

Pitoëff thus based his entire conception of *Saint Joan* on that aspect of Shaw's play which had seemed the most deficient to the French critics who had seen or read the work in English. His emphasis on the saintly and miraculous represented a complete departure from the London performance and Shaw's intentions.[26]

Pitoëff constructed his production around his wife in the role of Joan; for him, she was Saint Joan.[27] As for Ludmilla Pitoëff, the identification was equally strong; Jeanne d'Arc had been for her a life-long obsession. She ultimately became so completely transported by playing the role of her favorite heroine that she underwent a religious crisis in which she was tormented by her own impurity and undertook religious pilgrimages in order to commune more closely with the saint. Finally, to come closer to the real Jeanne d'Arc Ludmilla also appeared in a strictly historical version of Joan's career taken directly from the transcripts of the trial.[28]

It is clear that Ludmilla Pitoëff's personal attachment to the historical Jeanne d'Arc and her husband's conception of the play as a mystic religious drama explain the singular way in which she interpreted Joan, going counter to the English and American performances and to Shaw's own view of the role. Further, Ludmilla's usual style of acting and stage presence were such that she invariably transformed all her roles into something unreal and dreamlike, whether it was Shakespeare or naturalistic drama; she was even able to turn Shaw's play into a dream.[29]

Every one who saw the play was overwhelmed by the tremendous emotional force of Mme Pitoëff's acting and by her complete identification with Joan. The trial scene which Gabriel Marcel and other French critics had found cold and academic in the English text, became so moving that it wrung tears from the spectators.[30] In the trial, Ludmilla produced this overpowering effect because she appeared so slight and frail, animated only by an interior flame, and seemed so childlike in her

26. *Ibid.,* 212.
27. Georges Pitoëff, 12–13.
28. Aniouta Pitoëff, 138–39.
29. Robert Brasillach, "Animateurs de théâtre: II. Georges et Ludmilla Pitoëff," *Revue des deux mondes,* XXXV (September 1, 1936), 152.
30. Martial Piéchaud, *"Sainte Jeanne,"* *Revue hebdomadaire,* June 13, 1925, p. 226.

innocence and weakness before the unrelenting tribunal that condemned her.[31]

The French critics, especially those who had seen the English or American productions of *Saint Joan,* recognized that Mme Pitoëff's interpretation represented a distinct departure from the author's intentions, but they felt that she had improved the play by transforming the character which Shaw had originally conceived. In comparison, the English actress Sybil Thorndike had appeared vulgar, stressing only Joan's exterior traits of energy and will power. According to Lenormand, the English Joan was indeed the forceful warrior that Shaw wanted to depict, but Ludmilla Pitoëff made the role yield spiritual qualities superior to anything that Shaw had been able to imagine. Lenormand also suggests that Shaw's later hostility to the Pitoëffs can be explained by his feeling that Mme Pitoëff had surpassed his own intentions and become his rival in artistic creation.[32] For others, Ludmilla was less Shaw's rival than the true creator of the character, showing the English playwright how he should have written his play.[33]

In particular, it was Mme Pitoëff's interpretation of the trial scene which changed the entire significance of the play. She sat facing the audience with the court behind her so that the interrogation appeared an irrelevance and her judges seemed of a different world than Joan's spiritual universe of voices and inner light. Mme Pitoëff had totally eliminated from the role the breeziness and public-spirited energy so much in evidence in Sybil Thorndike's performance. In the trial scene the French actress was above all a pathetic Joan and appeared as "a piteous little waif in her misery."[34]

Shaw himself had an opportunity to see the Pitoëff's production of *Saint Joan* when the French company came to London before the opening in Paris.[35] The dramatist made quite clear that he liked neither the acting nor the staging, and at a reception for the French and English casts, Shaw told Pitoëff that he had upset the balance of the

---

31. François Mauriac, "Sainte Jeanne," *Nouvelle revue française,* XXIV (June 1, 1925), 1051.
32. Lenormand, 124-25.
33. Claude Berton, *"Sainte Jeanne:* les visages de la comédie parodique," *Nouvelles littéraires,* May 16, 1925, p. 7.
34. Desmond MacCarthy, *Shaw* (London: MacGibbon & Kee, 1951), 172.
35. Ambrière, *Les Annales,* October, 1951, p. 51.

play by giving too much importance to Joan.[36] When André Maurois, who saw the performance with Shaw, ventured to praise Ludmilla's performance, Shaw exclaimed:

> What! That frail, delicate woman is your idea of Joan of Arc? NO. Joan of Arc was a strong peasant who could take a soldier by the scruff of the neck and throw him out the window. Your Mme Pitoëff is charming, touching, but she would never have driven a single Englishman out of France.[37]

However, it was undoubtedly just this divergence from Shaw's conception of his play which made the Pitoëff's version of Saint Joan so popular in France in the mid-1920's. The war had redirected French popular sentiment to Jeanne d'Arc, as had happened in all difficult periods in French history. Yet the subject matter alone will not explain the success of Shaw's play; over a hundred plays about Joan had appeared in France since 1890,[38] but none of these achieved a lasting place in the theatre or any enduring literary fame. Shaw's play, on the other hand, was immediately accepted as the definitive treatment of the French heroine. What were the special qualities and characteristics of Shaw's play, as interpreted by the Pitoëffs which enabled it to succeed completely where so many other plays on the same subject had failed, even though they had been written by worshipful and patriotic Frenchmen, properly respectful of the saint?

After opening night, the critics hastened to assure their readers that not only was Shaw's play in no way shocking or offensive, but rather was full of surprising reverence for the French heroine. Joan remained historical and heroic, unscathed by the dramatist's usual irony, and the French critics were left to speculate how it was possible that their beloved saint had stayed undefiled in the hands of the author who had already debunked Napoleon, Caesar, and other heroes of the past.

The first explanation given of Shaw's unwonted adoration of the heroic was in terms of the inspiration of the play. Joan of Arc had inspired Shaw and wrought yet another miracle.[39] "Once more the

36. Aniouta Pitoëff, 142.
37. André Maurois, "Le Théâtre de Bernard Shaw," Les Annales (Conferencil), January, 1957, p. 23.
38. Pierson, 3.
39. Robert de Flers, "Sainte Jeanne," Le Figaro, May 11, 1925, p. 2.

formidable saint vanquishes the enemy."[40] In fact, it was as though Joan herself were the real author of the play, taking it right out of Shaw's hands and raising it to a height beyond his usual reach. From the French point of view, not only Mme Pitoëff but Joan of Arc herself had improved on Shaw's original conception. Shaw clearly appeared to be losing the battle to educate the French and have them sit submissively at his feet. The heroine herself and the actress who interpreted her were praised for creating the play, and later on in a conversation with Jean-Jacques Bernard, Shaw discounted the success of the French production, saying, "*Saint Joan* is not a play by me . . . She already existed!"[41]

Nonetheless, the critics did praise Shaw for the good use which he made of this inspiring subject matter and particularly for his handling of the dramatic structure of the play. Even though the real impetus came from Joan herself, Shaw at least knew how to arrange the material in order to display the saint adequately. The French were impressed with Shaw's dramatic technique; he had cleverly emphasized Joan's nobility and purity by reserving all his satire for the other characters whom he debased and ridiculed.[42] Such a belittlement of the surrounding figures made the glory of the saint shine more splendidly; this use of perspective was a standard technique of hagiography.[43] Shaw's application of this principle of contrast to the story of Joan of Arc was considered his masterstroke in *Saint Joan*. There results a perpetual contrast between Joan's noble purpose and devotion and the world of greed, ambition, and deceit in which she must live and to which she is finally a sacrifice. Juxtaposing the saint and the almost farcical world of Shavian satire seemed an amazing technical feat whereby Shaw avoided sullying Joan as the French had feared and instead glorified her as never before by exercising his ironic wit on her opponents.[44]

By shifting the dramatic center of interest in this fashion from Joan

40. Piéchaud, *Revue hebdomadaire,* June 13, 1925, pp. 222-223.
41. Jean-Jacques Bernard, *"César et Cléopatre," L'Europe nouvelle,* Jaunary 5, 1929, p. 10.
42. William Speth, *"Sainte Jeanne," Revue mondiale,* CLXV (May 15, 1925), 198.
43. Gillet, *Revue des deux mondes,* XXII (August 1, 1924), 688.
44. Berton, *Nouvelles littéraires,* May 16, 1925, p. 7.

to those about her, Shaw was able to create a new type of Joan of Arc
play in which the heroine's opponents and their worldly struggles play
a major role and become the subject of satire and humor.[45] In his review
of Porché's *La Vierge au grand coeur,* Pierre Brisson had already
suggested that a new and original play about Jeanne d'Arc would have
to make just such a shift in the center of interest. By establishing a new
center of interest in the contrast between Joan and the people surrounding her, Shaw not only gave his *Saint Joan* an original structure
which liberated the subject from the stereotypes of its traditional
treatment, but he also solved the major problem of the Jeanne d'Arc
play: how to make it amusing, and not merely edifying. At the time of
Porché's *La Vierge au grand coeur,* the critics had regarded the subject
itself as virtually impossible; worthy intentions could never bring to life
in the theatre the saint's noble history which was at once too well-
known and too sublime to entertain the public. Shaw's great accomplishment was to have discovered how to make this forbidding subject
lively and entertaining.

By presenting the characters in Joan's time as no less petty or foolish
than human beings as we know them today, Shaw succeeded in animating the historic past and making it live again on the stage. The people
in *Saint Joan* are those of any age; for this reason they seem alive and
akin to us.[46] The French critics repeat again and again as key terms in
their explanation of how Shaw renders history amusing the words
familiar and *lively.* Rather than elaborate historic reconstructions based
on weighty documentation, Shaw presents living history, and instead of
conventional figures from the Middle Ages, men of all time. Shaw's
anachronistic technique of making historical figures think and speak as
if they were our contemporaries explained in large part why *Saint Joan*
was so much more interesting than the usual history plays which
attempt to make the characters' thought and speech peculiar to their
age.[47] As a result of this technique, Shaw avoided the common pitfalls
of the historical play about Jeanne d'Arc.

Most significantly, Shaw did not make the mistake of trying to give

45. Pierre Brisson, *"Sainte Jeanne,"* Annales politiques et littéraires, LXXXIV (May 10, 1925), 495.

46. Henri Bidou, *"Sainte Jeanne,"* Journal des débats, May 4, 1925, p. 3.

47. Lucien Debech, *"Sainte Jeanne,"* Revue universelle, XXI (June 1, 1925), 655.

his plays a simulated religious inspiration, as Porché had done with *La Vierge au grand coeur*.[48] Shaw's portrayal of Joan was quite the opposite of such official pomp and pious platitude. He presents a Joan who is simple, human, and intensely alive. Shaw is able to reveal both her human and her divine character, whereas the French had been so awed by the Saint that they were unable to make her sufficiently human. By presenting a simple Joan of Arc, Shaw banished from his play the kind of false rhetoric that marred Porché's play and was the chief fault of most works on the subject.[49]

The objections raised by the French critics of the English text, that Shaw failed to present Joan's religious inspiration, vanished in the criticism of the performance. In Mme Pitoëff's Joan, the divine inspiration no less than the human character of the saint was made manifest. This was Joan as she actually was, a simple peasant, almost a child, directed by divine light. Shaw's treatment of Joan's voices and miracles, which the critics of the English text had regarded as the superficial explanation of a rationalist, impressed most of those who saw the performance as the most effective means of dramatizing the supernatural. Joan's voices were all the more real in that she alone heard them. The fact that no angels appear on the stage and no wonders are performed before our eyes increases our belief in the spiritual forces animating Joan.[50] Indirect presentation of the miracles seemed an ideal solution to the problem.

Yet in all this praise, there is not a reference to a single specifically Shavian characteristic. On the contrary, Shaw is commended for strictly subordinating himself to his material and keeping discreetly out of the way of Joan and Ludmilla so that they can dominate the scene. The French critics found Shaw's Joan true to life because the dramatist limited himself to the known facts of her life and kept his own personality out of the creation. Accordingly, the trial scene seemed outstanding since at that point Shaw followed most closely the historical records. In fact, the enthusiasm of the critics for the trial scene as played by Mme Pitoëff was boundless. Not only was it the best scene in all of Shaw, but it represented one of the great moments in the entire history

48. Mauriac, *Nouvelle revue française*, XXIV (June 1, 1925), 1048.
49. Flers, *Le Figaro*, May 11, 1925, p. 2.
50. Rivoire, *Le Temps*, May 4, 1925, p. 3.

of the theatre. To some it was Shakespearian, and to others more than Shakespearian.[51]

Thus, for the majority of critics, what was best about *Saint Joan* was what was least typical of Shaw. Only Gabriel Marcel, who admired Shaw's most characteristic work, refused to consider *Saint Joan* his masterpiece for the very reason that the play's merits were strictly impersonal, but its defects peculiarly Shavian.[52]

Even those critics who considered Joan and the trial as Shakespearian in stature agreed with Marcel that the least successful portions of the play were the least accurate historically and thus the most freely invented by Shaw and the most typical of his usual methods. Almost all the adverse criticism of the play was directed against unhistorical episodes and minor characters that revealed Shaw's customary techniques of parody and humor. Even though these unfavorable opinions were no more than slight qualifications to the high praise accorded to the play by most critics, such objections focus upon the unique features of Shaw's *Saint Joan*, whereas the praise is most often based on aspects of the story and of the performance that might well be common to other dramas dealing with the same subject matter.

The epilogue in particular struck all critics as thoroughly Shavian and quite uncalled for and inappropriate in a work about Joan of Arc. Everyone agreed that the play would have been better without the epilogue. Despite the recognition of Shaw's serious purpose in the epilogue, the critics felt that its bizarre form, combining fantasy and humor, was provincially English, a kind of music hall revue.[53] For the French, the tone of the epilogue was false and jarring. The intrusion of humor at this point was unwelcome, and the half-burlesque, half-fantastic treatment seemed forced and unnatural.

After the epilogue, the most questionable aspect of *Saint Joan* was judged to be the excessively farcical depiction of Charles VII and his court. Dunois, the Archbishop, La Trémouille, Gilles de Rais, and especially Charles himself appeared to be gross caricatures and mechanical puppets. Such a treatment of Charles and the court seemed

51. Flers, *Le Figaro*, May 11, 1925, p. 2.
52. Marcel, *L'Europe nouvelle*, May 9, 1925, p. 620.
53. André Billy, *"Saint Jeanne,"* *Mercure de France*, CLXXX (June 1, 1925), 489.

exaggerated, even though it was part of Shaw's fundamental technique of contrast. By debasing the characters who surrounded Joan to the level of burlesque figures who said just the opposite of what such historical figures would actually have said, Shaw put his saintly heroine in the company of buffoons.[54] For the French, such a procedure raised questions about Shaw's mixing of genres. Clearly *Saint Joan* was a mixture of several different genres; it was alternatingly comic and serious, a gay tragedy full of satire and clowning.[55] The critics who investigated most fully Shaw's treatment of genre came to the conclusion that *Saint Joan* was fundamentally parodic in its design and that the presentation of the royal court was in the manner of Offenbach's burlesque of history, a kind of comic operetta without music. Shaw was credited with inventing a new type of play, the philosophical and historical vaudeville which utilizes the techniques of many different genres for the purposes of parody.[56]

The ironic treatment, the mixing of genres, and the prominence of caricature, burlesque, and parody were further indications of the way in which Shaw was able to make an historical play about Jeanne d'Arc amusing. Because of the skillful combination of these diverse elements, *Saint Joan* never ceased to interest and to entertain. All the critics recognized the amazing theatrical qualities of the work and exclaimed enthusiastically, "C'est du théâtre!"[57] Shaw's juggling with dramatic form and technique was seen as a mark of rare theatrical skill, and his success in placing the saint uncontaminated into a burlesque setting was regarded as a technical *tour de force* of great difficulty. His omission of the traditional scenes between Joan and her family at Domrémy was an interesting innovation designed to center the entire drama on the contrast between the saint and the worldly forces of religion and politics.[58]

On the other hand, the French had little use for Shaw as a thinker. Although they recognized his intentions in *Saint Joan*, the critics mini-

---

54. André Beaunier, *L'Echo de Paris,* April 29, 1925, p. 4.
55. Speth, *Revue mondiale,* CLXV (May 15, 1925), 198.
56. Berton, *Nouvelles littéraires,* May 16, 1925, p. 7. Dubech also calls the play a philosophic vaudeville [Dubech, *Revue universelle,* XXI (June 1, 1925), 654], and from this point on the expression is commonly used to describe Shaw's plays.
57. Rivoire, *Le Temps,* May 4, 1925, p. 3.
58. Piéchaud, *Revue hebdomadaire,* June 13, 1925, p. 223.

mized the importance of the historical and philosophical ideas which Shaw tried to express through his characters. The value of the play for the French did not lie in its intellectual content, but in its artistic qualities. For example, Shaw's attempt to explain the opposition to Joan as an alliance of the feudal state and church was considered interesting not for the ideas themselves, but for the characters who represented them.[59]

Since Shaw cleverly put his philosophical ideas into the mouths of thoroughly human characters, Shaw's mastery of dialogue and dramatic movement was acknowledged even by those who questioned the validity and reasonableness of his ideas.[60] What seemed particularly questionable to those critics writing from a Catholic point of view was Shaw's presentation of Joan as a protestant and his rehabilitation of Cauchon. Of the protestant Joan, Claudel simply exclaimed, "What a Monstrosity!"[61] For François Mauriac, transforming Joan into a protestant and justifying Cauchon were characteristic of Shaw's method of saying the opposite of what the public expects. Both of these transpositions are intellectual feats that appeal to Shaw's love of paradox. However, such tricks betray Shaw's limited understanding of Joan's purely Catholic inspiration and also his deliberate ignoring of the evidence that condemns Cauchon of bad faith.[62] Shaw suppresses facts that show the trial to be a conspiracy in order to make Cauchon a more effective contrast to Joan.[63]

For the great majority of critics, however, the ideas in *Saint Joan* were not offensive, but neither were they significant or important in explaining the play's success. The preface was not translated into French at the time of the performance and is not mentioned by any of the critics. Several years later Pierre Brisson contrasted the play and the preface, showing how the ideas central to the preface assumed little importance in the actual performance.[64] For Brisson and for all the other French critics, Mme Pitoëff was the real heroine of *Saint Joan.*

59. Billy, *Mercure de France*, CLXXX (June 1, 1925), 488.
60. René Salomé, *"Sainte Jeanne," Études*, CLXXXV (October 5, 1925), 79.
61. René Groos, Esquisses: *Charles Maurras, poète; Marcel Proust; Bernard Shaw* (Paris: Maison de Livre Français, 1928), 54, footnote 1.
62. Mauriac, *Nouvelle revue française*, XXIV (June 1, 1925), 1048-50.
63. Lucien Debech, *"Sainte Jeanne," L'Action française*, May 3, 1925, p. 2.
64. Pierre Brisson, *"Sainte Jeanne," Le Temps*, June 27, 1927, p. 3.

The French estimate of *Saint Joan* is in large part based on a single actress's personal interpretation of Joan's character and disregards or minimizes those elements which Shaw felt to be most important and original in his work. Thus, the great critical and popular success of *Saint Joan* in France was due less to the peculiar nature of Shaw's genius than to the play's subject and to the circumstances of the production. Shaw's long-awaited triumph in Paris was not the success which he had wanted and once expected. However, the play's lasting reputation and influence did in part vindicate Shaw; *Saint Joan* proved ultimately to have some educational effect on the French.

Until the outbreak of the Second World War, *Saint Joan* remained Shaw's most popular and famous play in France. It was revived at least twelve different times by the Pitoëffs in Paris between 1925 and 1934, and constituted the most permanent and dependable play in their repertory. Yet the play remained inseparably linked with the Pitoëffs' production, and Mme Pitoëff for the French was Saint Joan. The only other production took place under the German occupation in December, 1940, and then it was used for an ulterior political purpose. It was one of the first plays staged under the occupation for its value as covert propaganda. Under these circumstances, *Saint Joan* contained two possible meanings: one for the German censors who considered it anti-English, another for the French patriots who considered it anti-occupation, and thence anti-German.[65]

Since the war, the play has not held the stage, but it has continued to be highly esteemed. Gide considered it marvellously intelligent and superior in every way to Schiller's play.[66] At the time of Shaw's death in 1950, *Saint Joan* was still cited as one of the few plays of Shaw destined for immortality.[67] With the passing of twenty-five years, the Catholic magazine *Études,* which had attacked the play as anti-Catholic when it first appeared, praised the work in 1950 as a noble tribute to the Saint.[68]

Besides its unusual success and lasting fame, *Saint Joan* was the first

65. Beatrix Dussane, *Notes de théâtre: 1940-1950* (Paris: Lardanchet, 1951), 121–22.
66. André Gide, *Journal: 1942-49* (Paris: NRF, Gallimard, 1950), 28. The entry is dated September 29, 1942.
67. René Lalou, "George Bernard Shaw," *Revue de la société d'histoire du théâtre,* 1951, I, 48.
68. Marius-François Guyard, "Bernard Shaw," *Études,* CCLXVII (December, 1950), 339.

and only play by Shaw to exert any appreciable influence on the development of twentieth-century French drama. Prior to *Saint Joan,* Pirandello had been the major influence on French dramatists in the 1920's;[69] for the French, the Italian playwright had introduced a new conception of character.[70] With *Saint Joan,* Shaw for the first time appeared to several critics as a significant innovator opening up new possibilities for the drama.[71]

In particular, *Saint Joan* suggested the possibility of a new direction in the writing of historical drama. In the second half of the 1920's there was much discussion of possible new directions for the French theatre. To some it seemed that the historical drama offered an approximation of those dynamic qualities of pure theatre to which many felt the modern stage should return.[72] Jean-Richard Bloch, in his book *Destin du théâtre,* discusses *Saint Joan* as a model of what the new historical drama might be.[73]

The humor, fantasy, and anachronisms that the critics had found in *Saint Joan* became accepted characteristics of the new genre of historical drama which was best represented in the works of Giraudoux. In a review of Giraudoux's *Judith,* Alfred Mortier detects Shaw's influence in the liberty and fantasy with which the French dramatist treats even a Biblical subject.[74]

Ultimately, the real originality of Shaw's *Saint Joan* and the source of its influence in France lay in Shaw's application of comic irony and modern psychology to a historical subject which had previously been considered entirely serious. None of the earlier plays about Joan of Arc had ever departed from the strictest gravity and piety. No irony had ever intruded. If, in some of these, Joan appears after her death, it is

69. Jules Marsan, *Théâtre d'hier et d'aujourd'hui* (Paris: Editions des Cahiers Libres, 1926), 259.

70. François Mauriac, *"La Galerie des glaces; Chacun sa vérité," Nouvelle revue française,* XXIV (January 1, 1925), 84.

71. William Speth, "La Saison 1924-25," *Revue mondiale,* CLXVI (August 1, 1925), 304.

72. Benjamin Cremiéux, "Chronique dramatique," *Nouvelle revue française,* XXVII (August 1, 1926), 235.

73. Jean-Richard Bloch, *Destin du théâtre,* (Paris: Librairie Gallimard, Editions de la Nouvelle Revue Française, 1930), 85-86.

74. Alfred Mortier, *Quinze Ans de théâtre (1917-1932)* (Paris: Albert Messein, Editeur, 1933), 356.

only to comfort her parents or to help France win the First World War.[75] Shaw's break with the old tradition constituted his innovation.

Thus, the characteristically Shavian traits of humor, fantasy, and anachronism account for the play's lasting influence in France. As has been seen, these were not precisely the features of *Saint Joan* which produced its success with the public and with most of the critics. The conventional elements of the play, the pathetic martyrdom of Joan, explain the drama's great appeal in the Pitoëffs' performance, but the more indirect and enduring effect on the French drama and on French dramatists lies in Shaw's creation of a new type of historical drama based on a comic view of human nature.

75. Pierson, 19-22.

XXIII/A People's Heroine

Crime is the basis of a series of Shaw's dramas, but not the crime of an individual before society and not that of an individual before mankind. Instead it is "society's crime," as the dramatist himself has put it. This crime of society toward an individual or toward mankind is evidenced especially in *Saint Joan* and his plays written after the First World War. Of course Shaw did not limit himself to subjects of startling social strength. He was also interested in the romantic delusions of his time, and the struggle against these illusions. But the crimes of society in relation to the individual or mankind stood in the center of his best and most widely known dramas. If Shaw's hero even dies, and that happens very seldom, as in *The Doctor's Dilemma* or later in *Saint Joan*, the reason for the hero's death is not a personal clash with some concrete antagonist, but with a wider and deeper general law of life.

Thus the theme of justice all the more actively enters into the dramatic work of Shaw. True, it is never the conventional theme of justice; in several plays, as in the epilogue of *Saint Joan*, or the conclusion of *The Simpleton of the Unexpected Isles*, there appears a tragic or tragifarcical image of justice. Almost without exception the plays written after World War I concern some concept of justice, and each play reflects the intention of the author to expose his ideas on justice in differing ways to the judgment of the audience. So the audience at a debate is changed—literally in *Joan*—into an audience in a courtroom, and the action itself reminds us of a judicial process.

A. Obraztsova, *Dramatturgicheskii Metod Bernarda Shou,* (Moscow, 1965). Trans. by Kaaren Page and adapted by the editor from pp. 35–38, 78, 130, 140–46, 209–10, 241–74.

When Shaw went into history for his plays he did so for the sake of taking his heroes out of the usual, everyday situations of capitalist reality yet accommodating them within a perfectly workable and contemporary atmosphere of sharp political disputes. Joan was thus put to death because of "political necessity." Through her, Shaw summed up the results of his many years of reflection about a particular type of realist, creating the tragic figure of a realist-hero in the form of a folk heroine and incorporating in her his own enormous faith in the reason and strength of man, while honestly recognizing that what even the strongest and most intelligent person can do alone is insufficient in order to change society. For Joan there could not have been another end than public burning.

Majestically and mightily, yet with special austerity and simplicity, Shaw expressed his faith in man's reason in the character of Joan, who is free from all the illusions that dominate society. Such freedom from illusions does not necessarily come only with age. Although Shaw's Caesar was past fifty, Joan had not even reached twenty when she was put to death. As Shaw wrote in his preface to the play, "At eighteen Joan's pretensions were beyond those of the proudest Pope or the haughtiest emperor.... She lectured, talked down, and overruled statesmen and prelates. She poohpoohed the plans of generals, leading their troops to victory on plans of her own. She had an unbounded and quite unconcealed contempt for official opinion, judgment, and authority, and for War Office tactics and strategy."

Imagination, and reason free from illusions, merge in the character of Joan. In the stage direction anticipating her first appearance Shaw writes of an "ablebodied country girl . . . very confident, very appealing, very hard to resist." The strength of Joan is the strength of the people. "I am only a poor country girl," she tells the Dauphin Charles; "I know the people: the real people that make thy bread for thee." After the scene in Rheims Cathedral, Joan announces to the King and Archbishop, "I will go out now to the common people, and let the love in their eyes comfort me for the hate in yours. You will all be glad to see me burn; but if I go through the fire I shall go through it to their hearts for ever and ever." And ringed by judges in the last hours of her life Joan observes, "If we were as simple in the village as you are in your courts and palaces, there would soon be no wheat to make bread for you."

Joan's common sense is her God, only she did not know it: the right decisions quickly surfaced, but in her confession she was ready to attribute them to private voices, about which Shaw remarks in his preface, "Joan must be judged a sane woman in spite of her voices because they never gave her any advice that might not have come to her from her mother wit exactly as gravitation came to Newton." What is thus specially important is that Joan's reason is also the mind of the people.

Because he had been considering for many years the possibilities and limits of human reason, Shaw felt a moral responsibility to depict in the character of the hero-realist a people's hero, to show her strength as the strength of the people, and her reason as the reason of the people. This was noteworthy. Joan is a people's heroine, but also in a special sense Shaw's heroine. Images of ordinary people interested Shaw very little in his plays. Rather, individuals began to interest him only after they broke through from the bottom to a greater or lesser height; and some characters in his plays already led a secure life as well-to-do people, as with Sartorius in *Widowers' Houses,* Undershaft in *Major Barbara* and Mrs. Warren. The author had an attitude of contempt mixed with compassion toward the jobless and self-pitying Peter Shirley in *Major Barbara,* understanding the economic causes behind Shirley's humiliating position. Undershaft, however, despised the poverty he had once known, considering it a terrible crime. Shaw's constant reflection about the strength of man's reason, and his faith in it and hope for it in earlier plays, before *Saint Joan,* compelled Shaw to dwell on this theme—the common sense of the people, the innate temperance of the people (not bourgeois common sense or bourgeois temperance and prudence, but something completely opposite to them), the sharp wit of the people, and the humor of the people. In this sense the characters of Eliza Doolittle and her father in *Pygmalion* are notable.

The proximity of Joan to the people is relative. In his play Shaw does not make the people an active, real force, and here, as always, he does not believe in people as a creator of history. However Joan's common sense is not a peasant's reason but the collective wisdom of people, wisdom which is comprised in the understanding of people and their pain. None of Shaw's heroes does as much for the people—for life and society—as his Joan. She crowned the Dauphin Charles in Rheims and freed her country from the English. Everything she did was accomplished logically and prudently. But from the first her victories provoked organized hatred against her. In Shaw's preface he explains, "Now it is always hard for superior wits to understand the fury roused by their exposures of the stupidities of comparative dullards." From the very beginning the path of Joan is the difficult path of a realist. Every action, every step makes the bearers of officially accepted views furious. "Why do all these courtiers and knights and churchmen hate me? What have I done to them? I have asked nothing for myself except that my village shall not be taxed; for we cannot afford war taxes."

Joan's reason and imagination, as created by Shaw, are inseparable. Her thought develops in lofty poetical forms, and from the poetical forms Joan reaches logical conclusions. Her speech is simple, expressive, and to the point. Yet there are many analogies between her attitudes and Caesar's freedom from convention, from false conceptions of honor and benevolence, and from self-sacrifice and self-denial. Shaw's Joan, despite her death, is extremely far from sacrificing herself, or even from understanding what it means.

Also, nothing human is unnatural to her. In this she is almost as a child. As Dunois relates, when she is wounded in the throat near Orleans, she cries in pain as children do, and continues to fight. Joan is also both child and woman. "I wish you were one of the village babies," she tells Dunois, because "I could nurse you for a while." She could bring up many children, this strong country girl Shaw depicts. But he could not permit her any tenderness of heart toward men, any deviation from the main theme of the play.

The humanism of Shaw's Joan is real and elevated. Shaw distinguishes her from all previous literary depictions of Joan for she is endowed with military and political genius to a greater degree than her literary predecessors, yet not once does she herself kill anyone on the stage or off. Her care about people is like Caesar's self-confidence prompting him to do what he must. "Minding your own business," Joan says to the Dauphin the first time she meets him, "is like minding your own body: it's the shortest way to make yourself sick." She even dies at

the stake worrying about others, compelling Ladvenu to acknowledge
to Warwick, "My Lord: a girl who could think of another's danger in
such a moment was not inspired by the devil."

The theme of the loneliness of the hero-figure appears almost for the
first time in Shaw in the character of Joan. The ardent, highly ideologi-
cal public debates, so tenacious and original in Shaw, usually united the
heroes of his plays with their antagonists so that loneliness seems in
effect impossible. Caesar did not know an equal, but he was not alone.
Shaw's Joan also did not have an equal. But she was alone. The
irreparable, catastrophic loneliness of Joan contributed to her tragic
experience.

The play is the tragedy and failure of a hero-realist. Joan, as a matter
of fact, is tragically cut off from her people. The masses in *Saint Joan*
are Philistines, not able to understand a lonely realist. Even the soldier
who gave Joan a cross, two sticks bound together, when she stood at
the burning stake, did not understand her. Even the good-hearted
Dunois did not understand her. (But it is necessary to mention that
Shaw's thinking, as always, was dialectic: if someone could do something for Joan at the last minute, then it would be the simple English
soldier, a debauchee by appearances and mannerisms, who in all his life
had accomplished only a single good deed. It was this cross of sticks
that Joan hid on her breast, standing in the bonfire, and the homemade
cross burned with her.) Shaw's tragic conclusion is strict. "Yes, I am
alone on earth," says Joan: "I will always be alone. . . . Do not think
you can frighten me by telling me that I am alone. France is alone; and
God is alone; and what is my loneliness before the loneliness of my
country and my God?"

Did Shaw himself believe so fully as before, having experienced a
world war, that a sane, sober, illusion-free personality could accomplish
something alone in contemporary society? His works demonstrate that
having overcome his own bourgeois democracy, he was inclined to
oppose the dictatorship of personality.[1] His Joan was the acme in the
evolution of the realist character, but his search in this direction,
although it continued further, evidently went into a slump. On the

1. This was apparently written at the time of post-Stalin emphasis upon the evil of
the "cult of personality." [Editor's note]

medieval stake burned the playwright's ideal heroine, his most cherished dream. The artist in Shaw had enough courage to throw into the bonfire his background of Fabian socialism, and he foresaw to the end how from his ideal nothing would remain except the ashes.

The tragedy of Joan is not so much her being burned alive. The tragedy above all is the impossibility of her resurrection either twenty-five years after her death or five hundred years later. Her canonization in 1920 is tragically absurd. However much her former enemies and friends vied with each other in glorifying her (in Shaw's epilogue), no one wants Joan to return to earth. "Forgive us, Joan," apologizes Dunois: "we are not yet good enough for you." Cauchon explains, "The heretic is always better dead. And mortal eyes cannot distinguish the saint from the heretic." Warwick insists that although all sincerely regret their mistake regarding her, "political necessities, though occasionally erroneous, are still imperative." The spokesman for Vatican views, appearing in the year 1920 to report Joan's elevation to sainthood, is equally adamant, telling her, "The possibility of your resurrection was not contemplated in the recent proceedings for your canonization."

Alone, Joan asks, "O God that madest this beautiful earth, when will it be ready to receive Thy saints? How long, O Lord, how long?" In the Europe of the year of Joan's canonization, which was covered with blood from a world war, yet was preparing for the march against the land of the Soviets, which had just come into existence, there was no place for a heroine who expressed the heart and reason of a people. In a series of prefatory notes to the play, Shaw directly linked what is happening in the play with the present, heading several sections "Credulity, Modern and Medieval," "Toleration, Modern and Medieval," and "Cruelty, Modern and Medieval." Like Brecht's *Mother Courage,* Shaw focused the attention of his contemporaries upon the tragic clash of man with reality in the form of the conventional laws of development of capitalist society.

Shaw's realist heroes seldom died; they remained living to energetically continue the struggle with life. Only once, in *Joan,* did he aim at the height of true poetic tragedy. Western theatre criticism sometimes classifies as tragedy the work of dramatists who depict life that is inconsolable and sometimes denies the possibility of the existence of a modern tragic play. "Tragedy died," maintains John Gassner in his book *The Theatre in Our Times,* although he calls *Saint Joan* and several other modern works tragedies. Eric Bentley in *The Playwright as Thinker* indicates two directions in the development of twentieth century tragedy—"tragedy in modern dress" and "tragedy in the dress of fantasy." *Saint Joan* is contemporary tragedy in yet another sense, for it summarizes the tragic experience of the lives of the European peoples in the tragic previous decade. The critics were puzzled, calling it a "play of ideas," and "comedy of ideas," a "gloomy comedy." Shaw wrote simply that it was a chronicle. But the play is a tragedy, an historical tragedy.

Nowhere did Shaw have such a compulsion toward the reconstruction of actual events as he did in *Saint Joan.* However he did not intend to charm his audiences with battle scenes, or think to show the coronation of the king or the burning of Joan. The "medieval air" in the play is severe; all the action is austere and handled with restraint. In the early scenes specific expectations concerning justice are set forth. From the very beginning the action proceeds steadily to the courtroom session where the outcome has been decided beforehand. The atmosphere of hatred encircling the heroine thickens; the ring of enemies tightens all the more. The atmosphere of the unjust court darkens. Yet if her judges had been subjectively unjust and dishonest, the fate of Joan would not have been tragic. The true tragedy of Joan is that honest judges tried her and the grave crime committed by them was not the result of individual villainous acts. The crimes were the ideas which they defended and in which they piously believed. The hostile ring tightening around Joan in Shaw's play is a ring of hostile ideas. For Shaw wrote *Saint Joan* not solely to show how a heroine of the French people was tried, and to show the inevitability of her path to the bonfire. He also created his courtroom scene in order to explain the thinking of similar courts in all times up to the era in which the play was written.

Shaw's Joan, in even greater measure than her literary predecessors, belongs to the playwright's own time, with all its solvable and insoluble problems. The allusions to the world war are a constant undercurrent in preface and play. The mockery over contemporary English militarism is relatively subdued. "Have you ever seen English soldiers fighting?" Robert de Baudricourt asks Joan in the first scene. "Have you ever seem them plundering, burning, turning the countryside into a desert?" Later the Earl of Warwick apologizes for seeming "to take the [proposed] burning of this poor girl too lightly. When one has seen whole countrysides burnt over and over again as mere items in military routine, one has to grow a very thick skin. Otherwise, one might go mad. . . ." Here Shaw resorts to the subtle comparison of the medieval epoch with the contemporary one: more sparingly than elsewhere in his historical plays (as in *Caesar and Cleopatra*) does he make use of the method of direct teasing of his contemporaries. But in the preface to the play the author is more open in his comparisons. He compares the process of justice with respect to Joan with the trial and condemnation of nurse Edith Cabell in a German court and with that of [Irish rebel] Roger Casement in an English court. (Edith Cabell dared to declare, "Patriotism is not enough.") The basic method by which Shaw relates history to the present in *Saint Joan*, however, is that he forces her to directly step into 1920 to realize that there is still no place for her. History openly encroaches upon the present.

Saint Joan is the most Shakespearean play of Shaw's in the sense of its wide historical background. The combination of various human types here is especially whimsical yet complex. In his dramatic art Shaw formulated a method of characterization that is opposite to the principles he saw operative in Shakespeare. Shakespeare's characters to Shaw were individuals ungoverned by forces beyond them, "completely satisfied that if they would only to their own selves be true they could not then be false to any man . . . as if they were beings in the air, without any public responsibilities of any kind. All Shakespeare's characters are so: that is why they seem natural to our middle classes, who are comfortable and irresponsible at other people's expense, and are neither ashamed of that condition nor even conscious of it." Shaw therefore provided his audiences with "not only the visible and human puppets, but the Church, the Inquisition, the Feudal System, with divine inspiration always beating against their too-inelastic limits: all the more terrible in their dramatic force than any of the little mortal figures clanking about in plate armor or moving silently in the frocks and hoods of the order of St Dominic." There is a complex junction of history and the present, owed greatly to Shaw's ability to combine

living characteristics with the functions of orators, polemicists and
irreconcilable antagonists in a huge debate. In bitter skirmishes they
oppose not only simple ideas, but express the various nuances of these
ideas. Every idea appears to be expressed by various sides, in all its
aspects.

The French royal court is represented in farcical, buffoon-like tones.
Dauphin Charles dresses in such rags that he is a match for a country
beggar. All shout at him. All scheme against each other. The satirical
intonation of the play changes when the author passes on to an outline
of the judges of Joan. Satire becomes severe and rigid. It acquires an
epochal character. The shapes of Joan's enemies and judges are openly
symbolic. Yet the author explains in his preface that he would have to
make a twentieth century audience "conscious of an epoch fundamentally different from its own" by making his characters intelligible to
themselves although they were as unconscious of the peculiarities of
their time "as of the atomic formula of the air they breathed." Shaw
keeps his promise.

Before the Church and the Law appears Shaw's people's heroine.
Their solid, inexorable strength opposes the heroine although her
judges could argue with each other and even quarrel among themselves. The Church's judges condemn Joan because she placed her
country over the holy Catholic Church, because she encroached on the
Church's authority and might, and because she saw God herself and no
one came between her and God. To Cauchon she is a heretic. And her
heresy was dangerous because she could enthrall every nation in
the direction of national independence and away from obedience to the
dogmas of religion. The worst would be if the people escape from the
influence of the holy Church. And this is fully possible because Joan
embodies the wisdom and genius of the people and she is a natural part
of the people. Secular interests oppose Joan because she wants to make
the king a sole and absolute autocrat [as opposed to direction from his
nobles], and that thought almost drove even the king himself out of his
wits. Warwick rules effectively, as he explains, "only as long as the
people follow their feudal lords, and know the king only as a travelling
show, owning nothing but the highway that belongs to everybody." So
the real state of affairs beneath the violent struggle of the Law and the
Church with Joan was their fear of losing their influence over the

people. The tragedy of Joan was an epochal unresolved tragedy of the people. Two powerful forces—the Church and the Law—crushed Shaw's heroine.

Medieval justice proved specially significant in the perspective of the situation of postwar Europe. The judgment upon Joan reflected the fear always experienced by the Church and the secular power, for they are always being tested by the people. Did Joan die? Could she die? "She is more alive than you, old man," says the Executioner to the priest, de Stogumber, in Shaw's epilogue. "She is up and alive everywhere."

XXIV/Bernard Shaw's Other Saint Joan

Had Lawrence of Arabia—of all people—anything to do with Bernard Shaw's conception of his Saint Joan? It seems, on the surface, hardly likely, but nevertheless a study of the record brings out some remarkable relationships. Some plays appear the product of a flash of inspiration; others—Shaw's *Saint Joan* is one of the great modern examples— have had gestation periods of a decade or more, awaiting that incident or experience which triggers them into birth. *Saint Joan's* conception can be traced at least as far back as a visit Shaw made in 1913 to what he called "the Joan of Arc" country. From Orleans he wrote a series of picture postcards to Mrs. Patrick Campbell (who would shortly become his Eliza in *Pygmalion*). On the back of one concerning Joan he prophesied:

> I shall do a Joan play some day, beginning with the sweeping up of the cinders and orange peel *after* her martyrdom, and going on with Joan's arrival in heaven. I should have God about to damn the English for their share in her betrayal and Joan producing an end of burnt stick in arrest of Judgment. "What's that? Is it one of the faggots?" asks God. "No," says Joan "it's what is left of the two sticks a common English soldier tied together and gave me as I went to the stake; for they wouldn't even give me a crucifix; and you cannot damn the common people of England, represented by that soldier because a poor cowardly riff raff of barons and bishops were too futile to resist the devil."

> That soldier is the only redeeming figure in the whole business. English literature must be saved (by an Irishman, as usual) from the disgrace of having nothing to show concerning Joan except the piffling libel in Henry

South Atlantic Quarterly, LXIV (Spring, 1965), 194-205.

VI, which reminds me that one of my scenes will be Voltaire and Shakespear running down bye streets in heaven to avoid meeting Joan. . . .[1]

Exactly ten years later, Shaw was writing a Saint Joan play which did include—as a wry epilogue—one of the scenes he had described on the picture-postcard. But, according to well-authenticated legend, it took enormous prodding from his wife, and from his friend Sydney Cockerell, to get him to begin. They suggested the subject, offered him books about it, and left them lying conspicuously about the house until he actually began work on the play. However true, the story overlooks the fact that until the well-publicized canonization of Joan took place at St. Peter's in Rome on May 16, 1920, Shaw's memory could not have been effectively jogged by any number of well-placed books into the shaping of the wry epilogue upon which the play is built. Further overlooked is another well-placed book, and the ramifications of a new Shavian friendship based upon it, begun in 1922. To T.E. Lawrence, Shaw wrote late that year, " . . . perhaps I shall put you into a play, if my playwriting days are not over." Shaw could not have realized then how soon he was going to put Lawrence in a play, or write any play at all, for at sixty-six he felt written-out, barren of new inspiration.

As I have described in *Private Shaw and Public Shaw* (New York and London, 1963), ex-Colonel Lawrence became a close friend—almost surrogate son—and soon not only offered the Shaws the unpublished chronicle of his desert campaigns to read (and later to edit for him), but took the Shaw's name on joining the Army as a private in March, 1923. Thus as G.B.S. began researching and drafting his stage chronicle of a military commander even more unorthodox than Lawrence, he had at his elbow Lawrence's *Seven Pillars of Wisdom,* in many striking ways the chronicle of a modern Joan. The coincidence may have been of vital importance to the play.

Visitors to Ayot St. Lawrence during 1923—the year in which G.B.S. began and completed *Joan*—usually were treated to an admiring display of, and lecture on, Lawrence's epic, and the more customary reading of a fragment from the current Shavian work-in-progress. Sidney and Beatrice Webb, for example, were accorded the dual honor,

1. Shaw to Mrs. Campbell, September 8, 1913, in Alan Dent (ed), *Bernard Shaw and Mrs. Patrick Campbell: Their Correspondence* (New York, 1952), 163.

and Beatrice duly recorded the episode in her diary. Meanwhile, Shaw, busy with preliminary reading and planning of *Saint Joan,* had little chance to finish *Seven Pillars* himself. That his enthusiasm for the book survived both sporadic reading and Charlotte's missionary zeal for it is a key to the playwright's real feelings about the literary merits of Lawrence's book. He took it in brief nightly stints when he was at Ayot that winter and spring, for the Oxford edition of the book (five copies, set in newspaper type) was too massive to be regularly carried about for reading in railway carriages (a favorite practice of Shaw's). By mid-April, just as he began the actual writing of *Saint Joan,* he still had forty pages of *Seven Pillars* to go, but was convinced, even apart from his wife's panegyrics, that Lawrence had written one of the era's great books. Sydney Cockerell, patiently waiting to read the Shaw copy, had to be put off by a G.B.S. note that the book had to be finished to the last morsel before it could be released.

In May, Lady Gregory, Yeats's great friend, arrived for a stay with the Shaws and carefully noted all the details in her diary. They provide a most important contemporary link between the personality of Lawrence and Shaw's conception of Joan:

> *May 19, 1923.* Came down to Ayot by train. . . .
> G.B.S. drove me home and talked of his Joan of Arc play. He has not read Mark Twain, is afraid of being influenced by him. He has read a little of Anatole France and is reading the evidence at the trial, it was published some years ago. He does not idealise her as Mark does, and defends the Church, "it didn't torture her." I think there will be something good about the English soldiers. He tells me that Lawrence, who fought in Mesopotamia, had been to see him, is an extraordinary man, very small, living as a private in the army, having resigned his command, and has written a wonderful book, has had five copies linotyped, and lent him one. "It will be one of the great books of the world. He describes every blade of grass and flower and noxious insect, and all the fighting and the terrible crimes of the Turks and the terrible vengeance he and his men took on them. He has not a religious mission like Gordon but must have a touch of his nature. His brother is a missionary in China, or wants to be one, and his mother has the same desire." He thinks (G.B.S. hears) that all his family will die out because they are all mad.

> *May 20, 1923.* He showed me in the evening this book, and I read a few sentences and said, "It seems as good as Doughty," and G.B.S. said, "Lawrence is a great admirer of Doughty." This probably gives him his style.
> G.B.S. has been working at Joan without talking [further] about it. . . .

G.B.S. says he chose Joan of Arc because of Bernhardt and others having played so many parts turning on sexual attraction, he wanted to give Joan as a heroine absolutely without that side. . . .

I am reading the Lawrence book, it is enthralling, each sentence rich and complete.

Charlotte says Lawrence was a Don at Cambridge. . . .

He had come to lunch with the Shaws while (as he still is) a private, but dressed extremely well, and although he said that a couple of weeks ago he had been washing plates for the sergeants' mess, she could hardly believe it because his hands were so well cared for. He was charming, but one hears of his thrusting away approaches of friendship with some rudeness. . . .

May 21, 1923. We have been to Cambridge. . . . Cockerell met us at the Fitzwilliam Museum. . . .

Then we had lunch at "The Bull," ordered by G.B.S. . . . There was a good deal of talk of Lawrence and his book. Cockerell says it (the book) is to be kept secret, but G.B.S. says, "When Lawrence gets into a secret place it is in the limelight. If he hides in a quarry, he puts red flags all around."[2]

While G.B.S. was attempting to pull strings in Whitehall to get Lawrence—Private Shaw—pensioned out of the army, he was completing *Joan,* finally writing on August 27 to the young American expatriate, Molly Tompkins, "Saint Joan is finished (except for polishing): a magnificent play,—and I thought I should never write another after Methuselah! I am certainly a wonderful man; but then historical plays hardly count: the material is readymade." By September, 1923, only the arrangement of the stage business remained to be done, and by early October he was staying with Barry Jackson at Birmingham, planning for rehearsals of the new play early in the following year.

As Shaw researched, plotted, and wrote *Saint Joan,* he may have sensed the uncanny resemblance which the work in progress (however much a religious play) bore to the book at his elbow—*Seven Pillars*—and its enigmatic author. Whether the coincidences helped shape the play and its preface can only be surmised, but striking parallels *are* there and perhaps represent Shavian perspectives upon both the legendary Maid and the living legend of the ascetic former knight of the desert. As Shaw lived with the records and chronicles of one, and with the chronicle and person of the other, their figures seem in many ways to have merged into a single image, reinforcing for the playwright the timelessness of Joan's experience: the experience of having the spirit

2. Lennox Robinson (ed), *Lady Gregory's Journals* (New York, 1946), 192, 193-94.

within—adventurous, imaginative, ascetic, contemplative—made use of
and then destroyed by a world unready for idealism except as an
instrument to serve the purpose of political realities.

The great Dutch medieval historian Huizinga[3] has described Joan
from contemporary details—the scanty data preserved by her cohorts,
who were little interested in personal descriptions. These were documents Shaw read in researching *Joan*. Much of the picture of the Maid
formed by her contemporaries strikingly fits Lawrence—Joan's short-
ness of stature, her eating and drinking sparingly, her avoidance of
physical contact and generally asexual behavior, her combination of the
laconic with the lighthearted, her "superior, irresistible, and infectious
bravery."[4] Even her delight in beautiful horses and armor, and the rich
raiment she wore, which offended Church authorities, can be visualized
in the contemporary terms of Lawrence's fascination with the flowing
dress and ornaments of an Arab sheik—which scandalized other English officers—and (in the days G.B.S. knew him) his infatuation with
his mechanical steed, a Brough motorcycle, which T.E. named as would
a medieval knight his charger.

In many cases, except for the personal pronoun, it would be difficult
to separate the personalities of these two figures, medieval and modern,
with their immense appetites for glory, their abilities to put people in
their pockets, their knack for unconventional strategy unconventionally
set forth. "She lectured, talked down and overruled the plans of generals, leading troops to victory on plans of her own," Shaw wrote in his
preface to the play. "She had an unbounded and quite unconcealed
contempt for official opinion, judgment, and authority, and for War
Office tactics and strategy. . . . There were only two opinions about her.
One was that she was miraculous: the other that she was unbearable."
Observers and associates might have also said of Joan what John Buchan did about Lawrence, and what G.B.S. certainly saw: "His qualities lacked integration. He had moods of vanity and moods of abase-
ment; immense self-confidence and immense diffidence."

In both cases we find the campaign's central figure in the grip of a

---

3. Johan Huizinga, *Men and Ideas* (New York, 1959), esp. pp. 218-19.
4. Shaw, Preface to *Saint Joan*.

nationalistic impulse to create a unified state from a feudal order, and
to set a monarch representative of that unity upon the throne of the
nation-state. Joan's France under the Dauphin (later Charles VII) may
have had as its contemporary parallel Lawrence's more naïve dream,
dashed at Versailles, of a Pan-Arabian kingdom under Feisal.

By the time Shaw had begun *Saint Joan,* T.E. had already ascetically
retired to his hoped-for obscurity in the ranks, once saying of himself in
a letter to Lionel Curtis in May, 1923, when he was still attempting to
adjust to Tank Corps life, that his was a strange form of lay monasti-
cism:

> I want to stay here till it no longer hurts me: till the burnt child no longer
> feels the fire. . . . One used to think that such frames of mind would have
> perished with the age of religion: and yet here they rise up, purely secular.
> It's a lurid flash into the Nitrian desert: almost seems to strip the sainthood
> from Anthony. How about Teresa?[5]

What might Joan have done, had she lived? In his Preface, dated
May, 1924, Shaw pondered, "Had she escaped she would probably
have fought on until the English were gone, and then had to shake the
dust of the court off her feet, and retire to Domremy. . . ." We may
ponder further that Joan, "a young girl, pious and chaste; [whose] . . .
excesses have been excesses of religion and charity and not of worldliness and wantonness"—as the Inquisitor points out in the play's trial
scene—might have found her postwar world depressing and unsatisfy-
ing and sought fulfillment instead with the walls of a convent, a medieval equivalent, perhaps, to Private Shaw's refuge. In 1927, quoting an
anecdote about Marshal Foch, G.B.S. wrote that Lawrence's self-im-
posed retirement after the First World War saved England a delicate
problem—the question of the young colonel's future. The Marshal, the
story went, was asked how Napoleon would have fought the war.
"Superbly," he said; "but what the devil should we have done with him
afterwards?" Flatteringly equating Lawrence's achievement with Napoleon's, Shaw added, "The Prince of Damascus solved the problem for

5. Lawrence to Lionel Curtis, 14 May 1923, in David Garnett (ed.), *The Letters of
T. E. Lawrence* (London, 1938), 416.

Britannia. He simply walked away and became a nobody again under another name."[6]

It is remarkable that Shaw, several years after connecting the Foch anecdote to Lawrence's situation, reapplied it to St. Joan. The occasion then was a B.B.C. radio talk delivered on the five-hundredth anniversary of the burning of Joan at the stake, May 30, 1931. The question of what is to be done with them after their period of accomplishment, Shaw pointed out, arises with many people of extraordinary ability. He went on to pick a case from the newspapers—that of Leon Trotsky. Stalin's former rival—a civilian whose military exploits from his railway car headquarters, Shaw thought, rivaled those of history's great commanders—was then in precarious exile in Turkey. There were many reasons why, in 1931—if the omission from the anecdote were a conscious one on Shaw's part—it were best for him to leave Lawrence (for the moment) publicly unmentioned. Still, interestingly enough, we sense a labyrinth of relationships in Shaw's mind in the St. Joan anniversary talk, for G.B.S. had just completed the section of his play *Too True to Be Good*, in which T.E. is affectionately caricatured as the infuriatingly undisciplined military genius, Private Napoleon Alexander *Trotsky* Meek.

"The Conflict between Genius and Discipline" is the title of one section of Shaw's Preface to *Saint Joan*. In it Shaw discussed the charismatic quality of the Maid's personality:

> Outside the farm she had no authority, no prestige, no claim to the smallest deference. Yet she ordered everybody about her from her uncle to the king, the archbishop, and the military General Staff. Her uncle obeyed her like a sheep, and took her to the castle of the local commander, who, on being ordered about, tried to assert himself, but soon collapsed and obeyed. And so on up to the king.

Lawrence, too, Shaw knew, had his equivalents to Bertrand de Poulengy and Jean de Metz, as well as to Joan's General Staff. A fellow officer in the Middle East, John Buchan (Lord Tweedsmuir), called Lawrence the only authentic genius he ever knew and confided, "I am not a very tractable person or much of a heroworshipper, but I could

---

6. Shaw, Preface to the *Exhibition Catalogue—Catalogue of an Exhibition of Paintings, Pastels, Drawings and Woodcuts Illustrating Col. T. E. Lawrence's book Seven Pillars of Wisdom.*

have followed Lawrence over the edge of the world." There was no question about the compelling power of T.E.'s wartime leadership, however unmilitary and informal his Arabian operations were. Still his irregular status needed administrative sanction, even if ex post facto. G.B.S. embellished the facts slightly: "As to the British Army, its feelings when, after having to make Lawrence a colonel rather than be ordered about by a nobody, it found him leading his hosts to battle on camel-back in a picturesque Arab costume, can be more easily imagined in messrooms than described by me. Even the camel did not get its regulation meals."[7]

Not only was Lawrence "unbearably irritating" to his military superiors (to quote again from Shaw's prefatory comments about Joan), but was regarded "as a liar and impostor." Shaw went on in language strikingly applicable as well to Lawrence:

> It is hard to conceive anything more infuriating to a statesman or military commander, or to a court favorite, than to be overruled at every turn, or to be robbed of the ear of the reigning sovereign, by an impudent young upstart. . . . Not only were the envy, snobbery, and competitive ambition of the baser natures exacerbated by Joan's success, but among the friendly ones that were clever enough to be critical, a quite reasonable scepticism and mistrust of her ability, founded on a fair observation of her obvious [military] ignorance and temerity, were at work against her. . . . she must have seemed, to all who were not infatuated by her, so insufferable that nothing but an unbroken chain of overwhelming successes in the military and political field could have saved her. . . .

His charisma even manifested itself regularly during T.E.'s final incarnation as "Shaw," when he was in a rank technically remote from command level. An incident of 1929, recorded by Mrs. Clare Sydney Smith, wife of Lawrence's commanding officer then, indicates as much. Flight-Lieutenant Brecky, who was in charge of R.A.F. marine craft at the Calshot station, and Mr. Robertson, of the Air Ministry's Press Section, had gone down to the slipway, discovering there a corporal transmitting some orders about a boat. "Who gave you those orders?" the officer inquired.

"Mr. Shaw, sir."

"Who is Mr. Shaw?"

7. *Ibid.*

"Well, sir, Aircraftman Shaw."

"And why should you, a corporal, take orders from an aircraftman?"

"Well, sir, it seemed perfectly natural to take orders from Mr. Shaw."[8]

Mrs. Smith drew from the incident what she considered a key to T.E.'s "unconscious power of leadership," referring to Chapter XXV of *Seven Pillars*. There Lawrence had written,

> . . . the work suffered by the creation of . . . a bar between the leaders and men. Among the Arabs there were not distinctions, traditional or natural, except the unconscious power given a famous sheikh by virtue of his accomplishment; and they taught me that no man could be their leader except he ate the ranks' food, lived level with them, and yet appeared better in himself.

It is unlikely that these lines escaped G.B.S. in 1923. Shaw's Joan, perhaps out of the same instinctive power of leadership, insists (as play and Preface point out) on having a soldier's dress and arms, horse and equipment, and on treating her escort of soldiers as comrades, sleeping side by side with them on the floor at night as if there were no difference of sex (or rank) between them. Yet both youthful warriors, medieval saint and medieval scholar, were essentially unmilitary individuals—novices at war yet in love with its trappings and its heady thrills. To the village girl whose sole military experience has been to see the soldiers pass by, Dunois comments, "You have the makings of a soldier in you. You are in love with war." So too, in 1916, was the young archeology student from Oxford.

How both Joan of Arc and Lawrence of Arabia were able to triumph as military tacticians has puzzled historians and encouraged skeptics. And as Shaw realized about Joan, as early as her rehabilitation trial and for centuries thereafter, there were evasive answers to questions about the quality of her military genius and its actual tactical effect: whether her role was more moral and emotional than strategic, arising from the example of her undoubted courage. G. B. S. assumed that both warriors had real military skill. The facts of accomplishment and the testimony of comrades-in-arms were both plentiful. The Duke of Alençon had praised Joan, Shaw read, as being "in war . . . very expert, whether to

8. Clare Smith, *The Golden Reign* (London, 1940), 109.

carry a lance, to assemble an army, to order a battle, or to dispose artillery." But Shaw knew that neither Joan nor Lawrence needed, in the relatively uncomplicated military situations of Joan's day or the primitive conditions which were Lawrence's stage, more than a pick-up knowledge of the simple weaponry, penetrating common sense, spectacular courage, and a charismatic personality. Lawrence's war, E. M. Forster suggested in a review of *Seven Pillars,* was "probably the last of the picturesque wars . . . waged under archaistic conditions . . . the last effort of the war-god before he laid down his godhead and turned chemist."[9]

What was quite apparent to those as close to Lawrence as was Shaw, was that the reports about his disinterest in such conventionalities of living as love and marriage were borne out by his choice of friends and his monastic barracks life as much as by his letters. The "conflict of sex," as Shaw put it in his description of Joan, was given little encouragement to manifest itself:

> The evident truth [Shaw wrote of Joan] is that like most women of her hardy managing type she seemed neutral in the conflict of sex because men were much too afraid of her to fall in love with her. She herself was not sexless: in spite of the virginity she had vowed up to a point, and preserved to her death, she never excluded the possibility of marriage for herself. But marriage, with its preliminary of the attraction, pursuit, and capture of a husband, was not her business: she had something else to do.

Shaw comprehended Lawrence's design for living only in part—the part represented by what Shaw called moral passion in an individual, such as he saw in Joan. This kind of hero does not control his passions by any rational process. His physical passions are overwhelmed by a greater passion, the passion of virtue, which is a passion of the mind. For Shaw, thought is a passion, as he demonstrated to his own satisfaction in many of his later plays, from *Back to Methuselah* (completed shortly before Shaw met Lawrence) to the play of Shaw's ninety-third year, *Farfetched Fables.* It is at the close of the *Fables* that Raphael insists that there are passions far more exciting than the physical ones: "On the contrary: intellectual passion, mathematical passion, passion for discovery and exploration: the mightiest of all passions." To Shaw's

---

9. E. M. Forster, *Abinger Harvest* (New York, 1936), 146.

discomfort, however, he sensed in another part of Lawrence's design—
his choice of the ranks—a quest for a living martyrdom rather than a
quest for an ascetic way of living. To Shaw martyrdom was

> a waste of vitality and a triumph of illusion over reality, since it produces a
> sort of hypnosis upon its witness. Men develop fixations upon the cross, the
> act of martyrdom itself, while doing their best to ignore the implications of
> the martyr's ethical conquest. As Joan remarks, "It is the memory and the
> salvation that sanctify the cross, not the cross that sanctifies the memory and
> the salavation. . . . I shall outlast the cross."[10]

A possible Shavian reflection of this attitude is the evidence that as
Shaw worked on *Saint Joan* he pressed his efforts—against Lawrence's
own wishes—to pension T.E. out of the service and into creative
literary work. The outcome was another of T.E.'s tactical successes.

There is even some internal evidence in *Saint Joan* that Lawrence or
his chronicle influenced some of the play's dialogue, particularly in the
fourth scene, in the exchange between Warwick and Cauchon. Cauchon paints Joan as a Mohammed, with her own collection of Arabs,
who follow her through force of her personality. "What did the camel
driver do at the beginning more than this shepherd girl is doing?" he
warns. Warwick, the Englishman, is unimpressed: "I am a soldier, not a
churchman. As a pilgrim I saw something of the Mahometans. They
were not so ill-bred as I had been led to believe. In some respects their
conduct compared favorably with ours." Cauchon, displeased, answers
sharply: "I have noticed this before. Men go to the East to convert the
infidels. And the infidels pervert them. The Crusader comes back more
than half a Saracen. Not to mention that all Englishmen are born
heretics."

It may not be so, but it is easy to imagine that the dominant metaphors of the dialogue were unlikely to have occurred to G.B.S. before
his friendship with the young man who wrote an Oxford thesis on
"Crusader Castles" and a personal memoir of his leadership of a motley
Arab camel corps, during which he described having discovered Arab
ethics as comparing favorably with those of his native England.

Although both Lawrence and Shaw enjoyed the discipline of sitting

10. R. F. Dietrich, "Shaw and the Passionate Mind," *The Shaw Review,* IV (May,
1961), 9.

for portraits and busts, and the reflected glory of looking at them, it is unlikely that either playwright or subject ever saw Lawrence of Arabia in the Joan of Arc which G.B.S. shaped. Shaw appears to have modeled Joan's superficial physical appearance after the woman who then managed the Fabian Society Summer Schools. When the play was published he inscribed her copy: "To Mary Hankinson, the only woman I know who does not believe that she is the model for Joan and the only woman who actually was." T.E. received several copies of the play over the years, the last inscribed "To Shaw from Shaw to replace many stolen copies until this, too, is stolen." An earlier one, which disappeared from T.E.'s barracks, had been signed, "To Pte. Shaw from Public Shaw." Had G.B.S. realized it, he might have written instead, "To Bernard Shaw's other Saint Joan."

 A. N. KAUL

XXV/Shaw's Joan: The Hero as Saint

Saint Joan (1923) is Shaw's best play if only in the sense that it is his one completely serious play, with all his characteristic wit and humor and freedom from humbug, but without any of that equally characteristic humbug of Shaw's own manufacture which he so often substituted in place of the humbug he exploded—without, that is, any of those intellectual sleights of hand, twists of argument, and promotion of novel theories which have the brave air of revelations that no one will believe, not even their author. *Saint Joan* is a serious play because in it the bourgeois artist and the Marxian student of political and social history can unite without difficulty, and Shaw is at one with himself. Or we can say, using Chesterton's two main terms for Shaw, that the Puritan and the Progressive can unite without one tugging at the sympathies in one direction and the other constantly nudging the intellect in another.

   Saint Joan can be read as a tragedy, although Shaw himself called it not a tragedy (as he did *The Doctor's Dilemma*) but only a "chronicle" play. But if it is a tragedy, it is the tragedy of a historical hero rather than a saint. Louis Martz discusses it as the latter in an essay entitled "The Saint as Tragic Hero: *Saint Joan* and *Murder in the Cathedral.*"[1]

Originally titled "George Bernard Shaw: From Anti-Romance to Pure Fantasy." Extracted from *The Action of English Comedy: Studies in the Encounter of Abstraction and Experience from Shakespeare to Shaw* (New Haven, 1970), 321-26. Retitled by the editor.

   1. *Tragic Themes in Western Literature,* ed. Cleanth Brooks, (New Haven, Yale University Press, 1955).

But this rather brilliant tour de force succeeds only at the cost of sacrificing altogether that historical dimension which is of no particular interest in Eliot's play but constitutes, it is worth insisting, the very life and substance of Shaw's. Shaw's Saint Joan is, indeed, less "The Saint as Hero" than "The Hero as Saint"—comparable, if a comparison must be made, to Shaw's own other historical heroes rather than to Eliot's Becket. The importance of a play's or a novel's historical theme should not be confused with the far less interesting question of its historicity, meaning the adequacy of historical research and the authenticity of each character, event, or statement that has gone into the work. Nor can Shaw's own observation which Martz cites—"I deal with all periods; but I never study any period but the present, which I have not yet mastered and never shall"—be construed as a denial of that importance.[2] It is not only that Shaw made this remark years before he wrote *Saint Joan,* but that there is no contradiction involved in recognizing the centrality of the play's historical theme and at the same time granting Shaw the claim that he never studied "any period but the present." For though there are many ways of studying a period, the historical or genetic is basic to them all. At least that was Shaw's own persuasion. And while none of his historical plays is an antiquarian piece, and all bear the burden, however large or slight, of contemporary issues, in *Saint Joan* he was doing nothing less than dramatizing the historical origin of the present period. Of course, he made Joan a nationalist, a Protestant, a champion of the individual conscience and the inner light, before either Protestantism or nationalism was formally inaugurated, and he knew exactly what he was doing. Without these things Joan's tale, to use his own words from the note in the program, "would be only a sensational tale of a girl who was burnt" while the "true tale of Saint Joan is a tale with a glorious ending."[3] For Shaw she stands for an early and divinely inspired heroine of the long crisis out of which was born a new culture—his own. He sees her as a historical hero all the more because she is the instrument of forces which she

2. For Shaw's remark, see Preface to *The Sanity of Art* (New York, B. R. Tucker, 1908), p. 5.
3. Archibald Henderson, *Bernard Shaw: Playboy and Prophet* (New York, Appleton-Century-Crofts, 1932), p. 546.

does not herself fully understand, except as her voices, but whose emergence she nevertheless both manifests and advances—for this is precisely what being a historical hero means.

Even that pride which is in a way the immediate cause of her personal defeat—as against her historical triumph—is not so much a personal failing of hers as again the manifestation of a general tendency. It is not the same thing as vanity, of which Joan has some ("the cloth of gold surcoat"), nor is it in the last analysis the traditional sin of pride. Of course, the Archbishop tells Joan that "you have stained yourself with the sin of pride. The old Greek tragedy is rising among us. It is the chastisement of hubris." But if Joan's pride can bear this traditional analogy, the play also defines it elsewhere as a new phenomenon, part of a larger force breaking out at several spots to challenge all traditional authority. It is that "pride and self-sufficiency" (as Brother Martin calls it at the trial) which makes the individual a threat as much to the power of the Catholic Church as to the interests of the feudal aristocracy, to Warwick as much as to Cauchon, as each of them realizes from his own side. The Archbishop himself, for all his traditional habits of thought, recognizes the far-reaching importance of what is being witnessed: "There is a new spirit rising in men: we are at the dawning of a wider epoch."

Thus Shaw is able not only to admire the bourgeois hero in Joan but to endorse her triumph without reservation. She is his perfect hero, representing as much the values he admired as the cause of historical progress which he championed—engaging, in short, all his serious but none of his frivolous interests. Indeed, of all his heroes her case calls least for Shaw's habitual hedging and dodging and special pleading, although it cannot be said that the habit has disappeared even here as completely as its cause. For instance, it is unfortunate that Shaw thought it necessary to underline the triumphant quality of Joan's tale, its glorious ending, by writing an Epilogue, which he not only wrote but defended against all objections. With its fantasy tableaux, its flip jokes, its common soldier (on a day's parole from Hell) railing against "kings and captains and bishops" and telling Joan that she has "as good a right to your notions as they have to theirs"—even with Joan's famous last cry: "How long, O Lord, how long?"—the Epilogue mostly brings back the Shaw so admirably absent from the play itself. It is Shaw's theme bereft of the historical sanction of its own time, and one is struck though not surprised by the uncertainties of tone and intellectual argument alike that accompany the shifting of the mental perspective to the present period. Of course, the Epilogue, being only an epilogue, does no damage; but it is worth insisting how much more effectively this same idea of future vindication is expressed within the play, especially at the very end when Warwick says: "I am informed that it is all over, Brother Martin," and Ladvenu, just back from the execution, replies: "We do not know, my lord. It may have only just begun." Warwick himself, thinking of what Ladvenu has said, answers the Executioner's "You have heard the last of her" with "The last of her? Hm! I wonder!"

Within the play itself, likewise, Shaw is neither unfair to those who sent Joan to her death nor contemptuous of their position and beliefs. It is in view of the historical construction he put on the case that he took to task previous writers on the subject, Mark Twain among them, for seeing Joan's judges as corrupt men who tricked and trapped her into false submissions. So far from this being the case, said Shaw, "Joan's judges were as straightforward as Joan herself," and "it cannot be too clearly understood that there were no villains in the tragedy of Joan's death. She was entirely innocent; but her excommunication was a genuine act of faith and piety; and her execution followed inevitably."

What this means—and it is a point with which I should like to conclude the whole essay—is that Shaw understood perfectly that in a period of historical crisis there are no easy solutions, and it is erroneous to assume that the entrenched beliefs and institutions of a culture are mere chimera or foolish aberrations that a simple show of reason and ridicule can put to flight. Yet when it came to his own time, it would not be inaccurate to say that he both recognized it as a period of crisis and approached its problems somewhat in the easy spirit of the above assumption. Some such assumption was inevitably the basis of his comedy, and it had something to do likewise with all those fantasies by means of which he persevered in The Serpent's "Hope. Hope. Hope" against the misery and the uncertainties of Adam's "Fear. Fear. Fear." The same Shaw who realized that death and tragedy were the inevitable price Saint Joan had to pay for her adhering to the "inner light" and even just so much as "wearing male attire" makes it all sound rather easy when he has Undershaft ("Saint Andrew") declare in *Major Barbara:*

> Well, you have made for yourself something that you call a morality or a religion or what not. It doesnt fit the facts. Well, scrap it. Scrap it and get one that does fit. That is what is wrong with the world at present. It scraps its obsolete steam engines and dynamos; but it wont scrap its old prejudices and its old moralities and its old religions and its old political constitutions.

And here we see again the reason behind Shaw's interpretation, or rather his misinterpretation, of Ibsen. For what Shaw failed to see in his account of Ibsen as a realist at war with idealists is what Ibsen himself saw only too clearly: that certain ideals are so inseparably a part of the present-day culture that it is not easy to "scrap" them, and that scrapping them would involve nothing short of scrapping that culture's foundations. He thus wrote not Shavian comedy but what is increasingly called today tragicomedy. Shaw himself in his 1921 essay on Tolstoy described Ibsen as "the dramatic poet who firmly established tragi-comedy as a much deeper and grimmer entertainment than tragedy."[4] In this respect most significant recent drama is with Ibsen rather than Shaw. True, it is not realistic drama but, at least in its outward trappings, more farce and fantasy in the Shavian mode. Likewise, it can be called Shavian in its desperate recognition of the constitutional absurdity of man and the utter hopelessness of his state on this earth— that is, if we see only this aspect of a play like *Back to Methusaleh,* as is indeed done by most of Shaw's modern admirers. But this is not the only aspect; there are others more visible and persistent: the easy escapes, the many solutions, the constant hopefulness, in short, the insistence on comedy at all costs. Of all this recent drama has completely and quite self-consciously purged itself. It has in fact redefined the very content of the comic vision. "As the 'comic' is an intuitive perception of the absurd," as Ionesco puts it, "it seems to me more hopeless than the 'tragic.' The 'comic' offers no escape."[5]

4. Bernard Shaw, "Tolstoy: Tragedian or Comedian," *The London Mercury,* 4 (1921), p. 32.
5. Eugene Ionesco, *Notes and Counter Notes: Writings on the Theatre* (New York, Grove Press, 1964), p. 27.

Notes on the Critics

John Mason Brown was a dramatic critic for *Theatre Arts Monthly,* the New York *Post* and *World Telegram,* and the *Saturday Review.*

John Fielden, a critic and teacher, taught for many years at Purdue University.

Jeanne Foster was an American journalist.

Daniel C. Gerould, a drama translator and critic, teaches at the City University of New York.

James Graham was an American journalist and translator.

Johan Huizinga was a distinguished Dutch medieval historian and author of *Erasmus and the Age of the Reformation* and *The Waning of the Middle Ages.*

Edith J. R. Isaacs, American drama critic, was for many years on the staff of *Theatre Arts Monthly.*

A. N. Kaul is a professor of English at Yale and author of *The American Vision* as well as a study of English stage comedy.

Desmond MacCarthy was an English literary critic and editor whose associations were with the Bloomsbury Group.

Louis L. Martz has written primarily on seventeenth-century English religious literature and is a professor of English at Yale.

A. Obraztsova is a Russian literary scholar who has worked under the Russian Shaw critic A. Anikst.

Luigi Pirandello was the major twentieth century Italian playwright, author of *Six Characters in Search of an Author* and *Henry IV.*

John Mackinnon Robertson was an English journalist and critic who had been friendly with Shaw in their earlier years.

Charles Sarolea was a Belgian critic and scholar who taught for many years at British universities.

J. I. M. Stewart is an Oxford don who has not only written a number of literary studies of 19th- and 20th-century Englishmen but writes mystery stories under the pen name of *Michael Innes.*

Hans Stoppel was a German literary scholar with a special interest in the drama.

Walter Tittle was an American magazine illustrator and writer.

Arland Ussher, an Irish critic and journalist, specialized in writing about modern Irish literature.

J. van Kan was a Belgain historian with a special interest in the medieval period.

Alick West, an English Marxist critic, remains best known for his study of Shaw, *A Good Man Fallen Among Fabians.*

E. J. West, a theater scholar and critic and editor of *Shaw on Theatre,* taught for many years at the University of Colorado.

Edmund Wilson, perhaps the most distinguished American literary critic in the twentieth century, was the author of *To the Finland Station, Axel's Castle,* and *The Wound and the Bow.*

T. C. Worsley, English journalist and critic, reviewed plays for many years for the *New Statesman.*

A *Saint Joan* Checklist

There is an enormous literature on Bernard Shaw. The following selected bibliography emphasizes studies which contain material relating
especially to *Saint Joan*. The standard texts of Shaw's plays are those of
the Collected Edition published by Constable of London beginning in
1931 and added to thereafter; and the successor *Bodley Head Bernard
Shaw* (1970-74), seven volumes including the prefaces, self-drafted in-
terviews about the plays, and dramatic fragments. For books and
articles about Shaw and new publications of his works, see "A Continuing Checklist of Shaviana" in *The Shaw Review*, published three times
a year by the Pennsylvania State University Press.

1. BIOGRAPHY AND LETTERS

Ervine, St. John. *Bernard Shaw: His Life, Work and Friends.* London
and New York, 1956. A biography by a fellow playwright with a
playwright's insights into Shaw's plays. The *Joan* section usefully
reviews contemporary critical reaction.

Henderson, Archibald. "Bernard Shaw Talks of His *Saint Joan.*" *Literary Digest International Book Review*, II (March, 1924), 286-89. An
interview.

_____. *George Bernard Shaw: Man of the Century.* New York, 1956.
The third and most compendious life of Shaw by his "official" biographer.

————. *Table-Talk of G.B.S.* London and New York, 1925. Contains some pages of Shavian comment on *Joan.*

Langner, Lawrence. *G.B.S. and the Lunatic.* New York, 1963. A chapter on *Saint Joan* details Shaw's long-distance involvement in the first American production of the play, with much useful biographical and background material, including many Shaw letters and cables.

Pearson, Hesketh. *George Bernard Shaw: His Life and Personality.* New York, 1963. Pearson's lively, anecdotal, Shaw-guided narrative of 1942 (then titled *G.B.S.*) together with a postscript of thirteen additional chapters published in 1951 after Shaw's death.

Shaw, Bernard. *The Listener,* June 3, 1931; reprinted in "Saint Joan," Dan H. Laurence, ed. *Platform and Pulpit. Previously Uncollected Speeches.* New York, 1961. B.B.C. radio talk, delivered on the 500th anniversary of the burning of Joan of Arc.

————. *Saint Joan. A Screenplay.* Edited by Bernard F. Dukore. Seattle, Wash., 1968. The full text (with alternate matter) of the screenplay Shaw wrote in the thirties for a production never filmed. Also many illustrations from productions of the play.

————. "*Saint Joan* Banned: Film Censorship in the United States." New York *Times,* September 14, 1936; and London *Mercury,* XXXIV (October, 1936); reprinted in E. J. West, ed. *Shaw on Theatre.* New York, 1958. This is Shaw's protest against the Catholic Church-inspired demands by the Hays [film censorship] Office in Hollywood to eliminate anything in his film script which made his play "a satire against Church and State which are made to appear stupid and inept." No film was then possible.

Tittle, Walter. "Mr. Bernard Shaw Talks about *St. Joan.*" *Outlook,* CXXXVII (June 25, 1924), 311–13.

Weintraub, Stanley. "Bernard Shaw's Other Saint Joan." *South Atlantic Quarterly,* LXIV (Spring, 1965), 194–205. On T. E. Lawrence ("of Arabia") as Shaw's living model for Joan.

————, ed. *Saint Joan.* Indianapolis, 1971. A volume in the Bobbs-

Merrill Shaw Series which includes play, preface, five additional Shavian discussions of Joan and his play, and extracts from *Trial and Rehabilitation Transcripts* (published in 1841–49) in the 1902 English translation from which Shaw extracted some of his action and dialogue.

2. GENERAL CRITICAL STUDIES

Bentley, Eric. *Bernard Shaw.* New York, 1957. Amended edition based upon the 1947 text. Includes a consideration of *Joan* as Shaw's "most ambitious drama."

Chesterton, G. K. *George Bernard Shaw.* London, 1935. A new edition with an additional chapter. In a brief concluding chapter, "The Later Phases," G.K.C. is pleased at "the wind of refreshment . . . to find one anti-clerical who is clever enough to base his case on defending the clerics. . . ."

Crompton, Louis. *Shaw the Dramatist.* Lincoln, Neb., 1969. Includes a chapter elucidating *Joan* through the play's social, philosophic, and intellectual backgrounds and sources.

Irvine, William. *The Universe of G.B.S.* New York, 1949. One of the fullest analyses of Shaw's intellectual background, with a detailed section on *Joan.*

Kaul, A. N. *The Action of English Comedy: Studies in the Encounter of Abstraction and Experience from Shakespeare to Shaw.* New Haven, 1970. The chapter, "George Bernard Shaw: From Anti-Romance to Pure Fantasy," discusses *Joan* as "the tragedy of a historical hero rather than a saint."

Meisel, Martin. *Shaw and the Nineteenth-Century Theatre.* Princeton, N. J., 1963. A consideration of *Joan* as "a direct-line descendant of a characteristic species of the nineteenth-century historical drama with which Shaw was entirely familiar: the heroic history play written for a woman star."

Morgan, Margery. *The Shavian Playground: An Exploration of the Art of George Bernard Shaw.* London, 1972. A chapter on *Joan* examines the play among Shaw's "histories."

Nethercot, Arthur H. *Men and Supermen: The Shavian Portrait Gallery.* Cambridge, Mass., 1954. An analysis of Shaw's characters and character types throughout the canon.

Stewart, J. I. M. *Eight Modern Writers.* Oxford and New York, 1963. The chapter on Shaw considers *Joan* "conceivably the finest and most moving English drama since *The Winter's Tale* or *The Tempest.*"

Weales, Gerald. *Religion in Modern English Drama.* Philadelphia, 1961. Includes a staunch defense of the *Joan* Epilogue, with its ambivalences and ironies, as the "heart" of the drama, dependent "for its irony on the Shavian assumption that Joan's death is an unnecessary horror. Yet for Joan the Catholic, her death is not a misfortune, but a triumph."

West, Alick. *George Bernard Shaw: "A Good Man Fallen Among Fabians."* New York, 1950. A Marxist analysis of the major plays, including *Joan.*

3. REVIEWS AND CRITIQUES OF *SAINT JOAN*

Ayrton, Michael. "A Performance of *Saint Joan.*" *Fabrications.* London, 1972, and New York, 1973. Pp. 44-51. Ostensibly a review of early performances of *Joan,* and in particular a repertory performance in Southampton in 1940, this study reveals itself inevitably as a work of fiction in which the real Gilles de Rais ("Bluebeard") takes his own part in the play and adds lines Shaw never wrote.

Bentley, Eric. "The Road from Rouen to New York." *What Is Theatre?* New York, 1968. Pp. 254-56, 460-61. In this review and in a 1956 afterword Bentley sets out his position (as well as that of Richard Hayes in *Commonweal*) that Shaw was less than fair to the Church in his play.

Boas, Frederick S. "Joan of Arc in Shakespeare, Schiller, and Shaw." *Shakespeare Quarterly,* II (January, 1951), 34-45.

Brown, John Mason. "The Prophet and the Maid." *Saturday Review of Literature,* XXXXIV (October 27, 1951), 27-29.

Eliot, T. S. "Shaw, Robertson and 'The Maid'." *Criterion,* IV (April, 1926), 389-90. A derogatory review which belies the fact that Eliot would crib from the play in his own *Murder in the Cathedral.*

Fielden, John. "Shaw's *Saint Joan* as Tragedy." *Twentieth Century Literature,* III (July, 1957), 59-67. A careful analysis of the play and Shaw's aims from the perspective of classical tragedy, a point of view the author feels Shaw must have intended.

Gerould, Daniel C. "*Saint Joan* in Paris." *The Shaw Review,* VII (January, 1964), 11-23. A survey of French press reaction to the first performances of *Saint Joan* in Paris in 1925, as well as of the play's continuing reputation and influence in France.

Graham, James. "Shaw on *Saint Joan.*" New York *Times,* April 13, 1924, Sec. 8, p. 2. Report of Shaw's reaction to advance criticism of *Joan* in France, including full text of Shaw's letter to the London correspondent of the Paris theatrical publication *Comoedia.*

Griffin, Alice. "The New York Critics and *Saint Joan.*" *Shaw Bulletin* [afterwards *Shaw Review*], I (January, 1955), 10-15. A thorough analysis, with extracts from reviews, of press reaction to the first New York production and two subsequent revivals.

Huizinga, Johan. *Men and Ideas.* New York, 1959. Pp. 207-39. A translation of a two-part review by the great Dutch medieval historian which first appeared in *De Gids* in 1925. It remains the best analysis of Shaw's treatment of the historical Joan.

MacCarthy, Desmond. *Shaw.* London, 1951. Pp. 162-75. Reprint of a two-part review originally in *The New Statesman,* April 5 and 12, 1924, and a review of the French production of the play from the June 21, 1930, issue.

McKee, Irving. "Shaw's *Saint Joan* and the American Critics." *The Shavian,* II (February, 1964), 13-16. A rapid survey of New York press reaction to the 1924, 1936, and 1939 productions.

Macksoud, S. John, and Ross Altman. "Voices in Opposition: A Burkeian Rhetoric of *Saint Joan,*" *The Quarterly Journal of Speech,* LVII

(April, 1971), 140-46. An analysis of the play's dialogue according to the principles of Kenneth Burke's *Philosophy of Literary Form* to explain how Shaw succeeds in "making the audience tolerant of heresy."

Martz, Louis. "The Saint as Tragic Hero: *Saint Joan* and *Murder in the Cathedral*," in *Tragic Themes in Western Literature*. New Haven, 1955. Reprinted in R. J. Kaufman, ed. *G. B. Shaw: A Collection of Critical Essays*. Englewood Cliffs, N. J., 1965. Pp. 143-61.

Pirandello, Luigi. "Pirandello Distills Shaw." New York *Times Magazine*, January 13, 1924. Reprinted as "Bernard Shaw's *Saint Joan*," in *The Shavian*, II (February, 1964), 6-12, with an introduction by Frederick May. Pirandello's laudatory review of the play, anonymously translated.

Robertson, John Mackinnon. *Mr. Shaw and "The Maid."* London, 1925. A small and small-minded book by an old rationalist friend of Shaw's suddenly resentful at the playwright's reverent attitude toward Joan and stubbornly skeptical about Joan. Strangely, T. S. Eliot (see above) approved of Robertson's attack, probably because, although an Anglo-Catholic, he disapproved of Shaw.

Searle, William, "Shaw's Saint Joan as 'Protestant.' " *The Shaw Review*, XV (1972), 110-16. Discusses Joan as "irrationalist" and as "quite as much of an absolutist as her judges."

Stoppel, Hans. "Shaw and Sainthood." *English Studies*, XXXVI (April, 1955), 49-63.

West, E. J. "*Saint Joan:* A Modern Classic Reconsidered." *Quarterly Journal of Speech*, XL (October, 1954), 249-59.

Wilson, Edmund. "Bernard Shaw Since the War." *The New Republic*, August 27, 1924, pp. 380-81. A review of the first published edition of the play which turns into a retrospective analysis of Shavian drama.

Worsley, T. C. "An Irish Joan." *The New Statesman,* October 9, 1954, pp. 434–36. The Siobhan McKenna production reviewed.

Index to Writers and Critics